Praise for *Premoni...*

"*Premonitions in Daily Life* is a superb look at a very common experience—the sense of knowing a future event. Premonitions are our birthright, a natural endowment, a great gift. They exist for a reason, and we need to understand and honor them. Van Bronkhorst takes the mystery and confusion out of premonitions with this fascinating, reader-friendly book."

—Larry Dossey, M.D., author of *The Power of Premonitions*

"I highly recommend *Premonitions in Daily Life* to all those who are trying to make sense of premonition experiences in their lives. Sparked by a lifelong series of her own premonitions, Van Bronkhorst has researched relevant case studies on this topic as well as conducted intensive interviews with a variety of fellow experiencers. From this solid knowledge base and a background as counselor and social worker, she has compiled an in-depth series of guidelines for how to identify premonitions, how to normalize them, and how to integrate them in a sensible and useful way into your life. This is a book that extends beyond earlier case treatments, and one whose time has come."

—Sally Rhine Feather, Ph.D.

Premonitions
~ in ~
Daily Life

About the Author

Jeanne Van Bronkhorst experienced her first premonition at the age of five, and since then has had premonitions often enough to both trust their warnings and appreciate the questions they raise about free will, destiny, and the ways memory and imagination weave together. Those questions led her to graduate work in psychology and then social work, and a career in hospice social work. For the past twenty years she has helped people who face life-threatening illnesses.

She has given many lectures and workshops to healthcare professionals and hospice volunteers on topics related to bereavement and HIV/AIDS. She is a member of the International Organization for Noetic Sciences and of the International Association for the Study of Dreams. A native of Seattle, Washington, she now lives and works in Toronto, Ontario.

Premonitions in Daily Life

Working with Spontaneous Information When Rational Understanding Fails You

JEANNE VAN BRONKHORST

Llewellyn Publications
Woodbury, Minnesota

First Edition
First Printing, 2013

Book design by Donna Burch
Cover art: Swan: Fancy Collection/SuperStock
Cover design by Lisa Novak
Editing by Connie Hill

Llewellyn Publications is a registered trademark of Llewellyn Worldwide Ltd.

Library of Congress Cataloging-in-Publication Data

Van Bronkhorst, Jeanne, 1962–
  Premonitions in daily life : working with spontaneous information when rational understanding fails you / Jeanne Van Bronkhorst. — 1st ed.
    p.   cm.
  Includes bibliographical references.
  ISBN 978-0-7387-3475-0
1. Precognition. 2. Extrasensory perception. 3. Parapsychology. I. Title.
  BF1341.V36   2013
  133.8—dc23   2012041218

Llewellyn Publications
A Division of Llewellyn Worldwide Ltd.
2143 Wooddale Drive
Woodbury, MN 55125-2989
www.llewellyn.com

Printed in the United States of America

To Ann, my home, who makes all things possible

Contents

PART TWO: COMMON ASSUMPTIONS

PART THREE: MEANING OF PREMONITIONS

CONTENTS

Acknowledgments

My heartfelt thanks to Susan Simmons, my good friend and brilliant editor. You alternately encouraged and challenged me, and taught me how to write for an audience larger than one person. This comma "," is for you!

Many thanks to Charlie, Evelyn, Julie, Olivia, Phillip, and Roger, who took a chance in sharing their stories. Your warmth, humor, and many insights offer us a glimpse into the twisting, complex, splendid dance between memory and imagination in time.

I am grateful to Angela Wix, acquisition editor, and the Llewellyn staff for discovering and championing my book. I am grateful as well for the dedicated and passionate writers at the Canadian Authors Association, whose encouragement helped me hang in there, keep writing, and find a publisher.

And finally, my warm thanks to B. Alford for offering me a caring and honest appraisal of my first draft, may it rest in peace. Such friendships are rare and to be treasured.

INTRODUCTION

What Would You Do?

Imagine you are sitting in an airplane, dozing over the in-flight magazine as other passengers jostle past to their seats. All around are muted
conversations, the soft clicking of overhead compartments being shut,
engines idling. But as the plane backs away from the terminal, you wake
with a start. In your mind's eye you see one of the wheels wobble and
fall away as the plane rushes down the runway, and you know the plane
will skid and slide off the runway before it finally stops, with passengers
and crew—including you—shaken and frightened.

What would you do?

Most people understand that fear of flying happens at any time. Even
seasoned travelers know they will have occasional moments of anxiety,
and they treat those moments as just that—anxious thoughts that have
nothing to do with the actual flight. They push the feeling away, calm
themselves with safety statistics, and settle back into their seats.

But if you are reading this book you also know another possibility
exists. This sudden worry just might be a premonition, and that possibility brings up questions most people have not considered. What bit of

information lets you know this is a warning of imminent danger and not just anxiety in a new form? If you decide your vision is a genuine premonition, what do you do next? Do you notify the pilot, force your way off the plane, warn others to get off the plane with you? Or do you quietly prepare yourself for a frightening but ultimately non-lethal accident? If you trust the warning, can you trust the limited nature of the accident you just pictured? What do you do with an intense and disturbing experience that has no good explanation?

Most people in modern Western culture have been taught that premonitions are not real. Premonitions supposedly belong to a distant past, before the Age of Enlightenment, back when superstitions and magical thinking drove people's imaginations and beliefs. We have been taught premonitions belong to a pre-rational, pre-scientific time, and we are best off when we keep them safely back there.

It does seem that premonitions challenge everything this culture teaches about the forward direction of time, the law of cause and effect, free will, even what God has intended for us. Many people ask why they should throw away everything they already know about the world for such a rare, fleeting, random event that might never repeat itself.

The Problem with Premonitions

The problem with premonitions is not their rarity. Research has shown premonitions can happen to anyone: men and women, children and adults, scientists and artists, waiters, farmers, police officers, nurses and teachers, business consultants, students, engineers, and ministers, regardless of their personal comfort with them. Most people I know can tell at least one story of a moment in which someone—maybe a friend, maybe themselves—seemed to know what was going to happen before they should have known it.

In fact, surveys throughout the world have shown somewhere between half and three-quarters of the people report having had some kind of psychic experience, with about half of those events being premonitions, according to Dr. Richard S. Broughton, director of Intuition

Laboratories.[1] That is an enormous number of people acknowledging an experience our culture insists cannot exist. Even if researchers are correct when they estimate only 10 or 15 percent of the general population have experienced what some might call a premonition, that still adds up to tens of millions of people in North America alone.[2]

Stories about premonitions appear in every culture and in every time period, including our modern Western culture. In nearly every other culture premonitions are welcomed as significant events, but here they are often greeted with confusion and fear, or dismissed as so much nonsense. Still, our disbelief doesn't stop premonitions from showing up, pushing their way into our modern daily life regardless of our carefully reasoned arguments against them. Their intensity and irrational clarity challenge us to respond to them as if they are real. They push some of us to choose between everything we thought we knew and the reality of our direct experience.

The problem we face with premonitions is not their rarity, but our inability to talk about them. Premonitions may be one aspect of normal human perception, but without a common conversation about their value or their meaning, most of us have a hard time bringing them up with friends. We don't learn how to handle a premonition as we learn how to handle our dreams. We don't learn how to recognize a premonition in its initial moment, and then we feel shocked when a future event connects to our earlier impression. We don't learn how to distinguish a likely premonition from all the other ways we think about the future and then feel stuck with two rather extreme choices: Believe everything is a premonition or believe nothing is a premonition because premonitions can't exist.

No wonder so many people feel scared, overwhelmed, or even threatened by a premonition. Without a few basic skills to sort through the difference between a premonition and all the other ways we think about the future (such as a fear of flying), or a grasp of the choices still available, or the support of friends, many people have no idea what to do with a premonition's warning.

Another Way

We don't have to be so lost or confused. The example of the wheel falling off the plane came from my friend Phillip, who once found himself in the same situation while traveling home from a business trip. He was dozing in his seat when he was startled awake by the thought that a wheel was going to fall off as his plane gathered speed for take-off, causing it to skid and veer off the runway. He felt a wave of fear roll through his body as he tried to figure out what to do. Fortunately, this was not the first time Phillip had flown in a plane nor the first time he had experienced anxiety about flying. But most importantly, this was not his first premonition.

Phillip already kept a mental checklist to help him figure out if any unusual moment was a premonition or another instance of his occasional fear of flying. Now he went over that checklist, carefully noting the differences between his fears about flying and his premonitions. He noted this was a sudden, clear thought about a specific problem on the plane. He knew his usual anxieties crept up on him more slowly or were triggered by reading or hearing about accidents. His usual anxieties came to him as questions like, What if the wing falls off? or, What if the pilot falls asleep? His premonitions, on the other hand, often came with the calm, clear certainty of one particular problem, such as in this instance.

Phillip decided it was a premonition, and this decision gave him a new list of options to consider. Should he get off the plane? Prepare for an accident? Warn others? Tell the flight attendants? His options may seem boundless, but just as Phillip already accepted premonitions, he also already had a good idea about what his premonitions were for and how they worked for him. Phillip already knew premonitions *were his ability to see future events before they occurred.* From his own premonitions and from all he learned, Phillip trusted the future was already fixed in time, an inevitable event that cannot be changed. While others have experienced premonitions as anything but belonging to a fixed future, Phillip's belief helped him sort through his options quickly. He didn't worry about trying to change the inevitable. He also knew the plane was moving onto the runway and that passengers were all safely buckled in their seats for take-off. His understanding that premonitions help him prepare for an inevitable future helped him decide what to do next. He remained seated and prepared himself for a frightening (but not fatal) accident. He didn't raise the alarm, as he couldn't see how that would help. His decisions helped him remain calm in a moment of intense fear.

Was it the right decision? It clearly was the best decision for Phillip. Rather than panicking he questioned his experience and then sorted through his options. He remained calm and figured out what he could do next, which helped him feel emotionally ready for whatever was about to happen.

Phillip also knew every premonition comes in two parts. First comes the initial moment, followed by its future connecting event. A premonition doesn't really exist until the initial moment connects to some future event. When his plane easily lifted off the ground with all its wheels intact a few moments later, he felt his only real anxiety. Now he had no future event to connect back to his original fear. He felt relieved, of course, but also disappointed. He wondered if he had mistaken simple anxiety for a premonition after all, meaning he might not be as good at recognizing premonitions as he thought.

Later that evening Phillip heard on the evening news that a different airplane taking off an hour later from the same airport lost a wheel on its take-off and skidded onto a field, frightening crew and passengers. The details matched his earlier misgiving so closely he knew it was the connecting event to his premonition. He had been affected by a real event that had not yet happened.

Many people might want to stop reading right here, convinced by Phillip's story that premonitions bring nothing but bad news and put us into impossible, helpless situations. I know researchers and authors have focused primarily on those premonitions linked to tragedies, leading some to believe all premonitions will bring bad news. If we never hear about the more playful moments of premonitions, we might worry about those who go looking for premonitions and wonder if they might be putting themselves in real danger.

Despite their somewhat overwrought reputation, premonitions connect most often with small and personal moments that have nothing to do with danger. Rather than riding in on great tidal waves that threaten our lives, most premonitions play in the shallow waters close to shore, giving us glimpses of the intimate, casual details of daily life.

Premonitions can be delightful and playful, like gentle nudges in our lives. While it is true some premonitions bring people warnings of disasters, more often they bring glimpses of future events so trivial or benign that no warning is necessary. A woman suddenly knows two friends will meet each other and marry within the year. A man wakes with a song running through his head only to find the same song on his car radio an hour later. A little boy gets a strong feeling of anticipation just before the phone rings. A woman thinks of an old friend and the next day meets her friend walking down a busy street. These are all examples of the tiny paths premonitions can take through daily life. They are so small we can easily overlook them, but we don't have to ignore them.

The few people who have studied their own premonitions in a systematic way found the trivial moments far outnumbered the warnings, just as in daily life our moments of peace far outnumber our moments of terror. As far back as 1927 John Dunne commented in his book *An Experiment with Time* on how many premonitions of insignificant details wound their way through his dream images. Two different researchers duplicated what he found by tracking their own dreams closely, and they also found the majority of their premonition dreams connected to some trivial moment within the next twenty-four hours.[3] They never would have noticed those connections if they hadn't written down their dreams first; they only noticed the future events because they connected to earlier dreams.

Overview

The first step toward understanding premonitions—and so the first part of this book—is watching how premonitions appear in daily life. A rare premonition might appear as a spectacular vision suddenly popping up in front of our eyes, but most often premonitions are subtle and vague, like a sudden sense of conviction about what will happen in the next moment or a slow rise of adrenaline for no apparent reason. Even then, adrenaline and a sense of conviction can link to the future through more ordinary means like anxiety, intuition, or a prediction based on some earlier experience. This book lays out some of the questions people like Phillip ask before deciding that any specific moment is a premonition. We can learn how to use common sense to help sort out true premonitions from all the other ways we already think about the future. We can learn to prove the premonitions to ourselves, even if ordinary daily life can never meet the exacting standards of scientific investigation.

The second step—and the second part of this book—is making sense of a premonition. I explore the most common questions people who have premonitions ask: What does it mean? What does it say about me if I have one? Who can I talk to? What do I do with the information it gives me? I will look at how a premonition can affect self-identity and how community can help us understand and hang on to a premonition. Most importantly I will explore what options a premonition brings and so what choices we have when experiencing a premonition. What we each believe about premonitions will influence the decisions we make about them.

The Language of Premonitions

Premonition or *precognition* is one of the four extrasensory perceptions, or ESP, which is now more commonly called psi. Along with premonition, psi includes *telepathy* (perceiving someone else's thoughts), *clairvoyance* (perceiving an action or event that happens somewhere else), and *psychokinesis* (moving inanimate objects by thought). Clairvoyance has undergone some changes, and people now more often use the term *seeing at a distance* or *remote viewing*. Premonition, telepathy, clairvoyance, and psychokinesis are four different ways of perceiving that take place outside of our usual five senses. The idea of premonition gets so little attention that the words to describe it are not yet stable. Some people use premonition to mean only a physical sensation of fear right before some dangerous event, as opposed to *precognition*, which means a thought or idea of a future event. Others use premonition and precognition interchangeably. I see the word precognition used most often in experiments, so I use the words premonition, psi, and *psi event* to emphasize the place of premonition in daily waking life.

My Interest

This book grew out of my questions and my hope that premonitions can be explored as a human experience as vital as our emotions, imaginations, and dreams. I have had premonitions often enough to delight in their connections and even trust their occasional warnings, even if I don't know how they work within time or my cause-and-effect world.

The subject of premonitions didn't come up very often in my family when I was growing up. When it did, my parents dismissed it as casually as they dismissed bad dreams. The idea of a future event somehow influencing the past was too far removed from my father's engineering background or my mother's Catholic teachings. Premonitions didn't fit with their beliefs about the world or with their common sense or with the wider cultural assumptions in which we lived.

The first premonition I remember happened when I was six years old, the summer my family took me to Sea World for (what seemed to me) the second time. Even then I knew that people and events should not—must not—repeat exactly, and I felt confused and more than a little scared. In the next two decades I watched premonitions jump out from my ordinary time like small tornadoes, churning up memory, facts, knowledge and imagination, time, and question upon question. How is it possible for a moment to repeat itself? How can I find a premonition before its connecting event, and how do I weed out all the other ways I think about the future? Does a premonition mean I am doomed to repeat the same moment, or do I have free will to change it? How do I live with the knowledge of a future event I can neither control nor avoid?

I studied psychology in graduate school and learned to appreciate the constant juggling we manage every day, keeping aloft the soft balls of perception, memory, and imagination almost without effort. I worked in mental health clinics, teaching hospitals, homecare agencies, and hospices and listened to people make sense of their losses, faith, family, and what makes for a good life. I've learned to appreciate how much of life happens outside the understanding of science or religion, more deeply rooted in family truths, the lessons of personal experience, and our own physical bodies.

And so it might be with premonitions. Premonitions may ultimately be a human experience. Whether we believe they originally descend from a higher guiding spirit or spark from the firing synapses in our brains, we all live through them in a similar human way. Premonitions are who we are—our imaginations, our dreams, our unconscious physical reactions, our memories—and they can't be separated from our daily lives. They *are us*, they are a part of being human, and it is time we paid attention to them. Premonitions can take us to the edge of what we know about time, life, and the transcendent. They can give us comfort and occasionally they offer us the most radical of all freedoms, the chance to choose our actions a second time and so possibly change our futures.

In writing this book I have learned four things are possible. It is possible, sometimes, to recognize a premonition before the future event comes along to confirm our impression. It is possible, always, to find a personal meaning for our premonitions that gives us better control and purpose in our lives. It is possible to act on the information we receive according to our values and beliefs and inevitable human limitations. And it is possible to integrate our experiences into a good life, balancing our intuition with our experience, knowledge, and common sense.

PART ONE

Inside a
Premonition

CHAPTER 1

How to Recognize a Premonition

Sudden, urgent, vague, confusing, physical. The initial moment of a premonition stands out more for its riot of conflicting impressions than for any coherent plan it offers. Some of these conflicting impressions are strong enough to pull us out of our routine thoughts, bringing an intensity that lingers for days, even weeks. Whatever form the premonition takes, we notice it. We hear a warning voice, feel a gut hunch, have a flash of intuition, or simply know what is coming next. We might not recognize it as a premonition, but we notice the moment as different from all the other moments surrounding it, as something unusual and even rare.

A premonition in daily life requires more than this initial rush of impressions. A true premonition needs two moments: the initial impression and also a later, future event that matches it in some way. These two moments might be separated by a few minutes, a few days, or even several years, but the future event must connect to an earlier moment for the two to become a single whole premonition. Without both of these moments, we cannot have had a premonition.

Most famous premonition stories have big initial moments and big connecting events. An initial moment of warning and dread connects to an unexpected tragedy, accident, or disaster. This emphasis has led many of us to assume premonitions nearly always bring information on life-and-death matters, but researchers know otherwise.

Researchers have long noted that many premonitions concern trivial matters rather than dramatic events. Smaller premonitions usually do not capture our attention in the same way as dramatic premonitions. Smaller premonitions are more easily dismissed, perhaps rationalized away because they don't pull us into matters of life and death.

If the initial moment is subtle or the connecting event nondescript, then we might miss it altogether. We can only remember what we notice. An initial moment that carries no weight may slide right past, and we will never see a connection to its future event. Likewise, if the connecting event fails to grab our attention, we will have no reason to pause and wonder if there had been an initial predicting event.

Our own sensitivity to danger helps explain, at least in part, why most premonition accounts have focused on accidents and tragedies. We tune into messages about approaching danger because of its potential to disrupt our lives, just as we are more likely to notice the sound of an approaching siren and miss hearing the chickadees twittering in a tree overhead.

My friend Susan invited family and friends to her house for a traditional Thanksgiving turkey feast this year, with everyone volunteering to bring something—wine, salad, green bean casserole, and pie. The day before Thanksgiving, she was walking through the grocery store picking up last-minute items when she noticed a faint, barely-there urge to pause at the bakery, even though all the bakery items on her menu were already accounted for. She almost rushed herself along, but then she decided to linger a moment to see if she could get a stronger signal. The faint urge sharpened into a new thought that she should buy an extra pie or two, but her rational brain quickly took over. She had no need for more pie, she told herself. Her friend had already confirmed she was coming with homemade pies. It would be insulting to have backup pies sitting on the counter, and she certainly didn't need four pies.

The next morning, Thanksgiving Day, her friend called in a rush. Her mother had suffered a mild stroke that morning and she needed to stay at the hospital so wouldn't be coming for dinner. After offering sympathy and support and promising to save a plate and some dessert for later, Susan hung up the phone, looked around her kitchen, and had to laugh. She had no pie.

Premonitions about life-threatening events get more attention from all of us, just as disasters and tragedies get more media play and the painful foot holds more of our attention than the other foot that feels fine. We can recount our tragedies in vivid detail, including any earlier warnings we might have noticed, while our easier moments slide by without a second thought.

The same holds true for how we talk about our premonitions. If I had to choose just one premonition anecdote to send the researchers, I would choose my most dramatic story. The dramatic ones are more compelling, more riveting, and show the importance and usefulness of premonitions.

Premonitions of tragic events demand more of our attention right from the start. I can brush aside any tiny connections I find between daily life and my imagination, precisely because they are so tiny, but a potential danger is much more frightening. People who take no notice of a trivial premonition's subtle cues may look up for a feeling of impending doom. I know I have had more pie-or-no-pie level premonitions in my life, but the ones I remember more clearly involve near disasters. The stakes are higher in these moments, making it harder to ignore the warning.

For all these reasons, the published stories don't deal so much with ordinary daily events such as work, family, hobbies, and missing desserts.[4] And for all these reasons we may be able to find more ordinary premonitions within our daily lives. If we allow ourselves to notice, we might find a steady trickle of tiny premonitions just like Susan's nudge to buy more pie, premonitions that do little more than brighten our days and make us wonder at the flow of time. If we know where to look, we might catch these friendly initial moments more often.

The first step in finding premonitions lies in figuring out which moments belong to ordinary time and which moments might be bringing a glimpse of the future. In a later chapter, I will outline the questions we can ask to make sure our glimpse is most likely a premonition and not something more common, like anxiety or our own educated guess. First, however, we have to notice them. We have to find them as they slip by in the background of our thoughts. Fortunately, researchers have found several patterns that can help us recognize the initial moment of a premonition.

How Premonitions Appear to Us

Dr. Louisa Rhine, scientist and wife of founding parapsychology researcher Joseph B. Rhine, and a researcher in her own right, built the single largest collection of psi anecdotes in North America.[5] Over the course of several decades she gathered over twelve thousand written accounts of telepathy, clairvoyance (or seeing at a distance), and premonitions.[6] Her work, first with her husband at the Parapsychology Laboratory at Duke University and later at the independent Institute for Parapsychology (now the Rhine Research Center), helped recognize spontaneous psi events as an important field of study.

Louisa Rhine was the first researcher to mark the patterns in all these anecdotes and categorize the premonitions people have in daily life. The first thing Rhine noticed was how personal the experiences were to the people who had them. Most premonitions didn't concern war or natural disasters but focused on the personal, daily lives of the experiencers. In other words, premonitions bring us information about tonight's dinner and tomorrow's commute more often than they point to life-changing events.[7]

Rhine noticed that all psi events first appear to us through one of four routes: (1) realistic dreams, (2) symbolic dreams, (3) intuitive impressions, and (4) hallucinations, such as a vision or voice. Regardless of whether the experience is telepathy, seeing at a distance, or precognition, we first become aware of it through one of these four pathways.

Realistic dreams are clear and specific, with details that mirror the future event so exactly there is no doubt about the connection. If you dream of a bassett hound puppy bouncing through your office and the next week your colleague brings in a bassett hound puppy she bought on a whim, you now have two exact images to compare: a dream puppy and a physical puppy, both bassett hounds, both tumbling through your workspace. Researchers love this type of premonition because the details are so easy to verify. Anyone can see your dream puppy and your colleague's actual puppy match each other.

Symbolic dreams use images that have meaning for the individual dreamer but would not be recognized by someone else as a close connection to the event. Say, for instance, your dream of a bassett hound puppy makes you think of babies in their bassinets and the next week a colleague tells you she is pregnant. Could your dream still be a premonition? Most researchers do not include symbolic dreams in their research. The two images—a bassett hound puppy and a colleague's pregnancy— do not have a readily apparent connection to each other, apart from the one you make and supply. Still, what counts in daily life is your experience. If your dream makes you think of babies at work right before your colleague announces she is pregnant, then it might be a premonition, regardless of whether you can prove it.

Intuitive impressions are gut feelings, hunches, or even sudden insights. They interrupt our waking life rather than make their appearance in a dream. They can catch our attention with surprising urgency, but these impressions may be the most vague of all premonitions. Sometimes they carry nothing more than an unexpected emotional or physical sense that something is about to happen. An intuitive gut feeling might look like you walking into your office and having a sudden wave of nausea that reminds

study he presented only thirty-five of them. All thirty-five were dreams that contained specific images of the disaster. Barker didn't include any waking premonitions because "the premonitions were so vague and indefinite that there was nothing to link them with Aberfan."[10] He needed to use only those premonitions that could clearly be matched, initial moment to event, in the eyes of his readers. His reluctance to publish the other premonitions didn't make them less real, or less meaningful to the people who had them. No matter how vague the initial feeling, the people who experienced them knew they were connected to the disaster.

While none of this proves waking premonitions are more common than precognitive dreams, it does help explain why so few waking premonitions show up in the research. They don't make good research material.

Markers for the Initial Moment of a Waking Premonition

So how to recognize a premonition among all the other passing fancies of daily waking life? The initial moments of premonitions have a similar core no matter how they appear or what the connecting event may be. Checking an experience against these six characteristics can help us recognize a premonition's initial moment as distinct from other ways we think about the future.

The first characteristic of waking premonitions is their sudden appearance. Unlike precognitive dreams, waking premonitions have a sudden, coming-out-of-the-blue quality. The second characteristic is the sense of certainty we feel, or, as Louisa Rhine called it, our "sense of conviction." The third characteristic is our own **confusion** about the moment. We are confused both by the unexpected information and by our certainty that the information is true. The fourth characteristic is a **sense of vagueness**, even when the information feels certain. The fifth characteristic is the jumble of physical sensations connected to the premonition, from a tingling down the neck to a sudden rush of adrenaline. This fifth characteristic has been reported only in passing by other researchers, as they had no way to verify it, but it remains an important characteristic nonetheless. Finally, we each will develop our own **personal markers** for premonitions, much like we each develop our own personal dream vocabulary.

....

MARKERS OF A PREMONITION

1. Sudden Appearance

2. Sense of Certainty

3. Confusion

4. Sense of Vagueness

5. Physical Sensations

6. Personal Markers

....

These six characteristics remain roughly the same, no matter who has the premonition or the importance of its future event. At the same time these characteristics are fluid and subjective, just like all human experiences; some people find them more often or more strongly than others. Alone they cannot prove any one moment is a premonition, but they can help us recognize the possibility of a premonition in the midst of daily life. These characteristics give us hope that we can learn to recognize premonitions when they first appear in the initial moment before its connecting event.

My friend Roger had one premonition that may have saved his life. Roger is a professional science writer. A friend of his, an accomplished pilot, called him one afternoon and invited him on a plane ride, something Roger had enjoyed several times in the past. Before he could accept the invitation, he suddenly felt a shivering, buzzing warning that told him he shouldn't go. Roger brushed the feeling aside and agreed to go anyway, sure he was imagining nonsense. At the last minute, he found a way to back out of the trip. His friend's plane crashed that day, killing everyone on board except the man who took Roger's place. Did Roger have a premonition? Roger respected the feeling he had and canceled his ride, but nearly thirty years later he still wonders about that day. Feelings such as Roger's are considered part of the set of markers used to identify the presence of a premonition. As we look more closely at the six markers of a premonition, we will see how Roger's experience fits the pattern.

1. Sudden appearance, out-of-the-blue. Waking premonitions come into our awareness suddenly and startle us out of our usual train of thought. They don't gradually dawn on us after careful thought or grow slowly out of our reasoning. We don't sit down and bring a premonition into awareness through sheer force of will. Instead, these initial moments seem like an intrusion of an idea (or feeling or insight) into an otherwise ordinary day. One minute we are talking to friends or driving home from work or waiting for an elevator, and the next minute we are startled by a new thought or feeling. The all-of-a-sudden quality can help us distinguish a premonition (completely unexpected thought) from our more usual predictions and anxieties (not so unexpected). Roger was on the phone with his friend talking about the upcoming trip when he suddenly felt something was wrong. As he describes it, "It was all of a sudden, like something switched on. I just felt a little voice telling me *No. Something is wrong here. This isn't right.*"

This out-of-the-blue quality, however, does not belong to premonitions alone. Many ghost stories begin with an ordinary moment being disrupted by whatever force is being described. Researcher Robin Wooffitt even wondered if the "all of a sudden" remark is a phrase people use to maintain their credibility while sharing something that seems unbelievable.[11] Describing an uncanny experience with the "all of a sudden" phrase reassures our listeners that we are rational people and therefore trustworthy.

While I understand Wooffitt's concerns, I have relied on my own sense of surprise to help mark my waking premonitions. Without that sense of interruption, I would never recognize a premonition. My thoughts that grow out of the previous thought and flow on to the next will not rouse me from my habitual state of mind or send my thoughts leaping into the future, like a premonition so often does. With a premonition the thought or feeling breaks into my awareness with its unexpected predictions.

2. A certainty beyond good sense. Roger didn't believe premonitions were possible and so didn't think of his concern as a premonition, but still he was uneasy. "When I thought about the [upcoming] plane trip I thought, *I really don't want to go on this flight.* I always assumed I would be going, but I didn't feel good about it." Whatever it is that we suddenly know or feel, we feel certain about it, even more sure than about our own rational assessment of the situation. In that moment we are not worried about a possible future or making an educated guess based on previous knowledge or experience. Instead we *know*—*we just know*—with a certainty that defies all attempts to rationalize it away that something is about to happen. The certainty feels important, clear, and urges us to pay attention.

Louisa Rhine called this characteristic a sense of conviction.[12] Whether they appeared in dreams or in waking life, many premonitions carried such a strong sense of conviction that people felt compelled to do or say something in response, such as warn a family member, check on a child, or change a plan to avoid danger.

Rhine studied this sense of conviction in depth and found it was stronger in the people who had vague, impression-like premonitions than in the people whose premonitions included specific details. A full 65 percent of the Rhine Collection's premonitions came as dreams, but less than half carried a sense of conviction. On the other hand, only a quarter of all premonitions came as a vague, intuitive impressions, but a surprising 84 percent of those impressions carried a strong sense of conviction. Waking or dreaming, people felt a stronger sense of conviction about vague information and less certainty when they had specific details.

At first these results appeared upside down to me. I am used to specific information bringing me more certainty, not less, and more confidence in my predictions. But premonitions are different. Premonitions that bring specific, detailed images invite my rational brain to take over and make educated guesses and predictions based on those images. When I can find other explanations for the images I usually take them, which makes me less sure the images will connect to my future. On the other hand, a persistent, vague feeling that does not carry detailed images is nearly impossible to dismiss, and my rational brain is caught off-guard. I can find no logical reason to think its message is true, which makes me that much more aware of its persistence and certainty.

Some premonitions feel so strong they override all our ideas about how we should behave. Many people have stories about doing something they don't unusually do based solely on the strength of a premonition. They turn down an unfamiliar street and miss the accident on their usual route; they move from one side of the street to the other and miss being run over; they linger over coffee and miss their commuter train, which crashes. Most of these people received no specific warnings other than a sudden conviction they should be in some other place.

The certainty is not always strong enough to push people into action; Rhine found nearly 15 percent of waking premonitions did not carry enough certainty to make people change their behavior. But the certainty usually was strong enough to catch their attention.

3. *How did I know that? Confusion.* Along with all the certainty a premonition brings, it also evokes in many people a sense of bewilderment and confusion. When people find themselves suddenly sure of something they know they shouldn't be sure about, they feel confused. Many people argue against themselves, scold themselves for being irrational, and question themselves closely. According to published anecdotes, most people remain puzzled about their irrational certainty or dismiss it entirely until some future event confirms their earlier feeling. Roger was quick to dismiss his initial warning. "I immediately crossed that [warn-

ing] off. I'd been in this plane several times and she wasn't a reckless pilot. I thought, *Oh, I'm just being paranoid. There's no reason for this.*"

Once the connecting event takes place, a new sort of confusion, called *cognitive dissonance*, sets in as people try to make sense of their experience. While a few people respond to the connecting event with relief ("Oh, so that is why I was so upset. I was just reacting to the future"), most are not so happy. The future event may help them make rational sense of their earlier misgivings, but only if they believe time can move backward. Most people find this solution worse than their original problem, however, which brings them a new level of confusion.

The concept of cognitive dissonance was first described by psychologist Dr. Leon Festinger as a psychological distress we feel when our behavior contradicts our beliefs about ourselves. For instance, I have worked with family caregivers for many years who often believe that a loving caregiver never feels tired, frustrated, or angry. When they inevitably do get tired, frustrated, and angry, because caregiving is incredibly hard work, they experience cognitive dissonance. Their actual emotions contradict what they believe they should be feeling. People resolve cognitive dissonance by either changing their actions to fit their beliefs or, in the example of caregivers, changing their beliefs to honor their experience.

With premonitions the connecting event challenges many people's long-held assumption that time can move only forward and never backward. Their personal experience directly contradicts what they know and believe about the flow of time, and they experience cognitive dissonance. People who already believe premonitions are possible don't often have this cognitive dissonance, but they can still have a momentary twinge of confusion when an initial moment feels odd, out of joint, or moving in the wrong direction.

4. *Vague and fleeting.* The initial moment of a premonition can feel sudden and sure, even important, but the specific details often remain maddeningly vague. We may dream of vivid and detailed images of an event

but we don't know when, or where, or how the event will take place (first form). Or we might notice an intense physical tension building up inside us until something happens and we see the connection between the event and our feeling, without ever having specific details to help us identify the event beforehand (second form). Lastly (third form), we can have a sudden understanding of the future as a whole and completed event, without any details.

You might think all this lack of detail would make people hesitate to call their experience a premonition, but just the opposite happens. Despite their shocking lack of details—maybe even *because* of their lack of details—premonitions feel important and emotionally compelling.

The first form—visual images without locating details—happens with dreams and visions. Dreamers find images from the center of the connecting event's action, but not from any action leading up to it. Dreamers feel immersed in the event without finding enough information to understand its context. The dreams often leave dreamers feeling overwhelmed and bewildered when they wake up. The images are striking in their vividness, but they do not carry the kind of detail that would let the dreamer predict when and where the connecting event will happen. The dreams may show fire, buildings collapsing, people crying out in pain, but no street signs or maps or dates to tell the dreamer what town or what year. Dreamers wake feeling like they have lived through a terrible tragedy, but they don't know when, where, or if the tragedy will occur.

One of the more famous examples of this form is Barker's study of the 1966 mining disaster in Aberfan, Wales, mentioned earlier.[13] Barker included descriptions of thirty-five dreams and visions that contained vivid, emotionally intense, and terrifying images. One person dreamed of screaming children buried by an avalanche of coal. Another dreamed of children in Welsh National costumes going to heaven. One person woke with the feeling of being smothered in "deep blackness."

These images were vivid and terrible to the dreamers, even before an avalanche of coal debris buried a school. Some dreamers woke up crying, and all were disturbed enough by these images to tell a spouse, friend, or family member and wonder about what the dream or vision might mean. At the same time, their perspectives were so terrifyingly close they could not see the larger picture of where or when this accident might happen. No dream or vision gave enough details to pinpoint what, exactly, was going to happen. No dream pointed to that specific school or that particular day. The dreams' images clearly connected to the mining accident, but just as clearly could not have predicted the tragedy. As one researcher later noted, "No one precognition would have given sufficient information to the percipient to locate and potentially warn people of the forthcoming tragedy. Taken collectively, however, all the basic details were, in fact, present."[14]

Sometimes a premonition is nothing more than a rising sense of anxiety, a need for caution, or an internal warning with no images or details about the trouble ahead. Along with the soft buzzing sensation, Roger heard a warning that was so clear it seemed almost like a voice. "It wasn't a voice but it was a verbal thought saying, *Don't do this. Something's going to happen.*" This is the second form of vagueness, and it can be frustrating, as those who experience it struggle to understand their rising dread from within the context of their daily lives. Often the connecting event brings some understanding to their earlier feeling; "I *knew* that was going to happen!" is a common exclamation, even if they could not have predicted it a few short hours earlier. They may not have known this exact thing would happen, but once it does, they can feel it connected back to their earlier discomfort.

The third form of vagueness is more cognitive. People become aware of a whole event without any images or details. They just know a future event as if it already exists as a whole somewhere. They know the event will happen and maybe even know who will be involved, but they don't know when it will happen or how they will transition from this present moment to that particular future. When I think about my first year of high school, for example, I remember the year as a whole, my overall impression of the entire year. I know I can remember specific events in greater detail, but more often I think about that year as a whole. My memory carries a great deal of certainty even without offering many specific details. This may be why premonitions can bring such certainty even in the fog of incomplete details. We can access the whole even without having access to the specifics.

5. *Physical markers.* Some waking premonitions bring distinct physical reactions as well. Roger's sudden warning came with a soft buzzing sensation. "It was like a little frisson, almost like a mild [very small] electric current, almost like a humming." It started in his abdomen and radiated out through his hands. A building anxiety, a sudden tension, or a rush of adrenaline can all mark a premonition. In his Aberfan study, Barker noted several premonitions that brought a physical sense of impending doom that he called "pre-disaster syndrome." He described the syndrome as a sense of vivid apprehension and a loss of concentration on other daily matters. The feeling caused a rising level of distress that was relieved only when the connecting event happened.[15] Barker didn't know what to make of such vague and distressing physical symptoms. They didn't carry the concrete images or specific details that he needed to verify accurate premonitions.

Leaving these physical markers out of the premonition discussion, however, has had an unintended consequence for all those who are looking for ways to sort through their personal experiences. Some premonitions do come on as a rush of adrenaline, a rise of anxiety, a tingling along the spine and back of the neck, or an ominous rumbling in our gut, and these physical sensations grow in urgency as the danger nears. Often no words accompany the sensations to tell us what exactly we should guard against.

6. *Personal markers.* One more set of markers to include here are the personal markers—the symbols and puns every dreamer uses that draw from our personal experience and life values. They are more than a symbolic representation of an inner fear or desire; they actually signal

us to pay attention to our dream or waking moment. They mark these moments and dream images as likely premonitions. When I was a child I used images of water to find my precognitive dreams. No matter what the dream images, if water was present in any form—a lake, a rainy landscape, a puddle, the ocean—I knew to pay attention. Water alerted me to the possibility of a premonition. It was not a perfect system. In college my dream meaning for water shifted from a marker for premonitions to a marker for important psychological events, with no premonitions attached.

I wouldn't include water as a general premonition marker because I haven't found it in the research or published anecdotes. The water images rose out of my own relationship with time and my unique life rhythms. But I can believe others have found their own unique markers for a likely premonition, just as everyone uses his or her own unique symbols in dream imagery. These markers will become more apparent with every premonition you find. They might be as dramatic as a dream's flashing neon sign or as subtle as a momentary physical stillness that settles over you in the midst of a busy day. The more aware you become of your own presence in the world, the easier it will be to find these personal markers. Even if you find your premonitions come without any additional markers, your added awareness will help you become more connected and attuned to your own movement through time.

The list of premonition markers makes a good beginning in helping us identify the initial moments of a premonition, but none of these markers are exclusive to premonitions. Each of these characteristics is a fairly common human experience in its own right. At one time or another I have experienced all of these thoughts and feelings, without any of them marking a premonition for me. I have had a sudden insight into a problem that came upon me like a flash. I feel absolutely certain about many things, most of which are not connected in any way to a premonition. I have felt a tingling, shivery feeling along my neck and arms when powerful music has moved me. At times I have felt confused by conflicting beliefs and ideas in my work and with my family. I have had intuitive hunches that felt like gut instincts. I have even felt completely sure of a gut feeling that helped me predict a future event without ever thinking of it as a premonition.

A slow-rising anxiety may mark a premonition, but it can also appear with no premonition attached; just another common anxiety of daily life. Likewise, intuitive leaps into the future can mark a premonition, but many people have a flash of intuition without it connecting to a pre-monition. Most people have an occasional nightmare without it connect-ing to a future event, so how do we learn when to cancel our plans and when to help ourselves relax because it was only a dream? Premonitions also overlap with other forms of psi, particularly telepathy and clairvoy-ance, leading some to question if they are the same phenomenon.

But when all of these characteristics come together and point to my future rather than my present or past, then I might wonder if I am having a premonition. The possibility of a premonition becomes more likely.

You might think I am being rather cavalier by advising you to have more premonitions, as if you have some control over when a premoni-tion will appear in your life. The fact is, premonitions are much more common in daily life than we have been led to believe and much more readily accessible to those who are willing to keep an eye out for them.

CHAPTER 2

Exploring Ordinary Premonitions on Your Own

The Challenge of Intense Premonitions

Evelyn, a quick-witted, energetic young woman who runs a daycare out of her home, experienced a wave of premonitions when she was just sixteen years old. One of those premonitions may even have saved her life. Evelyn's best friend's sister was getting her beautician's license, and Evelyn had agreed to make the trip to the nearby town to be the hair model. As the day of their trip approached, Evelyn grew increasingly uneasy. Something was telling her to stay home. "It was a nagging, aching feeling, like somebody yelling in my ear, *You're not going! You cannot go! This is not some place you need to be!* It was strong enough that I just physically couldn't go. I would have had a hard time crawling to the car."

Evelyn canceled at the last minute. She knew she was letting her friends down and disappointing her mother, but she couldn't make herself get in the car. Her friends invited their grandmother instead. On their way back home, their car spun off the road and overturned. Her friends' grandmother, the woman who had taken Evelyn's place and was sitting in the same seat Evelyn would have sat in, was critically injured and died a few hours later.

Evelyn was devastated and filled with guilt at the thought that maybe she was the one who should have been killed, not her friends' grandmother. It was not luck that kept her safe, but a warning she didn't understand, and one she was sure her friends' grandmother had not received. Talking about this accident nearly twenty years later, Evelyn still wrestles with the question of why she received a warning and her friends did not. Her memory of that day is filled with loss, her friends' grief, and her sense of guilt at surviving.

So many premonition stories we hear or read about contain these same incredibly intense elements. Premonitions of imminent danger have captured our imagination for centuries. The warnings are abrupt and intrusive or startle us awake with terrifying images. They warn us our safety is threatened, and they push, nag, and badger us to change our plans. The connecting events change our lives, whether or not we were able to avoid them. The connecting events make us aware of our mortality, the fragility of human life. Our natural response—shock, disbelief, astonishment, grief, and guilt—can twist around the warning we have received until the premonition itself appears to be the source of our suffering.

Premonitions of events that affect the larger community, such as assassinations, fires, floods, or acts of war, can throw us even further off our emotional balance. When we watch a personal dream connect to a public tragedy, we often feel deeply connected to that tragedy, regardless of our physical or geographical distance from it.

When the line between a subjective experience and the objective world moves so suddenly, some people have trouble sorting out their responsibilities. People may feel personally responsible for events that lie far beyond their control. What they once considered a private experience—their imagination or a dream—suddenly connects to an event that threatens the lives of people they have never met, and sometimes they feel culpable, as if the event was a direct consequence of their imagining it. Some feel guilty they could not stop the tragedies they foresaw or guilty for not warning the people they never met. Some have lashed out at their premonition because it didn't help or didn't help enough. The firm line our culture draws between what is a subjective experience and what belongs to the objective world suddenly shifts and we are left scrambling.

The Promise of Small Premonitions

Small premonitions, on the other hand, connect to future events that don't hold much significance in themselves, like a song we later hear on the radio or a small bunch of wilted lilacs held behind a friend's back or the color of an unusual coat someone wears on the subway. These small premonitions have a much smaller emotional impact on us as well. Even if I wake up with a particular song running through my head that later plays on my way to work, I know the song poses no threat.

Small premonitions give us a safe way to explore the occasional twists through time. This absence of danger is what makes the smaller premonitions so manageable. We can build familiarity with them without fear or regret, without the added torment of watching a terrible event come true. They give us the emotional room we need to handle the shock of seeing a future moment ahead of schedule. We can examine them up close and wonder at their improbability. With small premonitions we can learn how to keep our emotional balance in the face of the unknown, just as we accept the unknown quality of our dreams each night.

The same year Evelyn backed out of her road trip, she had another dream. In this second dream she came across a friend who was clutching a grocery sack in their high school's empty hallway. When Evelyn asked what she was doing, her friend replied, "I have friends in my sack." Evelyn woke feeling slightly disturbed by the idea that people could be stuffed into a sack, but she didn't feel frightened by the dream. That morning she arrived at school late and ran into her same friend in the empty hall. Her friend was carrying a grocery sack. Evelyn felt a rising dread and panic, and she ran up to her friend and blurted out, "What's in the bag? Got any friends in there?" The other girl showed Evelyn the bag, half-filled with candy she was planning to hand out. That day her friend was the most popular kid in school and Evelyn thought, *Wow, I guess you really do have friends in there.*

Evelyn's dream of friends in a bag challenged her belief about time without adding the fears and grief of a life-threatening situation. She had the emotional room to think about what having a premonition might mean. As she recounted this story, she easily explored how many other times she dreamed of that particular friend (none), other times her friend brought bags of candy to school (none), and how the connecting event was very much like but not identical to her dream. She didn't have to contend with an added fear or guilt or grief or confusion, which left her more emotional freedom to satisfy her curiosity. Rather than running away, she ran up to her friend to see if the bag was connected to her dream. She recognized her feeling came from her fear of premonitions and not from any fear of candy or hallways or being late to class.

In one sense these small premonitions are much less thrilling than the intense ones. But these smaller premonitions are also much more common than the intense ones, in much the same way ordinary days are much more common in most lives than days filled with tragedy. In any given life the small premonitions easily outnumber the occasional warnings of personal danger. Even the images of our regular dreams periodically come from our immediate future rather than from our immediate past.[16]

We aren't consciously aware of the small waking premonitions precisely because they are so small. A small premonition's initial moment can flicker past without attracting our attention and connect to a daily event that has no particular meaning, and we don't notice either one. We miss the initial moment and overlook the event as just another moment in our daily life.

I think these small moments can feel life-changing in their own way, without the added fireworks of high drama. No matter how routine their connecting events may seem, when we catch sight of time looping backward we still come right up to the edge of our known universe. All it takes is one moment twisting back on itself to bring us face-to-face with the unknown, even as we feel the certainty of our direct experience. Even a small premonition can bring a gut-wrenching recognition of how much we still do not understand about human consciousness or our place in time. We don't have to look any further than our evolving understanding of our nightly dreams.

Not too long ago we could divide the world into dreamers and people who never dream. People who didn't remember their dreams typically thought they simply didn't dream; no memory of a dream meant no dream happened. In the past forty years or so, we have learned all people dream several times each night, regardless of whether or not the dreams are remembered. The most recent research shows that the act of dreaming helps us remember and integrate new information from our waking day. Dreams have an integrated and functional role in our waking lives above and beyond the individual meanings they hold for each of us.

Our recognition of premonitions may take this same path. Right now we could divide the world between people who have premonitions and those who don't, but that distinction is fading with each new experiment. Research is finding premonitions at work in the way we learn new information, the way our reflexes respond to unexpected news, and even in the way we perceive the world.[17] Slowly the research is edging premonitions (and telepathy and clairvoyance) out of the supernatural realm and into a more natural—although still uncommon—human experience.

Premonition as a Skill

Taken as a whole, the experiments are painting a new picture of psi as something very much like an ability. Psi events may in fact be psi *skills*, something anyone can learn given enough attention and practice.[18] As with any ability—athletic, artistic, musical, mechanical—some people have more natural talent than others. And like any skill, most people can improve no matter what level of skill they begin with.

The talent for psi comes in part from our personality and in part from our personal beliefs. Volunteers who show natural talent on psi tests are more likely to have energetic and outgoing personalities. They pay more attention to their intuitive, gut instincts, and they spend less time thinking analytically through the test problems. High-scoring psi volunteers are more likely to be aware of their emotions on any given day. Perhaps most importantly, high-scoring psi volunteers believe psi is possible even before they begin the test. They are open to the possibility of psi. As a result they tend to be much more relaxed during the testing process than those volunteers who score lower.[19] Many people who do well on psi tests also practice some form of meditation or self-relaxation. Not every successful volunteer has all of these qualities, but when looking over large numbers of subjects and test scores, the people with these qualities tended to do better on the tests.[20]

As with any talent, psi skills improve with practice. When researchers looked at all the precognition experiments performed over the past century, they found four common elements in the most successful experiments: (1) the volunteers were relaxed enough to stretch themselves and try their best; (2) the researchers believed the volunteers could succeed; (3) the researchers encouraged the volunteers, making it safe for them to take a risk; and (4) the researchers gave the volunteers immediate feedback on their results. Some of the highest scores on psi tests come from research that included all four of these elements. Conversely, the studies in which none of these conditions were met—when skeptics tested people who also doubted psi existed, and then gave them no encouragement and provided no feedback—those experiments showed no evidence of psi at all.

These results may seem obvious, even anticlimactic. Athletes, performers, and anyone who has had to step forward and put their abilities on the line can understand the simple truth of these conditions. Positive encouragement works better than doubt and punishment. Immediate feedback helps people learn specific skills more quickly. A positive attitude helps calm nerves and keeps volunteers, athletes, and performers relaxed and willing to take a risk. The only new idea here is that psi testing, at least under experimental conditions, follows this same pattern. Psi behaves more like a skill, at least under certain testing conditions.

How to Find a Premonition

Finding premonitions is very much like finding dreams. Every book on dream interpretation includes a section on the best ways to consciously hold on to dream images because the authors know dream interpretation can start only when we remember our dreams. The following four premonition techniques, like dream recall, can help you find the premonitions that already exist by helping you become more aware of what already is happening. The techniques may not help you have more premonitions but can help you notice more of the premonitions you already have. By paying closer attention to your dreams, your imagination, and even your present moment, you can find these smaller premonitions bubbling merrily away, hinting at tomorrow's commute, a new job assignment, news from distant friends, faces in the crowd, and conversations you overhear at lunch. They are the smaller ripples of daily living, another color you can appreciate in the palette of your day.

....

FINDING PREMONITIONS
1. Meditation
2. Dreams
3. Imagination
4. Mindfulness

....

These four techniques can help you look more closely at your daily experience and become more aware of your waking moments. They may not have been designed specifically to find premonitions, but each one can help you become more aware of the premonitions in your life.

Meditation, for instance, entered the West as a spiritual practice and has become a common Western medical technique trusted by the medical profession for its health benefits. Consistent practice can lower blood pressure, calm anxiety, and help lift depression. The fact that it also increases our awareness of premonitions has long been considered an unintended side effect.

Most importantly, these four techniques can help you flex your psi muscles in a safe environment. Because their connecting events usually are too small to carry an emotional charge, you will have room to wonder over the beauty and mystery of time (occasionally) looping backward.

1. Meditation. In the past fifty years the Eastern philosophies of Buddhism and Hinduism have introduced millions of people in the West to the benefits and healing powers of meditation. Many people who consistently practice meditation have also become more aware of the subtle, delicate movements of time through their lives. In fact, meditation teachers often warn their students against getting caught up in psi events, as they see these events as another form of attachment to time and the illusory world.

Meditation opens our awareness to psi by helping us slow down the continuous chatter inside our heads. Most of us move through daily life filled with thoughts, ideas, memories, and feelings. We put our bodies on automatic while showering and dressing, driving, sorting through the business of the day, while we ramble—blissfully or fretfully—through an internal wilderness. We make plans for the future, consider ideas for work, get lost in physical sensations, react to other people and the world around us, ruminate on past conversations and what we should have said, then work our way back to what we want to do next, not to mention our daily concerns of money, work, home, relationships, and health. With all this internal chatter we easily lose track of the present moment.

A simple meditation practice can help you take a step back from all the internal chatter and let you focus instead on one single present moment. By doing nothing more than focusing on the present moment, you can clear a mental space of breath, peace, and clarity. Blood pressure falls. Breathing deepens. Muscles relax. And your mind slows, quiets, and clears.

The important part of meditation is not so much what you focus on, but your decision to focus solely on that one thing. Settle yourself into a comfortable position and pick a word that doesn't remind you of work or other obligations. You won't relax by meditating on a word like "office" or "testing." In fact, you don't even need a word. A meditation practice can be as simple as counting breaths. Breathe in to the count of four; breathe out to the count of four. When your mind wanders back into its familiar chatter, gently bring it back to the one thought over and over. That's all there is to it. That is meditation, the practice of focusing your attention on one present moment.

At first you might feel uncomfortable. You may notice new itches and muscle twitches. Scratch what you need to and return your focus to your one thought. As your mind quiets down you will notice a clearing of calmness amidst your usual chatter, like a small clearing in a forest. Stay with the quiet and let your thoughts and emotions drift through.

That mental clearing is where premonitions are most likely to show up. Over time you will begin to recognize the thoughts that pass through your mind. You will see which thoughts run along your familiar tracks and which thoughts arrive newly formed, unconnected to any others. And like any good practice you will carry this skill back into your daily life without any further effort. You will become more aware of thoughts that don't connect to your usual flow of ideas.

My friend Julie has practiced meditation for years as part of her spiritual life. She has found it helps her to find a calm center even in stressful situations. She learned to watch her thoughts and feelings drift through her clearing with a calm detachment, and it wasn't too long before she noticed a few thoughts, every now and then, connected to her future. Her practice also carried through to her daily life, and she has become adept at noting the difference between her habitual thoughts and the unfamiliar traces of premonitions. She tells me her premonitions have "become so much a part of my life, that they're almost not unusual anymore. It feels like something I just breathe with." Her premonitions most often come as gentle nudges in the midst of her day, helping her with the myriad choices each working day includes. Her premonitions give her a sense of being held through both hard times and good.

2. Dreams. Like premonitions, dreams come from an unknown source for reasons we do not yet understand. Unlike premonitions, dreams are a familiar and accepted part of human experience, even if we do still debate their importance and their meaning for waking life. Researchers have long known dreams incorporate details we have come across in the previous day or two, which they have dubbed *day residue*. What is less well understood is how our dreams are able to draw some images from our near future as well. The day residue becomes future residue.

As early as 1927, author John Dunne noted many of his dreams used trivial details that later showed up in his waking life—details he would not have noticed if he hadn't been watching closely.[21] The details were so small and the events so ordinary he doubted he would ever have noticed them if he hadn't been taking careful notes.

A few researchers have duplicated Dunne's efforts, including author and theologian Dr. Jeremy Taylor. For years Taylor wrote down every dream he remembered each morning, and he noticed his dreams often included images of small details he then ran across later in his waking life.[22]

The dream technique is fairly straightforward. Write down as many details of your nightly dreams as you can and then monitor your daily life for connections that might show precognition. This technique relies on two efforts from you: your ability and willingness to remember and record your dreams, which is no small feat; and your willingness to scan your daily life for the small connections that exist.

Remembering dreams takes some practice. Put a notebook and pen beside your bed so you can write first thing when you wake up. Some people use recorders and write it down later. If you wake up with no dreams in mind, then lie still for a few minutes, relax, and maybe some lingering images will come floating back to you. Write down any thoughts or fragments you have. Be sure to include the date on each entry.

The second step of paying attention during the day is much easier than it sounds. You don't need to stay on high alert or scan your environment for signs of premonitions. You can even forget about your dreams during the day. By writing down your dream images in the morning you have moved those images closer to your conscious mind, however briefly. If you do come across an image from an earlier dream, you will be more likely to recognize it because you wrote it down. Some people record their dreams on one page and any connections they find, past or future, on its facing page.

The trick is to become aware of these connections by whatever method works for you. You might want to review your dream notes before you go to sleep and compare your previous entries to the day you just had. You might find some interesting connections between your daily life and an earlier dream fragment.

This type of dream study is more time-intensive than meditation, depending on how many dreams and how many details of each dream you remember. But dream recall can feel safer than meditation for many people. With meditation we change the quality of our waking, conscious awareness, which helps us see connections we had previously hurried past. Dream recall keeps the line between our waking and sleeping awareness crystal bright and distinct. We may consciously recognize images from an earlier dream but that recognition won't change the quality of our waking awareness.

Physicist Dale Graff took this technique one step further in his own personal experiment. He cultivated his own precognitive dreams by setting an intention, meaning he reminded himself that he wanted to remember his dreams right before bed each night. As he drifted off to sleep, he reminded himself that he wanted to dream of pictures that would appear in one of his three local newspapers within the next five days. By the end of his experiment, he had honed his skill until he could dream of images that would appear on the front pages of these papers within the next three days. He writes, "Psi/precognitive dreams can be experienced by setting a firm intention to experience and recall them, and to not recall any other type of dream that night."[23]

3. Imagination. If mediation is clearing a mental space and passively observing the thoughts that wander through, then imagining your future is more like creating a new story within your own made-up environment. Using and stretching your imagination gives you a more active approach to premonitions. You can imagine yourself in your own personal future and then pay attention to all the little details your imagination automatically adds to each scene.

Using your imagination to find precognitive images of the future works because so much of imagining is unconscious. I can imagine myself at my writer's group next month. I can guess who will be there based on who usually shows up, and I know the topic of discussion and guest speaker from the announcement. But when I imagine myself at the meeting I am also imagining the clothes everyone wears, the faces of people I haven't yet met, the specific questions people may ask, and the exact time the speaker finishes. All these details come not from what I know but from what I imagine might happen. Some details come from my own plans, and some from my memory of past meetings. But some details I imagine may come from nothing I can discover and nothing I have learned. Some details may connect to the meeting in ways I didn't consciously direct, in ways that look more like a premonition.

I like this technique because I can imagine my immediate future in its most benign, ordinary form, filled with all the trivial details that make daily life so rich and exasperating. I can imagine trips to places I hope to visit some day, but I don't have to imagine anything more complicated than my next trip to the grocery store. I don't have to write down every dream or learn how to quiet my inner chatter. I can simply grab my inner chattering voice (metaphorically speaking) and face it toward my next day or my next trip.

My friend Charlie, who works as a county police officer, uses this method for his work. Before his shift he will go out on his back porch with a cup of coffee, relax in the silence for a few minutes, and then let himself imagine that night's work. He imagines his familiar moments, like entering the station, greeting colleagues, checking his equipment, even the nightly report. But while he is letting himself anticipate the evening work, he keeps one eye on his adrenaline. He doesn't look for detailed images; he imagines the evening and pays attention to how his body responds to his imagining, trusting that his nervous system can predict the relative danger he will face later on. If his system remains calm and relaxed, then he knows the evening will be quiet. If he feels his adrenaline kick in with its familiar rising anxiety, he knows the night will be busy and possibly dangerous. He prepares himself mentally for a dangerous shift. He knows he always has to be prepared, but his rising adrenaline gives him an extra warning to stay alert. He knows on these nights to follow his internal warnings without hesitation. He doesn't stop to ponder his decision but moves almost automatically, trusting his inner warning system to protect him and keep him one step ahead of the people he's chasing.

Like the other techniques, this one still only works if you use it. Even if you find no premonition, when you imagine your personal future you are exercising a set of muscles most people overlook, the muscles of imagination and memory that loop through time so effortlessly and anchor us into this expansive present. You will learn to trust and accept those moments when your subjective experience and objective reality seem impossibly entangled.

4. Mindfulness. Mindfulness is another method that can help us focus and direct the natural flow of our conscious thoughts. Mindfulness becomes our willingness to be fully present and consciously engaged with each moment in our lives. The term mindfulness was first popularized by Thich Nhat Hanh, a Vietnamese Buddhist and teacher, who described it as "keeping one's consciousness alive to the present reality."[24]

Thich Nhat Hanh explained that we spend much of our lives in a habitual mode of thought and action. We stop paying attention to our immediate surroundings and instead let our minds wander into day-dreams, plans, and our inner chattering monologue. When we leave our daily tasks to habit, we lose the beauty and expanse of our present moment. With mindfulness we return our attention to our present moment again and again, and fully experience the small moments of daily life. In one beautiful passage Thich Nhat Hanh described the qualitative difference between washing dishes in order to clean the kitchen and washing dishes in order to wash the dishes. If we wash the dishes in order to clean the kitchen, we fly through the work without noticing the dishes, the water, or our hands. We are intent on the larger picture of a clean kitchen, and we miss the importance of each moment within the task. Before we know it the kitchen is clean and we are on to the next task. But if we can focus our attention into the present act of washing each dish, then the moment opens up, becomes more spacious, serene, even beautiful. We become aware of our hands and the feel of water running over them and the beauty of each dish. We become aware of our belonging to this moment, this home, this life.

In these moments we become more aware of our thoughts and emotions. Instead of brushing away an occasional passing, unexpected feeling, we acknowledge it and settle into it. All we need is a willingness to pause and make note of the connections. My friend Susan did just this in the grocery store the day before Thanksgiving. She noticed her own tiny hesitation when she passed the bakery department and, rather than pushing on past it she paused, and observed what came next. She was rewarded when her hesitation stretched out into a new thought that she needed more pies.

These techniques can help you recognize premonitions in the initial moments. They will not give you more premonitions as much as they will help you notice the ones you already have. Call it practice in recognizing and accepting the small premonitions that flit through daily life. Call it practice in opening your eyes at the very edge of human knowledge (Western knowledge) of the universe. Just looking won't put you in any danger, but looking does take a certain amount of courage, especially when looking might reveal an unknown that challenges our Western assumptions.

If you decide to try one of these techniques, I assure you what you find will be worth the effort. You will learn to recognize passing thoughts that might have wandered in from your future. You will gain trust in your own ability to recognize these moments, as well as your ability to question your experience. You will see that you can emotionally handle something as culturally improbable as a glimpse of your own future. With enough trust you might find yourself building a kind of working relationship with your premonitions.

And if by some chance you do find a premonition of some dangerous event, you will have a solid foundation on which to build your response. You won't be paralyzed by the first question of whether or not it is possible. You will know it is possible. You will have had practice in watching, trusting, and questioning your present moment. You will have a new skill set, a new habit of paying close attention to your personal experience, and this skill will help you move to the next question of what you can do about it.

If you don't want to see the future anymore, if you find yourself too much in the company of moments that upset you, then all you have to do is stop paying attention. Finding premonitions takes a certain amount of work and commitment. These techniques all require your careful attention, which means you remain in control of what you notice. If you don't consciously imagine your immediate future, if you stop writing down your dreams, give up the meditation, and turn your attention back to the rush of daily life, then you will not be bothered by the premonitions that live in these spaces. The premonitions will fade once more into the background, like so much white noise.

Before you decide these ordinary premonitions are too far outside the comfort zone of your daily life, however, I want to revisit how much we all already know about managing unknown forces. We already know how to live comfortably with our nightly dreams, even though we don't fully comprehend them. We don't worry about dreams taking over our waking life because we have had plenty of practice waking up and getting on with things. We have an equally complicated relationship with intuition. We can ignore or pursue our intuitive insights, dismiss them, or rely on their directions, but we never forget that we are the ones doing the intuiting. For as many spectacular discoveries science has made about our brains in the past twenty years, we have not yet discovered the origin or the nature of human thoughts and emotions. We have no fear of our thoughts and feelings because they are familiar, common, and accepted by the culture. I can imagine a time when we will build a similar relationship with our premonitions, using them in our daily lives, and trusting and questioning them according to our needs and our values.

CHAPTER 3

What Else Could It Be?
Questions You Can Ask Yourself

Chapter 1 gave us a good start in identifying and naming an unusual experience as a premonition. The initial moment of a premonition often has a sudden thought or feeling about the future. It carries a level of certainty that surprises and puzzles the experiencer. It often feels very clear, even when its locating details are vague. Some premonitions come with a rush of adrenaline or a slow-building anxiety. Chapter 2 built on our ability to recognize premonitions by becoming more aware of our present moments. Now we need a method for sorting out premonitions from all the other ways we imagine, plan, and think about the future.

Phillip prepared for a possible airplane accident by using two separate mental checklists, not just one. First he looked for the premonition markers he had learned to trust. Was the moment a sudden and clear thought? Did it feel more certain than it should? Did it point to a future event? Did it bring a physical sensation, such as rising anxiety?

Second and just as importantly, he looked for all the other reasons he might be feeling so apprehensive at that moment. Even when he recognized the markers for a premonition, he knew he might not be having a premonition at all. He took a moment to compare his occasional but familiar fear of flying to his new apprehension, questioning every part of his experience. He wasn't about to let himself be injured in an accident he could foresee, but he also wasn't willing to miss his flight because of an instance of momentary anxiety.

Phillip had the right idea. We all need more than just an open acceptance for every premonition-like moment we recognize. We also need a critical eye, a willingness to question each moment, to keep it firmly rooted in our daily life. A slow-rising anxiety may mark a premonition, but it can also appear with no premonition attached, just another common anxiety of daily life. Likewise, intuitive leaps into the future can mark a premonition, but many people have a flash of intuition without it connecting to a premonition. How do we tell the difference between a new insight or prediction, and a premonition? Hindsight is the only way we can compare a connecting event back to its initial moment, but hindsight by itself cannot create a premonition. Sometimes we look backward from personal disaster and see all the tiny decisions that inevitably led to it and wonder how we ever missed their greater significance. Most people have an occasional nightmare without it connecting to a future event, so how do we learn when to cancel our plans, and when to help ourselves relax because it was only a dream?

If we never learn to rule out the more common ways of predicting our futures, then every anxious moment may look like a premonition and every bad dream a warning of death, which can make daily life miserable. If I consider my every present moment as a portent of some future moment, I will lose my ability to enjoy my present. I will focus so much energy into reading the hidden warnings I will forget how to relax and let the future take care of itself. I have to balance my belief in premonitions in general with my common sense, my natural (cultural) skepticism.

If I am going to trust a warning I cannot explain by other means, then I want to be sure I have looked at all other explanations. I don't want to prepare for a future event only to find I was reacting to a common anxiety. I need to learn how to rule out the more common ways in which I predict and imagine my future, and that will make it easier to trust those moments I can't otherwise explain.

OTHER EXPLANATIONS

1. Premonition or Chance

2. Premonition or Error

3. Premonition or Fraud

4. Premonition or Anxiety

5. Premonition or Intuition

6. Premonition or Nightmare

7. Premonition or Other Psi

8. Premonition or Hindsight

Recognizing the initial moment of a premonition and then sorting out the other possible explanations—maintaining both our openness and our common sense—takes patience and practice. We can develop a second checklist to go with the list of premonition markers. This second list holds some of the more common alternative explanations we might confuse with premonitions, like anxiety, intuition, or hindsight. Science can help us here. The scientific method requires the researcher to be aware of the human errors we all face when questioning an experience.

Frequently Asked Science Questions

Every scientific study runs the risk of mistaking wishful thinking for reality. In published articles, researchers must explain how they avoided chance, error, and fraud. Researchers know they may inadvertently mistake a random chance occurrence for something more significant. They know they might make errors in their calculations, their methods, or how they interpret their data. They also have to show how they have protected their work from fraud. They have to show they weren't lying or making it all up for their own ambition.

It's no surprise, then, that researchers look at any personal anecdote of a premonition with skepticism. They know anyone can make a mistake, especially when reporting a vivid personal experience. Astronomer and popular author Dr. Carl Sagan put it best when he explained why he rejects the many stories told to him over the years of UFO sightings and alien abductions. "People make mistakes. People play practical jokes. People stretch the truth for money or attention or fame. People occasionally misunderstand what they're seeing. People sometimes even see things that aren't there."[25]

Before moving into the more common ways we think about the future, we can begin with the three problems scientists face in every research article they publish: the problems of chance, error, or fraud. These three basic questions can help us begin to sort premonitions from all the other ways we draw ourselves (or push our way) into the future.

1. Premonition or chance. Ruling out chance in everyday life is not easy. Most of us are terrible at figuring the odds of any event happening to us.[26] We know random events happen every day, but we also know our lives have meaning and purpose. Some events arrive with such rich meanings for our personal lives we can't believe they occurred through chance. We even joke about the connection between chance and intentional events, as when we say if you want it to rain then plan a picnic, as if the weather responds to our plans. Sometimes thoughts and events coincide so clearly that the idea they could have occurred through chance doesn't seem right, but sometimes chance is exactly what is happening.

Some people use the idea of chance to discount all psi events. They point out that with six billion people dreaming every day, any connection between a dream and an actual event must be random. At some point a dream of a plane crash and an actual plane crash will naturally coincide, and they refuse to believe anything but chance was involved. I do think dreams of trouble need to be viewed in context, but from such a global perspective we lose more than just premonitions—we lose any ability to discover patterns of cause and effect. For instance, among six-plus billion people in the world someone is getting sick every single minute, but that doesn't make all illness a random occurrence. Medicine studies the causes of illness and the effects of their treatments on the assumption that something—a germ or gene or environmental pollutant or a drug—came first to cause the illness. If we decide that everything is random, then cause and effect become meaningless.

2. Premonition or error. The elimination of human error is just as difficult to transfer from the laboratory to daily life. Human beings have an unparalleled ability to find patterns among seemingly random events. Our memories and imaginations are elastic, creative, and absolutely capable of finding patterns in random events. Our eyes can be fooled even more easily. When I go to the movies I am shown a frantic succession of pictures, but what I see is fluid motion. With the creative powers of mind I can see the constellation Orion among the stars and even the face of my second cousin Patsy in a potato chip.

Human judgment is not much better. I have made my share of mistakes in judging almost every aspect of everyday life. I have felt insulted when no offense was meant. I have rushed to judgment when I needed to listen more carefully. I have been scared by noises in the middle of the night. I remember well the dizzying pains of first love, first crush, and first crushing disappointment when I realized the people I idolized had problems of their own. But none of my mistakes mean friendship is impossible. I have learned from my mistakes and found enormous joy in connecting with the people in my life.

Still, most of us have a tough time letting ourselves make mistakes with premonitions. A mistake about premonitions feels almost dangerous. Every mistake reinforces the skepticism of friends and family, making it that much harder for them to trust our judgment in the future. Of course, dismissing a genuine strong premonition as nonsense also carries a risk, that we might fail to protect ourselves or the people we love.

I think our fear of making mistakes partly explains why premonitions cause so much angst. Instead of holding on to our experience and testing it against what we know, we doubt our senses and reject the initial moments as not real. Then when a future event does connect back to that initial moment we feel shocked and frightened, forgetting that we refused to take the time needed to get to know it in the first place.

3. Premonition or fraud. The easiest question to answer is the question of whether or not we are lying. I can always tell when I am lying to someone else, even if I'm not willing to admit it out loud. Most of us know how to exaggerate our claims, bend the rules, or pretend to like unwanted gifts out of politeness.

The question of whether I am fooling myself is a little more difficult to answer. It reminds me of playing the game of Solitaire when I was much, much younger, when the game was played with a standard deck of playing cards instead of on the computer. I had to learn for myself the joys and hazards of cheating. I loved watching all the cards go my way, even if I had to reshuffle them a bit or move a card when I wasn't supposed to. But my victories by cheating made me lose interest in the game. Winning didn't mean anything when I cheated. I learned the only way I could enjoy winning was if I hadn't cheated first. I had to let myself lose, over and over, sometimes for weeks on end, in order to find the joy of a true win.

With premonitions we face the same temptation to nudge the facts a little bit. Some people will want to find a premonition even if they have to overlook the clues that told them what to expect. Others may want to dismiss their premonitions despite finding no other explanation for it. What matters is how well you know yourself. Do you sometimes cheat a little so you can win? Are you willing to ask the hard questions before you feel assured you are having a true premonition? Would you rather this moment be anything but a premonition? How hard will you look for an alternate answer? When will you be satisfied there is no other explanation?

These are arguably the most important questions you can ask your-self. The answer to every other question in this chapter rests on your judgment and your ability to name your experience accurately. I have been asked many times to validate someone else's premonition. Strang-ers have described their experience and then asked me if what they had was an actual premonition, and I find myself thinking about this ques-tion. I tell them why I know premonitions are possible, I help them com-pare their experience to the list of markers, and I give them this second list of other explanations. But I know I have no way to verify the truth of what they are telling me, just as I can't verify that any event or emotion in their life actually happened. They have to make up their own minds.

Questions for Daily Life

Of course, daily life isn't built like a scientific experiment. Daily life is more loose-fitting and more free, and therefore more prone to errors. We don't worry about proving gravity exists; we simply accept it and move on to more important matters. We accept a certain amount of squishi-ness in our perception, judgment, memory, and imagination because we understand ordinary time is complex enough. We are filled with thoughts, plans, emotions, ideas, memories, reactions, and connections between friends and family. Imagine if we had to prove that our likes and dislikes are consistent with our personality before making our breakfast each morning. Even scientists don't apply the scientific method to their daily life. Even so, their three basic questions can help us begin to sort premonitions from all the other ways we draw ourselves (or push our way) into the future.

Daily life is more complex than a scientific experiment. Our memories and imaginations swirl around the most ordinary of shopping decisions, blending into a delicate concoction of habit, desire, dreams, hurts, and relationships. We imagine ourselves at home with the new purchase, showing it off to friends, wondering what our parents or partners will say about it, and how it will work with our existing technology, or how long we've always wanted it. Our childhood lessons whisper in the background,

"It's too much, you can make do, why do you never get what you want?" Imagine a teenage boy and his fifty-year-old mother examining the same car. They will have different ideas about what the car should offer, what it should cost them, and what the car means to them socially. With practice and time we learn to balance our wants and limits with our dreams.

We need this same kind of practice sorting out our premonitions from all the other ways we move into our individual futures. We will make mistakes, but we can learn from those mistakes. A mistake doesn't mean we abandon the idea of premonitions, it means we keep learning. When we note which of the premonition markers are present and which are absent, we give ourselves a tool to examine our intuitive experience with openness, curiosity, and our common sense. When we consider chance, error, and fraud we give ourselves permission to make a mistake. Now we need to question whether this feeling might be connected to any of the other ways we think about the future.

4. *Premonition or anxiety.* If you have a sudden rise of anxiety or surge of adrenaline, when is it a premonition and when is it just anxiety? The answer to this question may help you settle into your seat more comfortably the next time you fly.

Most of us have moments of anxiety that don't connect to anything. Anxieties float around fears of real dangers (such as terrorist attacks, mad cow disease, or a new flu epidemic) and around daily life concerns (looking foolish, losing a contract, getting behind at work). Anxieties most often include the question "What if?" as in "What if the car runs out of gas?" "What if I left the iron on?" and "What if they don't like me at my new job?" My friend Jackie talks often about the anxieties she feels now that her children are old enough to drive. She worries about letting them take this next step into adulthood, even as she recognizes she can't stop them from growing up. Still, the world is full of dangers and she worries, "What if their friends pressure them to drink and drive?" and "What if they drive recklessly?" She worries about possible futures, imagined futures, but not specific futures that feel set in place. Her anxieties spring directly from her desire to keep her children safe and happy all of their lives.

The rising anxiety of a premonition is different. Instead of asking, "What if? What if?" a premonition anxiety feels more vivid, more focused on a particular moment, and more sure of itself. A premonition's anxiety brings a certainty that sharpens its edges. It often appears suddenly without a clear connection to an earlier moment, while ordinary anxiety tends to grow out of daily life situations.

Many people have a fear of flying, but their fear is so familiar to them they would never mistake it for a premonition. Phillip also knew he had worried about flying before, so he took some care in sorting through his usual anxiety from the anxiety of a premonition. He knew his usual anxieties about flying included "What if" questions, but this time his anxiety felt sure and focused on one specific problem with the wheel. He understood this new anxiety as different from his usual fears because it was specific, vivid, and very sure.

5. Premonition or intuition. Intuitive insights leap into our minds in a flash of brilliance. We may have been puzzling over a question or problem, when all the pieces suddenly arrange themselves into a new pattern. We are dazzled by the connections we discover and gripped by a sudden comprehension that makes sense of everything.

Most often this moment comes with relief and even triumph. People welcome intuitive insights with an "Aha!" or "Eureka!" or "So that's why such and such happened!" These intuitive insights come suddenly and feel certain and clear like premonitions, but they are anchored firmly and calmly in our past. We can look back from our new insight and find all the pieces we needed to complete our new picture.

A premonition, on the other hand, doesn't connect to our past. It feels connected solely to some unknown future. We have a flash of understanding, certainty, even anticipation, but when we look back we find nothing to connect to our insight. There is no earlier puzzle, no bits of data or environmental clues, nothing that helps make sense of the past.

Instead we find ourselves looking forward with the same clarity and certainty of a new insight that has no foundation. We have a sudden comprehension of something that has not yet happened. Instead of feeling relief and triumph, we feel confused and bewildered. Even after the connecting event has occurred, many people search for clues they may have overlooked and for puzzles they may have been unconsciously worrying about, but find nothing.

Another type of intuition, intuitive warnings, can also look and feel very much like a warning premonition. We feel a sense of danger and of something bad approaching, and we swing into action. Or we are suddenly shaken into a more watchful state of mind, but we don't consciously know why. Often we have very little time to consider all the possible reasons for our unease, and we act almost automatically.

In *The Gift of Fear*, Gavin de Becker explained how easily we pick up these subtle cues in our environment without being consciously aware of them and how much we rely on these subtle cues to keep ourselves safe. He praised intuition by saying that "the human brain is never more efficient or invested than when its host is at risk. Then, intuition is catapulted to another level entirely, a height at which it can accurately be called graceful, even miraculous."[27]

I experienced this type of intuitive warning a few years ago. I was buying gas early one morning when I began watching an impish, tow-headed four-year-old boy in the front seat of a dark green minivan parked beneath the gas station's sign near the street. I don't usually watch anyone when I'm filling up, especially when it's early in the morning and I'm half-asleep, but this particular day I stared mesmerized as the little boy crawled over to the driver's seat, leaned over and made a face at his little brother in the back, and then pulled down on the gear shift. In that split second I noticed the van's motor was running. It immediately started rolling backward toward traffic. Without thinking, I raced across the lot, jumped in the driver's seat as the little boy scooted out of the way, and stepped hard on the brake. The van stopped before it reached the street.

I took a second to breathe, then turned to the little boy, who looked as shocked at my sudden appearance as I felt. He had no idea the van was moving and no idea who this strange lady was. I waited outside the van until their mother returned a few minutes later, then went back and sat in my car until my heart calmed down. I wondered how on earth I knew to watch that particular minivan on that particular morning. It seemed like a miracle. I just knew something was going to happen.

The difference between this kind of warning and a premonition is again a difference of time and hindsight. My decision to watch the little boy didn't feel certain or include some idea of the future. My mind wasn't imagining or remembering a future, I was simply observing somebody else's children with a vague, still sleepy sense of needing to pay attention.

Over the next hour I pieced together what happened. The minivan pulled up after I was out of my car, and my ears most likely took note of a running motor. When the car door slammed while the motor was still running, and no accompanying sound of a parking brake being set, I looked over and saw the little boy jumping on the front seat. I paid conscious attention because my unconscious radar had picked up the clues—a car left running and a small boy playing by the steering wheel. A premonition might have felt like a vague unease beginning well before the car turned into the gas station, causing me to scan my environment for something dangerous. Or I might have imagined a child in trouble over breakfast, but neither of these things happened. My sense of warning started after the car arrived.

6. Premonition or nightmare. The most riveting premonition stories in print include vivid precognitive dreams of accidents and personal tragedies. People wake from a frightening dream of an accident only to find the very same terrible accident happening in daily life. With the rise of premonitions in the popular media and the acceptance of the scientific evidence for premonitions—however halting and uneasy—more people may wonder if their nightmares are pointing to something more than the emotional distress of their daily lives.

Even apart from premonitions, dreams often carry powerful messages. Dreams can bring to light emotions we have kept hidden, give us new perspectives on important relationships, and help us make decisions in our lives. Dreams also can bring us images from our future. Our nightly dreams often use images we have seen in the previous two days and mix them into a new pattern. Researchers have found that dreams use images from our upcoming two days as well, like a future-day residue.[28] Our dreaming minds don't seem to care which images come from the recent past and which come from the immediate future—both sets of images remain in service to the greater dream meanings. We find them only when we catch sight of a dream image during our waking life.

Nightmares bring their own challenges. Most nightmares are not premonitions, but they come with an intensity and vividness that makes them feel true. Terrifying images may cause us to wake up feeling shaken, frightened, sickened, or disgusted. Many nightmares include images of natural disasters, explosions, acts of war, floods, and other horrific events, but they are not usually premonitions. Most often they illuminate the emotional upheavals of our lives, our intense inner worlds of fears and longings. The Reverend Dr. Jeremy Taylor, founder of the Marin Institute for Projective Dreamwork, teaches that all dreams carry within them important messages for our own healing and growth, including nightmares.[29]

Sometimes nightmarish dream images come from the dreamers' personal memories of disasters or tragedies they have suffered through earlier in their lives. But more often the images come from movie, Internet, newspaper, and television pictures we have seen in the past day or two, day residue our dreaming minds use to help us understand our strong emotions. Most of us understand these nightmares do not mean we were responsible for the actual disasters. We can understand the power of such images without feeling personally connected to the disturbing scenes, other than how our dreams are using the images.

With the idea of future day residue we may have another way to understand our precognitive dreams. If our dreaming minds can pull nightmarish images from the immediate future as easily as from the recent past, then the future images we see might have two separate meanings: the future event, which may or may not connect to our personal lives in any way, and the deeply personal meaning of our dreams, which drew upon those future images to get our attention.

Whatever the reason for nightmares, the question of how to sort the difference between a regular dream and a precognitive dream remains problematic. Psychologist Mary S. Stowell, Ph.D., interviewed precognitive dreamers who described several features they used to identify precognitive dreams.[30] They looked for whether the dream had more lifelike qualities than symbolism. Their precognitive dreams had strong emotions that carried over into their next day and often had a level of certainty that pushed them into taking some sort of action in response. Lastly, they had more trouble understanding the psychological reasons for their precognitive dreams.

Other people are not so sure. Many emotionally charged dreams carry their emotional energy into the next day, and many feel quite vivid and realistic. Dreams in general are flexible enough to both offer psychological insights and connect to future events. When dreamers in other studies were asked to predict in advance which of their dreams would eventually connect to a future event, the dreamers couldn't find the difference between psi dreams and their more general dreams. Louisa Rhine noted dream images often carry less certainty than waking premonitions, probably for this same reason. A powerful image that helps us understand our lives could lessen our certainty about its connection to a future event.

7. *Premonition or other psi.* Premonitions have so much in common with telepathy and clairvoyance that researchers and experiencers have trouble telling them apart. If I suddenly know an old friend will call, am I having a premonition of her phone call, still in the future, or am I picking up through telepathy her intention to call me? Or perhaps it is clairvoyance that connects me to the phone call.

It is easy to see how the confusion happens between the different forms of psi. The information in all of these forms appears suddenly and seems disconnected from any previous train of thought. All three bring a strong sense of conviction about an event or information that experiencers know they could not have known in any other way. With all three—telepathy, clairvoyance, and precognition—people may have a sense of cognitive dissonance as they consider whether or not they can believe they know such information.

Andrew MacKenzie included an anecdote in his book *Riddle of the Future* of a woman who dreamed of living in a particular house while she and her husband were house hunting. A few weeks later she found the exact house, now for sale, and shortly after that they moved in.[31] Did MacKenzie's dreamer have a precognitive dream of her future life in that house or a clairvoyant dream of a house already in existence that might potentially be hers? The house certainly existed at the time of her dream, which could make it a dream of clairvoyance. Her dream showed her living in that house, something which did not occur for another several months, thereby making it possible to think of it as a premonition of her future living arrangement. It's also possible she and her husband decided to buy that particular house based on her dream, in which case her dream might not be a psi event at all, but rather the catalyst for the couple's later decision. What interests me is how quickly skeptics will latch onto clairvoyance or telepathy as a way to dismiss the idea of premonitions.

In fact, there may be very little difference in how we experience these three different psi events. All three forms of psi rely on the notion that our human minds can stretch beyond the boundaries of our human skulls. They may all be different aspects of the same muscle, the same internal stretching, with their only difference resting on what they imply about the direction of time—which is a big difference.

It is this sticking point in our Western minds—that time must move in one direction only and the future must remain open and unknowable—that seems to bother us the most when it comes to premonitions. The idea of knowing a future event before it exists can challenge our worldview so deeply that some people will latch onto the idea of telepathy and clairvoyance with relief. Even people who have had premonitions will sometimes first try to explain them as telepathy or clairvoyance. After all, receiving information from the mind of another person or across space from some event that has already occurred does not require us to reconsider the nature of time or the reality of free will, or the law of cause and effect, like a premonition might.

Some people have considered the role of psychokinesis in our apparent premonitions. In this view people who have premonitions unconsciously bring about the futures they see. Literally mind influences matter. In this theory if I have a sudden thought that my phone will ring and two minutes later it does, then I have not had a premonition of the phone ringing nor have I picked up on my friend's intention to call through telepathy. Instead, I have influenced my friend to call through my expectation. My apparent premonition (or telepathy) reached out and drew my friend's attention, encouraging her to call me.

I can understand this theory when it applies to my friends making a phone call. I have a harder time accepting it when thinking of bigger future events, such as disasters and community tragedies. Admiral Angelos Tanagras, past president of the Greek Society for Psychical Research, once explained how premonitions, even of disasters, could instead be examples of mind controlling matter. Tanagras stated if a man dreams of a plane crash he might then psychically sabotage the plane, through psychokinesis, in order to make his dream come true.[32]

While Tanagras clearly found this story more comforting than the idea of a premonition, as it maintains the open and unknown future, it moves me too close to a form of magical thinking that most of us leave behind in childhood, specifically the idea that our thoughts alone can wreak havoc on the world around us. I remain convinced our thoughts do not reach out and cause the awful accidents we sometimes see in premonitions.

Dr. Dean Radin, noted parapsychologist and author of several popular books on psi research, has proposed another theory. He wonders if precognition is actually the simplest explanation for all of the psi experiences. According to Dr. Radin, I might not be picking up my friend's intention to call when I anticipate the phone ringing but might instead be bumping into my own future of receiving the call. If all psi events need confirmation, then every psi event could be my premonition of when that event is confirmed, sometime in my future.[33]

In this theory telepathy becomes our premonition of what we later find out someone else was thinking. Clairvoyance becomes our premonition of the moment we find out about an event (or person or object) that happened. Even psychokinesis can be seen as our premonition of what the future state of a physical object will be.

Dr. Radin is echoing one of the observations of John Dunne. Dunne wondered why his dream images of events often mirrored exactly the pictures he later saw in the newspaper.[34] The newspaper images were taken from the exact same angle, often showing the same faces in a crowd of people, as the images in his dreams. Once he even dreamed of a newspaper headline about a tragedy in which hundreds of people died, and found out later the number he dreamed matched the headline he saw the next day, but not the actual tragedy. Dunne wondered if premonitions about community or global events are really premonitions of our own personal futures when we find out about the events. We may be dreaming about the moment we learn about a disaster through the news media, rather than about the disaster itself.

8. Premonition or hindsight. Most people who have a premonition don't recognize it at first. They notice the initial moment as unusual but they don't recognize it as part of a premonition until its future event comes along and connects back to it. Then they look back at that initial moment and suddenly understand it was not simply anxiety or a random certainty. They shake their heads and say in amazement or frustration or fear, "I *knew* this was going to happen!"

The belated recognition of a premonition, after the connecting event, feels both certain and confusing. Many people can hardly believe the event matches so well with their earlier trepidation, and they know without a doubt they are seeing a premonition. From the point of view of others, however, this moment looks very much like simple hindsight.

The possibility of hindsight masquerading as a premonition has distressed both skeptics and experiencers alike. Hindsight occurs when we look backward from a tragedy and see the path it took, winding through our decisions until it bursts upon us. We look back and see all the tiny moments leading up to this life-changing event and we wonder how we could have missed the clues. Too often we wonder if we should have noticed or should have done something different, and our memories change subtly to fit the tragedy. When Barker started his Aberfan study after that tragic event and then asked people to remember if they had an earlier premonition about it, Barker risked confusion between the initial moment of a premonition and our natural ability to see patterns through hindsight.

It is impossible for a researcher to distinguish a premonition from our more common hindsight. In both events a person looks back at the past from the wreckage of disaster and exclaims, *I knew that was going to happen.* But we can tell the difference in our own experience. The difference between the two lies in the initial moment.

The initial moment of a premonition feels puzzling right at the beginning and stands out from all the other moments as something strange, certain, and puzzling. I may not be sure what the significance of the initial moment is, but I know something unusual is happening. When the future event arrives, it feels deeply connected to that initial moment. It completes the initial moment.

With hindsight there is no initial moment—no surprise, confusion, or sense of certainty overriding what we think we should know. Hindsight feels merely inevitable. I look back and see all the decisions I made and actions I took that led directly to this moment, but I don't find an incongruous moment of knowing more than I expected to know. The future event might now look inevitable, maybe even foreseeable now that I know better, but it doesn't connect to an earlier warning.

In my work as a grief counselor I have heard many such fears from people who look back and wonder why they didn't catch the warning signs of trouble or why they didn't fight harder to get their loved ones to the doctor or why they didn't offer their friend a ride. Hindsight and grief turns any earlier question or hesitance into a certainty that was willfully ignored. But this terrible hindsight, fueled by grief, does not make a premonition. If no earlier moment stands out, distinguished from all other moments by a sudden sense of urgency or conviction that did not make sense at the time, then there can be no premonition.

What Will You Do?

Daily life needs our intuitions, our first impressions, and our impressive ability to recognize patterns amid the chaos of ordinary time. We have an immense capacity for intuiting connections, sensing dangers, creating patterns in the midst of random noise, even ignoring contrary evidence so we can push forward with our plans. The fact that sometimes we make mistakes doesn't slow us down in any other aspect of life and should not be used as a reason to stop us from looking for premonitions. Our mistakes come from our greatest strength—our capacity to make sense of the world around us.

Beyond all the reasonable alternatives and rational explanations lies a universe filled with mystery. Premonitions can bring us right up to the edge of what our best scientists and religious leaders understand about time, the universe, and our human limitations. Remaining on that edge requires a delicate balance between our openness to the possibility of psi, and our willingness to question our experience. Lean too far in either direction, and we lose the balance. Lean too far toward rational explanations and we might end up rejecting all psi events from our lives. Lean too far into openness and we end up calling everything we experience a form of psi and lose psi's distinct role in life. By remaining in the middle, balanced between rational skepticism and open curiosity, we can forge a partnership about those moments that lie beyond our rational understanding.

PART TWO

Common Assumptions

CHAPTER 4

Memory, Imagination, and Free Will

The summer I turned sixteen my parents moved our family from a quiet suburb of Seattle into the city. They invited my younger brother Tom and me, the last two children still living at home, to help them look for a new house, and even asked us what we wanted to see in a house. Tom and I filled pages with wild dreams, like a two-story library with built-in bookshelves and a winding spiral staircase, and maybe a backyard swimming pool.

But what we both wanted most of all was a bedroom far away from our parents. I had lived in the bedroom next to our parents for seven years by then and was looking to get a little distance. Tom had enjoyed those same years in a room downstairs and wasn't ready to give up his independence. At each prospective house, while our parents discussed square footage and plumbing with our real estate agent, Tom and I negotiated with each other for the best (most distant) bedroom. We finally agreed to alternate who got the first pick of bedroom at each new house we toured. When we entered an older, slightly rundown house in the sleepy neighborhood of Wallingford, it was Tom's turn to choose and I was thinking about the next house on our list.

I didn't think much of the Wallingford house at first. Besides being old, it was outdated, with mismatched color everywhere. But when I glanced out the living room window and caught sight of a vacant nine-teenth-century school building across the street, something clicked awake inside my brain. The school looked familiar. I remembered that school from somewhere, but I couldn't quite place it.

As my family followed the real estate agent up the stairs, I lingered in the living room, frowning. Now the room felt familiar but I couldn't think why. Had I seen this room before? I relaxed and let my sliver of memory widen until I remembered watching the school from the window of a small bedroom upstairs. I caught my breath. I was remembering this house as if I already lived here. Even though I had never seen this house before, I remembered it. I remembered hating my room upstairs—again, right next door to my parents. Or, I would hate that room in the future when I eventually lived here with my family.

I quickly ran through a list of other possible explanations. At age sixteen I already knew the most common arguments against premonitions. Our memories are faulty. Our imaginations run wild. Neither can be trusted. Maybe this house looked like one of the other houses we had toured earlier. Maybe I had overheard a conversation between my parents about this house, converted the conversation to a picture, and was now mistaking a memory for a premonition. Maybe I was having a moment of wishful thinking, although at this moment I actually wished I was wrong about the room upstairs. I knew I needed to see this bedroom and find out if it matched my memory.

I slowly climbed the stairs, crossed my fingers for luck, and stepped into the small bedroom. Even from the door I could see its window looked out over the school, with its young maple tree on the corner also looking too familiar, from the same perspective as my memory. This was the exact view. I had no doubt I was remembering some future moment when this house would be our home. I was standing in my future bedroom and I was going to be stuck here for years, right next to my parents. Again. I might as well start adjusting to it now, I thought sourly, and I wondered why I never got really cool premonitions about fun things.

But my parents came out of the master bedroom shaking their heads, and Tom looked bored. My father looked around and muttered, "Everything needs work." Back downstairs in the kitchen my mother sighed at the tiny roll-away dishwasher and the fifty-year-old cabinets. Then we all trooped down to the finished basement where Tom and I both gasped in wonder.

Nestled two entire floors below the master bedroom lay the crown jewel of teen bedrooms. It was virtually a suite with its own bathroom and outside entrance. Sure, I could touch the ceiling even though I was only five feet tall, and its only window barely cleared the ground outside. But someone living in this room could hear movement throughout the house, while no one upstairs could hear anything from down here. It was a cave, private and removed but still connected. Tom grinned at me, mouthing the word "mine" from behind our father's back.

My heart sank. With my premonition I knew the odds of us living in this house were now much higher than anyone else might suspect. Even though I had no rational reason to think my parents would buy this house, I knew the four of us most likely would be living here by summer's end.

As my family returned to the kitchen I stayed below and paced between the cave and the family room, sorting out my options. On the one hand, I knew I was destined for the room upstairs because that was what my premonition showed me, and who was I to argue with destiny? On the other hand, my parents could be right that premonitions are nonsense, which meant I was a fool for trusting myself, but also meant I still had a chance for a good bedroom in the next house. But on the other hand again, why wasn't I allowed to trust my memory? And if my memory was a premonition, why couldn't I change this one tiny aspect of which room was mine? My pacing brought me back to the cave's window. I looked out at the dirt and made my decision. I would trust my memory as a premonition about our real future in his house, and I would use that information to my advantage. I could do what I wanted, and what I wanted right now was this bedroom.

Back upstairs I took Tom aside and made him what must have looked like the offer of a lifetime. In exchange for me getting first choice in this rundown house (with the admittedly perfect bedroom), I would give him first choice in all the other houses we looked at, no arguments, no take-backs. Tom raised his eyebrows in surprise. We could hear our mother exclaiming that this house was not at all what she expected, and Tom laughed. "You are going to be so sorry," he said, and we shook hands.

We toured another ten or fifteen houses over the next month, and in each one Tom gleefully pointed out the coolest bedroom he was going to take. I smiled and agreed with him, yep, he could have whatever bedroom he wanted, a deal was a deal. I didn't see any need to tell him about my premonition. Besides, I might have been mistaken. I was taking a huge risk in giving up the chance at every cool bedroom in the city of Seattle. Except one.

As it turned out, the other houses weren't in the right neighborhood or didn't have enough bedrooms or were sold by the time we reached them. Most houses at that time were selling within days, but my house—*my house*—hung on the market for six more weeks, too rundown to attract much attention. Finally our parents circled back to it again. We took a second tour and this time my parents nodded as the real estate agent explained how easy it would be to remodel the kitchen and refinish the floors.

Tom and I stayed in the living room this second tour, eyeing each other in silence as the conversation upstairs turned to paint and wallpaper. I sat on the couch and watched him pace and scowl every time we heard laughter floating down. "They'll never buy this house," he insisted. "Just look at these colors. And the kitchen is all wrong."

Our parents made an offer on my house the next day, over Tom's futile protests. By the end of that summer we had moved in and I had settled into my private cave.

There can be no doubt that premonitions blur the line we have drawn so carefully between a cause and its effect, as well as the line between our imagination and objective reality. When any psi event moves the line, even nudges it just a little, many fear the line will be destroyed or lost altogether. They think, "Either reality exists apart from our perception of it, or there is no objective reality and everything we know about how the world works is false." No wonder so many people reject the idea of premonitions outright; allowing even the possibility of a premonition could endanger everything they know.

Dr. Carl Sagan, brilliant scientist and one of the country's most well-known astronomers, expressed his concern in his final book that an irrational belief in the paranormal might keep people from understanding the scientific nature of the universe. He worried that irrational superstition might somehow supplant logic and direct observation of the natural world, and science would be lost.[35] But Sagan was also willing to follow good scientific data wherever it led, and he saw promise in the research being done on telepathy and the possibility of mind influencing matter.[36]

Even parapsychology researchers become a little anxious when their experiments prove too successful. They worry the public will lose its ability to think critically if their findings are accepted at face value. John Beloff wrote in extravagant detail about this fear in a 1996 article titled "On Coming to Terms with the Paranormal." He suggested that if parapsychology validates spontaneous cases of premonitions, then ordinary people would lose the ability to tell the difference between fact and fantasy. Science would fall apart and a great irrationality would be released upon the world.[37]

Despite these fears, however, Beloff championed continued research into psi events, believing the risks are worth our discomfort if we can better understand the reach of the human mind. Beloff believed we have the best chance of understanding these events when we study them within the context of our daily lives.

I don't think accepting the possibility of premonitions needs to challenge our rationality. Accepting the strange (to us), winding reach of the human mind through objective reality is possible without losing the benefits of scientific research, our common sense, or our ability to think critically about our experiences. In fact, what we know about scientific research, common sense, and critical thinking can help us re-draw the line between acceptable mysteries and fantastical ones.

The study of premonitions may bring us right up to the line of our scientific knowledge, to be sure, but that line marks only the difference between what science can prove and what it has not yet proven. The line separating what we know from what we don't know is not only familiar, it is easily crossed. We may spend half our days involved in activities for which there is not a firm scientific foundation. Every time we accept the reality of our own self-reflective consciousness we cross that line, as science cannot yet explain how the matter in our brain becomes conscious of itself.

The rational explanations that people use to discount premonitions fall into a few habitual arguments. People who think they have had a premonition must be mistaking something ordinary for something unusual. They must be imagining a connection between two unrelated events. They must be mistakenly remembering the event or their first impression was wrong. They must be using hindsight to see connections that were never actually, objectively there. They must be miscalculating the odds, seeing connections where there were only coincidences.

These explanations are all reasonable. I know I can't always trust my memory; I forget details, names, and even entire days over the years. I don't always trust my imagination either. I have imagined things that aren't true, such as seeing a face in worn vinyl flooring. I know it is not a face, but my brain insists on creating familiar images for me to find within the random creases and smudges.

Faulty memory, faulty reasoning, and faulty imagination have been used to explain away many unusual experiences in this culture. Too often, however, we let these reasonable explanations divert our attention from the genuine mysteries in life. Everyone knows one naked memory is not sufficient to prove anything in science or in law, but we forget how often we hold on to experiences every day that we could never prove to anyone, including almost every small moment daily life holds. We forget personal experience doesn't need such exacting proof.

Science teaches us that any event experienced through our imagination or memory is less objective and therefore less real and less trustworthy than the things and events we know through our five senses. If we shut out every perception that science cannot explain, however, we will lose many important aspects of our lives, such as our intuition, creativity, emotions, and dreams.

Premonitions are carried within our memories, faulty as those memories may be. It takes memory to hold on to a first impression—that initial moment of a premonition—and carry it forward through time until the future catches up and connects with it. Premonitions come to us in the first place from within our imagination, regardless of their origin. In fact, any internal image of something not immediately in front of me, whether it is an object or an event, a feeling or thought, comes through my ability to imagine it. Any action I take toward an unknown future is possible only through my imagination, whether it's accompanying my parents as they tour prospective houses, angling with my brother to get the best bedroom, or recognizing a house I hadn't seen yet.

In the midst of daily life, memory and imagination are all we have to help us recognize and understand our premonitions. While scientists can and have devised experiments to prove the existence of precognition in general, most of us will never be part of those experiments. We will have to rely on our own judgment and common sense to recognize and sort out our premonitions from our other ways of knowing.

Memory

Almost thirty years have passed since I stood in the living room of that old house in Seattle, and I am reasonably sure my memory of that moment has changed. By this time it's more accurate to say I have a memory of a memory, which is another step removed from that first startled moment of recognition. I might be forgetting important details or even adding nonexistent facts.

As a social worker I learned to think of memory as a mental process of input, storage, and retrieval of information. This model works in most medical settings and gives doctors an important way to assess the impact of disease or injury to the brain. In my work I have asked people to recall the date and time, their name and where they are, and three random words which I ask them to repeat back to me after a few minutes. There is an elegant simplicity to this model. Memory becomes something like a big storage cabinet filled with experiences, thoughts, and feelings, ready for access on a split-second's notice. When we need the data— "What was the name of that guy in the movie we liked?"—we open the file drawer and retrieve it.

The problem with this image, though, is that no one has discovered where all this memory data is stored. Researchers don't yet know exactly how these memory input and retrieval functions work. Researchers don't know how we make memories or where we store them or even if memories can be stored.[38]

Another problem arose when researchers looked more closely at healthy, functioning memories and discovered that *what* our brains choose to store and retrieve does not always coincide with objective reality. Five people can each witness the same train wreck yet give five different descriptions; the details vary according to where they stood, what they focused on, and, most tellingly, what was important to each of them.

Some experts have reported that because memory is so malleable it is virtually impossible to trust any single memory as factual. Dr. Elizabeth Loftus, a psychologist at the University of Washington, found it was relatively easy to get people to remember seeing something they actually hadn't seen at all. Dr. Loftus's work provides the latest rationalization for why we can't trust our memories. In one study she showed volunteers a video of a car accident and later asked them to describe the event. When she gave them helpful hints of details that weren't in the video—like a stop sign—the volunteers "remembered" the details and incorporated them into their descriptions of the event. The longer the time lapse between showing the video and asking for a description, the easier it was for Loftus to change the volunteers' descriptions.

In another experiment Loftus asked volunteers to remember four events that had happened to them (the stories were supplied by relatives), including one event that was made up by the researchers, something that had never happened to them. She found that when asked about it later, nearly a quarter of her volunteers now remembered the fiction as an actual event. They remembered specific details about the event, and had trouble believing the researchers had given them a false memory. Loftus concluded, "People can be led to remember their past in different ways, and they even can be led to remember entire events that never actually happened to them."[39]

Loftus proved scientifically that human memory is not trustworthy in a court of law. Her work helped form legal opinion and has reached into popular culture. Now it is widely accepted that hypnosis can't be used in court testimony, false memories are possible, and even eyewitnesses may remember things that never actually happened. Loftus never focused her work on psi events like premonitions, but her work has been used to discredit the memories of people who report such events.

Loftus was not the first to notice and comment on the flexibility of human memory. Freud, Jung, and the mental health professionals that followed have also noted the ways in which memories shift over time. Mental health clinicians rely on this flexibility of memory to help their clients find meaningful change. To many clinicians, memory is an act of retelling our past from the perspective of the present moment, which can change as we change. When we remember our past from a new perspective, the past changes. We influence the past by reinterpreting what it means to us now. We may not change actual events, but by changing what those events mean, we are changing how they will influence us from now on. We can do this because human memory captures the meaning of events more than the events themselves. Even when we think we are recalling an objective image from a past event, we are actually remembering that event's meaning for us, right here in the present moment.

If human memory was any more objective, it would stop being useful. If I remembered the events of my life completely accurately, I would need as much time to remember each event as I took to live through it in the first place. For example, when I remember walking my dog last night I can see him in my mind's eye trotting along at the end of the leash. Remembering the walk takes me only a fraction of a moment, a visual flash in my mind's eye of what walking my dog looked and felt like on that particular day. My memory doesn't force me to follow us each step of the way, down the block, across the street, and through to the park. I can remember the people we met along the way, but I don't have to relive each exact moment I spent in their company. My memory doesn't bring me every thought I had during that walk or every object I noticed.

As psychologist Robert Sardello noted, I am influenced by the past, but what past I remember is influenced by what is important to me now.[40] How I remember the past comes from how I think of it right now. When I tell the story of any past experience, my tale is colored and even altered by what I think of that experience from my current perspective and by how I imagine it fitting into my future.

Our past can be shaped by the new meanings we give to it. We have the power, in each present moment, to shape and mold the past as the past shapes and molds us. We may not be able to change the facts of what happened, but by changing the meaning these events hold for us, we change what we think about who we are, how the world operates, and what it means to be us in this present time. By changing our perspective we change our present, which changes the past, which in turn changes our present again, opening up new possibilities in the future.

My memory of my parents' house in Seattle is new today, in the way all memories are new, and reflects my present thoughts about that day when I was sixteen. Details from that summer are fuzzy. I don't remember how many other houses we toured that summer. I don't remember what we had for lunch or what clothes I wore. I don't remember exactly what my parents said when they saw the tiny kitchen, apart from how wrong it was for them. In my mind's eye, Tom and my parents are walking through the house, peering at the moldings, counting closets, making comments, but they look and sound more like they look and sound now, and I know that's not accurate. A photo from that year reveals how much younger we all looked then.

Does that make my memory unreliable? Not really. I still rely on it and trust it every day. In its broadest sense, my memory carries not just my past but all my likes and dislikes, my friendships, and the ways I see myself as uniquely me. I can accept the fallibility of my memory (What was that phone number?) without giving up my past because I have found a way to live within memory's limits. I am not faced with an either–or decision; I don't have to either accept every memory as absolute or never trust my memory again. I can happily reminisce for hours about college days and still write down the phone number I want to remember because I understand and accept both the benefits and limitations of my memory.

Imagination

My premonition of the house, which felt so much like a misplaced memory, could also have been the work of my imagination. I even wondered if I was simply imagining a false connection to the house. Maybe I felt something familiar about the house and then proceeded to create an explanation to match my imagined experience. Or I might have dreamed about a similar house and forgot the dream, only to be reminded when I walked in the front door. Or maybe it was none of these things but simply my brain cooking up a connection where none existed.

As with memory, the reputation of imagination has frayed in recent decades. Imagination is often defined as not real. Certainly imagined events are not physical events, but too often "not physical" is interpreted as "not important," or "not effective." We confine imagination to the realm of play or fantasy.

Scientists are especially wary of imagination interfering with their experiments. They know their own imaginations may cause them to view data as evidence for their theories when the data actually does no such thing. Scientists are trained to hope for positive results and distrust those results at the same time. They remain wary of letting their imaginations misinterpret the data.

I see this tension between what we define as the objective world and imagination most often in my work as a medical social worker. In the objective world of the human body, medicines should work regardless of whether or not we believe in them. And yet medicines sometimes do work better when patients believe they will work, and medicines work better still when the doctors believe in them. Sometimes patients respond to new medications before the medicine has had time to work. This effect, called the placebo effect, has been described as our imaginations helping our physical bodies to heal, but it causes doctors distress as they try to figure out if the medicine is helping or not. Medical researchers try lessening the placebo effect in their clinical trials by discounting the data of study participants who get "too much" better too soon,[41] but placebos continue to work consistently across a variety of clinical trials. We imagine the medicine working and our pain goes away, our joints move more freely, our blood pressure goes down, our wounds heal more quickly, and even our brains function better. In fact, placebos have worked so well that some researchers are now studying how and why they work at all. Imagination may be less of an unavoidable hindrance that gums up an experiment; it may very well play a legitimate and important part in healing and in our overall well-being.

The placebo effect has a cousin in the experimental research for psi. Psi proponents (those who believe psi is possible) have achieved more positive results in their studies than psi skeptics (those researchers who don't think psi very likely), and no one knows why this is so. All researchers are looking for the most objective measurements they can find. The idea that their personal attitudes could influence the outcome of their tests despite their hard work has frustrated many of them. Most don't quite believe attitude could affect their tests. Skeptics who find consistently negative results wonder if the positive results come from tests that are not strictly objective. On the other side, psi proponents who find consistently positive results wonder if skeptics are avoiding the connections revealed in their studies. Two scientists—one a psi proponent and the other a psi skeptic—were so intrigued by the possibility that attitude could influence their experimental outcomes, they decided to conduct an experiment together. They agreed on the question and the methodology, they used the same protocol, chose their study volunteers from the same pool, and used the same methods to calculate the data. And like the previous experiments, their two results were significantly different. The proponent's experiment showed a positive result; the skeptic's experiment found no significance.[42]

Most of us live assuming that our imaginations are securely locked inside our heads and will not influence the physical world, but our best research reveals a different world. The line between subjective imagination and the objective world is more blurry than we might have believed. Imagination reaches out and mingles with the physical world in much the same way that memory winds back through objective events and changes their meaning.

If we dismiss imagination too quickly we will miss its most important capabilities, such as helping the healing process in some cases or improving the physical performance of elite athletes and performers. Researchers have found that simply imagining an event produces small but significant neural changes in our brains in much the same way living a direct experience does. Seeing a crowded subway and imagining a crowded subway affect the same neural pathways. World-class athletes use this knowledge to improve their performance by visualizing their races and routines, imagining as clearly as they can each motion of their sport. They know a vivid imagination will help their physical muscles respond as if they actually are moving (albeit on a much smaller scale). Public speakers and performers use similar techniques to picture themselves performing well, which both calms their performance anxiety and improves their actual future performance.

Memory and Imagination in Daily Life

I learned in graduate school that people live through time in a way that is both objective and subjective. Our bodies age one day at a time, of course, regardless of what we wish or believe. But our minds also engage with time in great looping arcs through present, past, and future. Daily living would not be possible without a constant swirl of memory and imagination to both anchor us in this moment, day, or year and pull us into the next. Memory carries our history, our family, our learning, even our personality. Imagination, in its broadest sense, is the only faculty we have with which we can anticipate the future, which is also a function of our present. We imagine the future, anticipate our vacations, and plan our careers. Even writing out the day's schedule takes a willingness and ability to extend our imagined selves into the near future. We can make dinner because we can anticipate what ingredients to use or plan a trip to the grocery store if we don't have what we need.

Something as simple as getting out of bed in the morning depends upon a conversation between imagination and memory. I may spring up out of bed because I anticipate a day full of opportunities or bury my head under the covers because I imagine boring drudgery. What I imagine the day will bring is based on my memory of other days like this one and anticipation for days even further into my future.

Consciously, I get up because I need to work for my future well-being, because I remember I like the work, and because I hope my work will make a difference in the world. Some days I get up simply out of habit, but even habit is grounded in the memory of the routine of previous days, my expectations and goals, and my picture of who I am. I get up because I remember my life well enough to know that getting up is the thing to do.

Exactly when I get out of bed is grounded in a different mix of memory and imagination. I imagine a future me who is late for work and regretting her past (my near future) after staying in bed too long. I remember a past me who did the same thing yesterday, and I mull over the consequences—was it worth the extra ten minutes? I imagine a future me who remembers a different past me who slept in another ten minutes and got to work on time, no problem, because she skipped her morning coffee. In my present I choose which of these times—my imagined future, my remembered past, the past of my future which is still my future, or the past that is also the past of my present—will propel me out of bed in this present moment.

What's more, I know how to get out of bed because of an even deeper, less conscious sense of memory and imagination. I remember how to stand and walk without effort; I think and plan out of habit. My present moment is infused with my memories and the meanings of my life. I am safe in my house because it's familiar, because I live from my memory of the day I bought it and the day I scraped the wallpaper off the kitchen walls and repainted them. I know my life—my self—without having to think about it consciously through this deeper level of memory.

Sometimes our imaginations frighten us with nonsense. Sometimes our memories don't always coincide with the stories our spouses and friends tell, and we argue about what really happened in our shared past. But through all of the mistakes and missteps and misunderstandings, most of us have learned how to keep ourselves balanced between past, present, and future. As deeply subjective as memory and imagination are, we know we can trust them as the foundations of our identity. Psychologist Dr. Ernest Keen showed how the interplay between memory and imagination, in his words anticipation, is the core of our personal identity. "I know who I am (now) because I know who I have been (in the past) and who I shall be (in the future). Knowing my past and future is knowing who I am."[43] (I am indebted to Dr. Keen for this example. JVB.)

John Horgan, an award-winning science writer, interviewed leading researchers on the study of the human brain and found that for all of the research in neurology, genetics, artificial intelligence, psychopharmacology, talk-therapy, and evolutionary psychology, the biggest questions of human consciousness remain out of reach.[44] Even now, more than ten years after his book was published, scientists have not discovered what consciousness is. Researchers don't know how human consciousness relates to the human brain or where feelings and thoughts come from or how they are contained in our physical bodies. This lack of scientific understanding has not stopped anyone I know from thinking or feeling. Most of us simply take for granted we live an intense, subjective life that can be shared and described but never duplicated or fully explained by research. Everyone knows that scientists can't predict our imagination, and we don't worry about it. Memories and imagination happen often enough to enough people that they have become part of our shared life experience. They may be difficult to measure and impossible to define or explain with today's science, but everyone knows they exist.

Free Will, Destiny, and Choice

When I was sixteen, I trusted a premonition enough to win the best room in our new house. I felt pretty sure (but not completely) that my parents would eventually buy that house and my success was sweet, but it raised questions that I didn't know what to do with. Did my premonition mean my parents had no free will to choose a different house? How many other people waited before putting their house on the market, making it impossible for them to choose something better? How many other people did the real estate agent show my house to, and how hard did she try to convince them it was the right house for them? I had no answers to these questions. All I had was the same theoretical paradox about time that has pushed at scientists and science fiction time travel writers for the past century. If the future is already fixed, then what becomes of our free will? If the future is not fixed, then what is a premonition?

Free will has long been held in Western culture as a human birthright, and premonitions seem to threaten this right to choose our own futures. Everyone knows time marches forward into new possibilities, not backward. When Doris Day sang "Que Sera, Sera," she was comforting herself (and us) with the knowledge that we don't have to know right now what is going to happen in the future. It is enough to keep ourselves anchored in the present, do the best we can, hope for the best, and then let go and let the future take care of itself.

This may be one of the reasons so many people decide to dismiss their initial moment of a premonition. They feel pushed to choose between trusting their (perhaps) one momentary instance of knowing the future or trusting what they have been taught about time, the law of cause and effect, and our human capacity for free will. With so many good reasons to reject a premonition, many find it much easier to ignore one than to consider its frightening implications.

This problem of free will versus a fixed future has almost stopped premonition research on more than one occasion. Premonition research gets stuck because researchers can't find a good theory to explain how we can keep both our free will and our premonitions. Even parapsychology researchers are wary of upending one of our most basic commonsense beliefs.

Back in my Seattle house I decided to bet a really good bedroom that my parents didn't have as much choice in life as they thought they did. A part of me wanted to see them break free, choose a different house just to prove we have complete free will, but I didn't want it enough to jeopardize my room. I knew if I told my parents about my premonition they might turn down the house just to teach me premonitions aren't real, so I didn't tell them. Without my information they didn't know a choice had already been made, somehow, by someone, and they relaxed into the illusion of linear time.

My premonition took that illusion away from me, at least for that moment, but then gave me new choices. My premonition didn't cause my parents to buy that particular house or influence their decision in any way. If I had not had the premonition, my parents still would have bought the house, but without the premonition I never would have considered that house as a serious match for them, Tom would have kept his turn for the best room, and I would have spent the next several years upstairs. The premonition gave me a way to recognize one potential future, now suddenly highly likely, and I was free to use the information in whatever way I wanted.

I found a way to move the line between the competing ideas of an absolute free will and a predestined future. I decided my premonition of that house was about a potential future, not a fixed future. The premonition gave me new information that I still had to evaluate for its usefulness. I knew I could have been wrong about the house. My brother was free to turn my offer down. Someone else could have decided to buy the house before my parents were ready to look at it again, and my parents could have bought a different house. My premonition didn't set any of their actions in stone, but instead gave me enough information to help me trust that the odds had somehow shifted in my favor.

You might wonder if I was so sure my premonition was accurate, why I didn't accept the premonition exactly and go along with living upstairs. But I didn't see it that way. I hadn't encountered any "supposed to" in my experience. I trusted my premonition enough to act on the information but didn't think I then had to follow its path at face value without question. I didn't believe the memory showed me where I should be living, as if the premonition knew what I needed better than I did. For me the premonition was more neutral, showing me the room where I very well might be living in the near future. I could use the information in whatever way I saw fit, even follow my own priorities.

Every day we confront the same choices. Trust or doubt our memory. Believe or reject who we imagine ourselves to be. Every day we make choices as if we have free will despite what science has taught us about genetics, biology, or social expectations. Even the language we use helps shape how we perceive the world. We value our right to choose our lives in the midst of all these determinants as we tell the story again and again of who we are, where we come from, and where we hope to go. Premonitions won't take away our free will any more than my premonition affected my choice of bedroom so many years ago. Instead, premonitions can give us more information which we can use to increase our options.

CHAPTER 5

Proof in Daily Life

The person in Western culture who exemplifies the problem of having a premonition and not being believed is Cassandra, a tragic figure in Greek mythology and the favorite daughter of the king of Troy during the Trojan War. As the story goes, the god Apollo fell in love with her, as gods often did in those days, and he promised her anything for her hand in marriage. Cassandra asked for the gift of prophecy, but as soon as Apollo gave her this gift she changed her mind and refused him. I imagine she was feeling quite pleased with herself at this point, having gained such a precious gift; she knew whatever the gods give to humans they can never take back. Apollo was furious. While he could not take back his gift, he could give Cassandra another gift. He gave Cassandra the "gift" of never again being believed. When the Greeks left a giant statue of a horse outside the city's fortified walls, Cassandra warned her father not to accept the gift, but he didn't listen. Instead he ordered the statue brought inside Troy's defenses. That night, Greek soldiers hidden in the statue opened Troy's gates to the rest of the Greek forces, leading to the fall and destruction of Troy.

Echoes of Cassandra's story are found in modern times in the ongoing argument about proof. Prove it to me, the skeptics demand, and I will believe you. But proof depends on someone willing to accept that proof. If the skeptics remain firm in their skepticism, they will find it difficult to accept any story, experiment, survey, or personal experience as proof of anything.

Why Worry About Proof?

Many people wonder why we should worry about proof, and for good reason. For those who have experienced premonitions, the connecting event is often the only proof they need. They already remembered an oddly vivid dream or noticed a feeling of caution that wouldn't go away. They knew their bodies and hearts were out of sync with the reality in front of them, and they knew they didn't have an explanation for it. When a later event connected to the out-of-sync feelings, the connection between the event and the initial moment was all the proof they needed.

Proving to friends or families that an experience was a premonition, however, is much more difficult. Most premonitions are spontaneous events. The initial moments vanish almost as soon as they are recognized, leaving experiencers to wonder whether they should pay more attention or let it go. Holding on to these fleeting impressions in the middle of everything else in life is hard enough, but proving such a moment existed to someone else is next to impossible. Premonitions are internal events; their power lies not in the event but in our memories and imaginations. To outside observers, a premonition anecdote is simply a story told by someone they may or may not trust.

I grew up with parents who loved me dearly but needed better proof than I could find before they would believe something as odd as premonitions. By the time I came along, number six of seven children, they were well aware their children could imagine scary monsters under the bed, exaggerate facts to make a story funnier, and lie through their teeth if it got them out of trouble. My parents had learned to believe only physical evidence and accepted any other story solely for its entertainment value. And I told my share of exaggerations and lies through the years. My mother was right to take with a grain of salt my announcement in the first grade that I was going blind in one eye. She told me to watch her finger, and as both of my eyes dutifully followed it all the way to my nose, she said, "Your eyes are fine" and went back to her visit with the neighbors.

My premonitions felt real to me, but still fell in the category of imagination for my parents. I realized if I wanted my parents' help in figuring them out, I would need to convince them I wasn't lying, exaggerating, or making a mistake. In my scientific-minded family that meant I needed some solid proof.

When I was twelve years old I carefully listed out the steps I would take to prove my premonitions were real. First, I would learn how to have a premonition when I wanted one. Next, I would point my premonition squarely at some important event my parents could see, so they could witness the premonition in action. Third, I would figure out what time actually is and how it works, in case they had questions about how I was doing what I was doing. Then they could compare my version of the event to the actual event and voilà! It was all so simple, so elegant.

It took years to finally understand the impossibility of my list. I couldn't complete even the first step. I never knew when the next premonition would come to me, and despite my determined efforts, I did not learn how to produce one on demand. Like most people most of the time, I recognized my premonitions through hindsight when an event connected with an earlier impression. Even when I did recognize what I thought might be a premonition, I usually didn't trust it enough to tell someone else until the connecting event proved it to my own satisfaction.

Early researchers didn't have laboratory tests for precognition. They relied on anecdotes rather than hard science but did their best to verify the stories they considered for publication. Dame Edith Lyttelton's *Some*

Cases of Prediction, which contains fifteen carefully verified accounts of premonitions, is an early example.[45] She recounts each premonition and its connecting event in a paragraph or two, usually in the experiencer's own words, along with the steps she took to verify its accuracy. She also includes letters from friends, colleagues, and family who can testify that the premonition happened just as the experiencer reported and that they had heard about the premonition before its connecting event.

Even with all of this work, researchers such as Lyttelton were not trying to prove the existence of premonitions. They knew the idea of a premonition is extraordinary and therefore requires not just pretty good evidence, but extraordinary proof, something their stories could not provide. They hoped only to gather enough of these well-verified premonitions to open up the possibility of premonitions' existence and maybe pique the interest of the general public. In their role as scientific investigators, they set a high standard for any anecdote to pass before they publicly endorsed it as a potential premonition.

This need for a proof that cannot be found leaves many experiencers in a quandary. They have the strength of their own convictions—but they know that is not acceptable science. And they have the ability to make sense of their personal daily life, which they depend on for every other part of their life—but skeptics have put that in doubt. For many people, trusting their sudden, irrational sense of certainty is hard enough. Finding ways to prove to someone else's satisfaction that that certainty will connect to a real event is nearly impossible. Still, the lure of a final, convincing proof is irresistible.

The Power of a Really Good Proof

Dr. Sally Rhine Feather, daughter of Joseph and Louisa Rhine, followed her parents in the research of psi events and wrote of the power the right proof can bring. In her book *The Gift*, she recounts the story of Becky, a woman who had several premonitions in her life but none that convinced her husband or children to take her seriously. For years her husband found ways to discount and dismiss her premonitions as chance, as coincidence, or as unrealistic fantasies. On September 11, 2001, the details of the attack on the World Trade Center in New York City matched one of Becky's premonitions. That horrible event matched enough details in her premonition that her husband could no longer remain skeptical. Rhine recounted the impact such proof had on Becky and her husband:

> In the end her frightening 9/11 premonition turned out to be a personal breakthrough for both herself and her marriage. She has finally come to accept her experiences. She no longer feels the need to hide or apologize for them. A great weight has been lifted off her shoulders. More important, her husband no longer looks at her strangely and disapprovingly when she talks about her intuitions. She can be herself and still be accepted by those she loves most.[46]

Dr. Rhine clearly understands the importance of unassailable proof to the well-being of experiencers and their family and friends. Becky's story shows us how a strong proof changed the dynamic of her marriage and her relationship with her husband. When I was a teen I also believed in the power of the right proof to change the hearts and minds of people I loved, and I searched for such an unambiguous premonition for years. I was sure the right premonition told at the right time to the right person could prove I was facing a genuine mystery and not getting lost in fantasy.

When I was in college it finally happened. I experienced a premonition I thought I could use to prove my reality to someone else. In the process I learned that even the best proof has its limitations. My friend Rob and I had been locked in the same argument for more than a year over whether premonitions were possible. Rob was older and sure he knew better. He was not going to abandon everything he knew about the world on my say-so alone, and my stories did not convince him. In the spring of 1981, Rob and I carpooled with two other friends, Tim and Carol, to Portland, Oregon, for a music festival. That was the weekend that Tim and Carol discovered they loved each other and spent all of their free time wound into each other's hair. By the time I dropped them off at Tim's dorm room early Sunday evening, I had no doubt they would spend much of the night together.

I had not yet put the car in gear to back out of the parking lot and Tim and Carol were still angling their way through the front door without letting go of each other, when I had a sudden flash of memory. In my mind's eye I saw myself standing in my parents' kitchen, seeing the kitchen clock hands pointing to nine thirty at night, and then laughing out loud.

For an instant I was going to brush this thought away as nonsensical, as I had no idea what made the clock so amusing, but then I paused. It seemed like a memory, but I knew I had never lived through a similar moment. I closed my eyes, relaxed my focus, and let the rest of the memory float back into my mind. First I caught a stray edge of the moment just before I saw the clock. I had stormed through my parents' house (my house), apparently angry at something, while trying not to disturb their visit with friends in the living room and had headed for the kitchen. Then I caught the moment just after laughing at the clock. I had called Tim and asked him what he was doing and had laughed again when he said he was alone and studying.

This imagined moment seemed improbable, unconnected to my past, unconnected to my relationship with Tim (friendly, but not that friendly), and yet clear and very certain in the way my premonitions could be. I didn't know why I remembered being angry or why my finding Tim hunched over his schoolbooks that night delighted me, but there it was. I ran down my internal checklist of other things these images could be. Could I have been letting my imagination run away with me? But why such specific emotions, such as anger turning into delight at the sight of the clock? Why was nine thirty so funny? Why was Tim studying? Everything I had witnessed in the backseat of my car that weekend led me to believe schoolwork was not on his or Carol's agenda.

My friend Rob was still smiling at the young lovers, and I realized it was still only seven in the evening. If this was a premonition, with its connecting event less than three hours away, I might be able to prove to Rob that premonitions are possible. So I bet him a dollar Tim would be alone in his room studying at nine thirty that night. I explained exactly what I remembered (or imagined) and he laughed when he took the bet, still believing his knowledge of college kids in love could trump any mixed-up fantasy he thought I was having.

I had no idea how my seven o'clock laughter would turn into anger or how I would stop myself from watching the clock, but at the end of the evening, it was one of Rob's housemates who helped me forget all about the bet. His political views were so plainly wrong that I had to argue with him. Somewhere in the heat of the argument I forgot about our bet completely and left their house still angry. I kept arguing with him in my head all the way back to my parents' house. They were in the living room with friends so I headed down to my room. I was still thinking of things I could have said and should have said when I glanced up at the clock on the kitchen wall and saw it was nine thirty at night exactly—and I started to laugh. Here was my premonition moment, the connecting event exactly as I knew it would be. My anger at Rob's housemate melted into delight and I called Tim, already sure of what he was going to say. Tim was studying for an early morning test he had just remembered. Carol had left a few minutes earlier. I laughed and then asked him to call Rob to help me settle a small bet and he agreed. I went to bed that night feeling vindicated, a little smug, and full of anticipation for when I saw Rob the next morning in class. He would have to believe me now.

The Perfect, Provable Premonition

The provable premonition is a thing of beauty and fragility. It requires just the right elements blending together at just the right time, in the right sequence, with just the right people to witness and record its appearance. If any of these elements are missing, the experiencers may be dismissed or discounted through any number of rational-sounding objections.

Over many years I refined my list of what I needed to do to prove a premonition to another person and eventually found a list used by early researchers that both helped and frustrated me.[47] The list did help me recognize my limitations and let go of my unreasonable need to understand the fundamental nature of time—which no one as yet understands—and my need to produce a premonition on demand. At the same time the list set standards that remain nearly impossible to meet in daily life. One researcher even remarked with some pride that, by using his criteria, he had successfully ruled out nearly every premonition anecdote he had ever come across. When I thought I had to satisfy this list before believing in my own experiences, I nearly gave up. I reminded myself this list was only about proving a premonition to someone else. Once I remembered I still could accept and believe my own experiences, I relaxed again.

I do not include the list here to warn people away from talking about their premonitions, but offer it as a kind of challenge, a quest to find the perfect, provable premonition. For those people who want to prove to a doubting friend that something unusual is happening, this list shows the hurdles they face. The first two criteria, recognition and insignificance, are my own additions to the list. Researchers had no need to consider these first two criteria because they evaluated only those anecdotes that were already complete; both the initial moment and the connecting event had already occurred. There was no question about whether or not the experiencer recognized it or how the experiencer would respond. The rest of the criteria come from early researchers and are included with my understanding of how they apply to premonitions in daily life.

··

PROOF CRITERIA

1. Recognition

2. Insignificance

3. Unique Details

4. Unpredictability

5. Lack of Control over Connecting Event

6. Witnesses

7. Timing of Connecting Event

8. Perfect Match Between Premonition and Connecting Event

··

1. Recognition. First, the experiencer must recognize the premonition before its connecting event appears. While this step may appear obvious, most researchers didn't consider spontaneous premonitions until after the connecting event, so they never thought about how to recognize one. In the midst of daily life, however, the experiencer first needs to recognize the initial moment so as to prove it later. This is no small task, as I discovered, but still possible.

When I suddenly remembered laughing at the kitchen clock that early spring evening when I was in college, I recognized a potential premonition. As soon as I became aware of the memory, I could tell it might connect with a future event because it did not match my mood or any past moment I remembered. It was a sudden thought, unconnected to my usual concerns, with unusual and unlikely details.

2. Insignificance. If I want to find a premonition in my own life that I can prove to friends and family, I want it to be about something insignificant. I want the freedom to hope it happens so I can prove the premonition without worrying that someone I care for will be hurt or put in danger. Researchers have no such concerns and use anecdotes of tragic events more often than any other kind of premonition in their studies. They can do so because they receive these anecdotes after the tragedies have occurred. The experiencers no longer have any option to avoid the events in question.

My sudden memory of Tim studying by himself at nine thirty on a Sunday evening was not a dangerous or tragic event, although disappointing for Tim and Carol. I had no fear I was endangering them by using their potential future to prove my point to my friend Rob.

3. Unique details. The connecting event must carry details that are specific, unique, idiosyncratic, or unexpected in some way. Premonitions that carry details that can match more than one event do not rule out the possibility of chance or coincidence.

My premonition included several specific details that convinced me of the premonition, but most were details my friend Rob would never see, such as my anger and then sudden delight. My seeing the kitchen clock would not prove anything to Rob. But the one detail of Tim alone and studying at a specific time was objective enough to satisfy even Rob's skepticism.

4. Unpredictability. The connecting event should be something the experiencer could not have otherwise known, guessed, or predicted from any other source. This is the only way to rule out inference, which is our sometimes amazing human ability to make accurate predictions based on very little information. The connecting event has to be something unlikely or improbable. If the connecting event could have been predicted in hindsight, the experience isn't a provable premonition. I could have known my parents would have friends over—even these particular friends—just from what I knew of them.

My premonition focused on something fairly improbable, at least for that year and those people. When Tim and Carol got out of my car that evening, studying seemed like the last thing they might end up doing. More to the point, Rob was so sure Tim would not be studying he was willing to bet good money that he knew more about college students in love than I did.

5. *Lack of control over connecting event*. The connecting event must remain out of our conscious and unconscious control. If we have no control over the event, then we cannot interfere with it, manipulate events to fit our needs, or commit fraud. On the other hand, if we are involved in any way with bringing the connecting event about, then someone could question whether we changed our actions to make the event fit our prediction. Rob knew I had no control over Tim and Carol's plans. He and I were together, arguing politics with his housemate until after nine that night, and I certainly had no time to contact Tim or Carol before nine thirty.

6. *Witnesses*. If the experiencer tells someone about the premonition before the connecting event, that person becomes a witness. A perfect witness is someone close enough to both hear the prediction and then actually see the connecting event happen. At the same time, witnesses should not be so close to the event that they could influence its outcome. If no witness is available, a dated journal entry can corroborate the premonition, but a written description in an email with an official time and date sent well before the connecting event is even better.

My witness was my friend Rob, who was also the person I most wanted to convince that year. I had told him other stories, but he didn't believe premonitions were possible, and I had not predicted anything to him before the connecting event. While he would not see the clock on my kitchen wall or know if I was truly surprised and delighted by it, he did know Tim well enough to trust his phone call, so we agreed Tim would be our referee. If my phone call interrupted his evening with Carol, I would pay Rob a dollar. But if Tim was studying at nine thirty, I would ask him to call Rob and tell him so.

7. *Timing of the connecting event*. Many researchers believe the time interval between the initial moment and its connecting event must be fairly short and often structure their studies to include only those connecting events that occur within a day or two of the initial moment. The time interval must also be long enough to rule out telepathy or clair-voyance. The connecting event should not be something another person was already planning to bring about. The length of time between initial moment and connecting event must also be short enough to reduce the possibility of a chance happening. I have had premonitions of events that didn't happen until years later, and I knew I could never offer convincing proof they were premonitions to someone else—too many other events had happened in between, including events that made my imagined future predictable and foreseeable.

My premonition came just a few hours before its connecting event, making it easy for me to place a small wager with my friend Rob, and that wager helped him remember the details. If the connecting event had come a few days later—if I had noticed the clock and called Tim on the following Tuesday, for instance—it would not have convinced Rob.

8. *Perfect match between premonition and connecting event.* Lastly, the connecting event must match the premonition closely enough for the witness to recognize it immediately, without help from someone else pointing out the details. If the witness cannot see the match between the two moments, he or she will not be convinced. This effectively rules out some forms of premonitions simply because of how they are structured. For example, a symbolic dream may be immediately understood by the experiencer, but unless the witness also understands the symbolism, the connecting event will have no meaning to him or her. My college pre-monition included specific details that convinced only me. I did storm through the house, still angry from the argument, and I did spot the kitchen clock at nine thirty and laugh with surprise and delight at see-ing my initial moment connect to this future event right under my nose. Rob didn't witness me forgetting the time until I saw the kitchen clock. For all of those internal states he would have to take my word they actu-ally happened. But Tim alone and studying was objective enough that Rob could witness it without me, which is why I asked Tim to call him.

A Perfect Premonition
Does Not Guarantee a Perfect Reaction

In 1981, I knew I had experienced a perfect, provable premonition. I was sure I had proven this one insignificant experience to one person, but I was wrong. The next morning my friend Rob paid me the dollar we had bet but quickly dismissed the episode as inconsequential. Rob didn't want to believe premonitions could exist and hinted darkly that Tim and I had worked together to tease him into believing in premonitions against his better judgment. His reaction was similar to that of many people who are sure that premonitions are not possible. When faced with something that looks so much like a premonition, they decide to suspect fraud.

In the meantime, our friend Tim was hurt and angry that we bet on his love life. He was not reassured when I told him the bet was about my premonition; he wanted to know why I was having premonitions of his love life, and I had no good explanation. I thought the premonition was reason enough, but for Tim, who also didn't believe in premonitions, there had to be some deeper psychological reason I was focused on him. I didn't know how to explain the beauty of this premonition or how much I wanted to prove its existence or that I wasn't interested in him personally—never an easy argument to win.

Tim considered himself an open-minded skeptic about premonitions, which to him meant my experience must have a more logical explanation. Any good scientist remains open to new discoveries, and so he assured me he might be persuaded with the right proof, but he would not be persuaded by this moment. He informed me that parapsychology had not produced one single verifiable claim of the paranormal, but when I asked him what research he had consulted, he looked surprised. He admitted he hadn't researched the topic; it was just what everybody knew. After all, wouldn't the scientific community be jumping with excitement if psi could be proven? No, he was going to wait for science to announce psi was real, and in the meantime he was not impressed or convinced by my bet with Rob. At twenty years old, without once looking into the research journals in the university library, he was certain no one had produced convincing proof of psi.

Cultural Pressure and Friendly Skeptics

Western culture is filled with friendly skeptics just like my friends Tim and Rob, who were both steeped in the scientific tradition and who said they were patiently waiting for proof while showing no interest whatsoever in examining the proof that was available in the research. Most people's first and often last response to personal anecdotes is distrust and a quick review of the difficulties with anecdotal data. They will say they are open-minded skeptics, but they show a great deal of skepticism and very little open-mindedness in this area. Most people know that if they do ever become convinced, they might have to identify with premonition believers, resulting in a loss of social status. So they choose to remain unconvinced, remaining more than happy to hear their friends' psi stories and point out all the possible alternatives, that is, rational explanations. If they cannot find a rational explanation, they will rest their arguments on the fact that science has not accepted these stories, so there must be some other explanation they haven't thought of.

I am not immune to the appeal of this friendly, rational skepticism. I listen to the stories of people I don't know, and I can feel the pull of alternative explanations I might find if I looked hard enough. A man told me he was driving one night and inexplicably paused at an intersection, thereby just missing being blindsided by a car that barreled through the intersection without stopping, and I thought about the little boy I watched playing in his mother's van with the motor running. I had reacted to a noise I hadn't consciously noticed, and I wondered if this man did the same. Perhaps he heard the approaching car without being consciously aware of it, and then took evasive action without thinking. Perhaps he saw a change in lighting on the street, suggesting headlights were approaching. Perhaps he didn't notice or perhaps he was so shaken from a narrow miss he can't remember the moment clearly. Perhaps he was mistaking his close call for a premonition in the way some people build up their personal experience into something it isn't to preserve their self-identity.

I have learned along with everyone else that the only proper response to a premonition story is open, friendly skepticism, in much the same way the only proper response to a pun is a good-natured groan. My skepticism marks me as an educated and upstanding member of this society. I have used this same friendly disbelief as a way to protect my own social reputation on more than one occasion, rather than trying to better understand the story.

What helps me pull back from this automatic search for other logical explanations is to remember it's not my job to prove the scientific validity of other people's daily life experience. In fact, I rarely ask for any kind of proof for any story that people tell me about their lives. If someone tells me he is in love for the first time in his life, I don't search his past for evidence he is lying or mistaken. I don't interrogate him on his criteria for true love or ask him to include short descriptions of every other time he thought he was in love but had been mistaken. I am under no obligation to remain open-yet-skeptical of his claim.

I can be so accepting of his declaration of love because I have no personal or social stake in his ability to identify his love life. I already know love exists, and I know everybody else knows it exists as well. I can live from my own experience of love no matter what he discovers about his own life. Science has conceded that love exists in some form, even as researchers look for the chemical, biological, and neuronal markers for the sensation of falling in love. With so much social and cultural acceptance, I don't need him to prove his experience is real in order to accept my own experience. This cultural acceptance gives me all the room I need to listen to his story with an open mind. I can let him explore what being in love means for him and how he will respond to his experience. If he is wrong I can trust he will learn soon enough the difference between the true love he desires and whatever he is feeling right now.

When I pull back and view premonition stories in this same way, I regain trust in myself and in the person I am listening to. I have experienced premonitions and at this point have talked with many people who have also experienced them. Unlike my friends who remain friendly skeptics, I *have* read the journals and books. Even without cultural permission I can listen to stories about premonitions without worrying whether or not they will prove or disprove my own personal experience. This gives me room to relax and focus on how the people I'm talking to at this moment will make sense of their own experiences and what they will do about it. I can focus on how they respond to their premonitions emotionally and how they let these feelings affect the rest of their lives.

Of course, cultural and social acceptance would be very nice, too. As the experimental designs have become ever more rigorous and still yield positive results, I half-expected more scientific interest and more information dispersed by the wider press. Researchers *have* proven precognition exists as much as anything has been proven in science, using established and accepted scientific methods. The results have been as clear and definitive as any research results, and what science knows now can be trusted as much as any other scientific understanding. In the future scientists undoubtedly will form new theories about premonitions because that is the way science works, but the evidence for premonitions is solid.

But skepticism digs in its heels. The fact that evidence alone is not convincing scientists, let alone the general public, sheds additional light on how cultures—including this one—change. Until people can examine the research or talk about their experience without being dismissed as irrational, most people will continue to look away. Right now that safety does not exist. Even well-respected researchers who choose to study consciousness can find themselves shoved to the outskirts of the scientific community.

The debate about climate change over the past three decades is a good example of the intersection between science, publicity, and cultural acceptance. For years the scientists who published alarming reports of warming trends were ridiculed as cranks. Former U.S. Vice President Al Gore gave his climate change talk for years to small, enthusiastic audiences, but without much fanfare. Right up until his movie *An Incon-venient Truth* opened, the public debate remained mired in the story that the scientific community was divided about whether climate change was real. People who believed climate change was a serious problem were called foolish and gullible, and accused of having seriously misplaced pri-orities. Then the movie became a hit and won an Academy Award. Gore and the scientists who worked with him won the Nobel Peace Prize. More money flowed into studies that showed mounting evidence, and now everybody is talking about the reality of climate change, how to slow it down or how to adjust to its inevitability. The movie made it safe for the general public to talk about climate change in a way that science alone could not.

This tells me that proof alone will never convince those who don't want to be convinced. The problem isn't with the proof; it is with our unwillingness to accept proof until we know it is safe to do so. If proof was all we needed for psi to be accepted, our newspapers and magazines would be filled with the evidence stacking up from laboratory experi-ments all over the world. But we aren't really looking at the evidence any more than we looked at the evidence for climate change fifteen years ago. The psi research isn't being published in national magazines, and psi researchers are not being invited to present their work at scientific con-ferences, because the scientific community hasn't decided to recognize the research as compelling. I think we are waiting, as a society, for some-thing to happen which mere evidence cannot provide. We are waiting for our cultural community to tell us it's all right to believe the evidence.

The scientific research for psi has been stuck for more than seventy years on proving the existence of psi. As long as researchers focus on the hard science of proof, the softer sciences of meaning and emotional integration are put on hold. There is not enough research into what these moments of psi might mean or how we can integrate the experi-ence into our lives. We don't know what our premonitions are good for, apart from their occasional warnings. All the proof in the world won't help us live more satisfying lives with premonitions. The personal, lived experience of a premonition remains vivid, compelling, and sometimes unnerving. When people cannot find ready answers through science or through their religious communities, many unconsciously turn to popular culture for answers.

CHAPTER 6

Premonitions in Popular Culture

Helen, an old friend of mine, recently told me about a premonition she had many years ago when she was still in college. One night she dreamed the older brother of a grade school friend had died. Helen didn't know the brother, and hadn't seen her friend in more than a decade, but six months later was astonished to read this young man's obituary in the newspaper. Apparently he had contracted an illness and died quickly.

In telling me about her dream more than twenty-five years later, Helen used the hushed tone of someone telling a ghost story and confided she lived in fear of another premonition haunting her. I asked her what it was that frightened her so badly, and she looked surprised. Hadn't I been listening? She dreamed a man was going to die and then that man died. But I was still perplexed by her intensity. Helen had been a hospice volunteer for ten years, and was more comfortable than most around the inevitability of death. I asked her to tell me more and together we went looking for what exactly had given her such a terrible feeling of dread.

Her answers were enlightening. She knew her premonition in no way caused her friend's brother to die, and she knew her dream hadn't given her any chance to protect her friend's brother from his illness. She had told her then-boyfriend about the dream right away and knew this gave her (and her boyfriend) proof that she was not making it up through hindsight. Her boyfriend believed her so she wasn't afraid of being seen as crazy or of being ridiculed, and she had no worry about being crazy. She did not have a strong emotional connection with her friend's brother and she wasn't in contact with her friend anymore, so she wasn't afraid her friend would stop liking her because of the dream.

But she still was afraid of the premonition. She still told the story with the wide-eyed intensity that often accompanies stories of the uncanny. Her premonition clearly upset her deeply, even though it didn't hurt her, didn't lead her into danger, and didn't push her to take any actions she might regret. Something about it unnerved her, and as a result she has taken defensive actions against any future psi experience. She shuts her eyes tight and keeps her hands over her ears and prays she will never again have to worry about such a terrible future event.

Helen has a deep conviction that people aren't supposed to know these things. To Helen, knowing the future violates the natural order of the universe. She knew twenty-five years ago, deep down where she didn't often look, that she wasn't supposed to know the future. She didn't know who had told her this but she knew it to be true, and she also knew everybody else knew it as well. She was speaking the language of culture; specifically, she was speaking the language of mainstream Western culture.

The mainstream culture in North America alternately has been described as European-centric, Western, post-Enlightenment, scientific, democratic, capitalistic, and Christian. A thousand other cultures live here as well—communities of people from all over the world who brought with them their own histories, traditions, values, and religious beliefs, but the mainstream culture holds the dominant voice in North America today.

Western culture is also one of the few world cultures that remain set against the idea of psi events as a matter of principle. In the middle of the 1600s, Western Europe entered what is now called the Age of Enlightenment. The next 150 years saw the newly emerging field of science shift the public conversation about reality from seeing it primarily as a spiritual realm to seeing a physical, natural, material landscape. Scientists questioned and then rejected long-held supernatural beliefs for nearly everything, and replaced them with rational explanations based on careful observation and experimentation. Slowly science became the new paradigm for Western Europe and the lands they occupied through empire. The Age of Enlightenment softened when Western culture turned to the passion of Romanticism in a backlash against pure reason in the 1800s, but science remains firmly grounded in Enlightenment ideals. Most scientists today continue to dismiss psi events as just another type of supernatural nonsense, and the subject of psi events or how to make sense of them are not taught in most schools.

Western religious values are rooted in Judeo-Christian traditions, which also view premonitions as supernatural but not from God, which means they could be spiritually dangerous, potentially evil. I was raised Roman Catholic and learned very early that pagan was another word for devil worship and that any unexplained event—premonitions, telepathy, even significant dreams—could not be considered part of God's work and therefore would never be considered good. Religious leaders may no longer preach about damnation as the consequence of psychic events, but neither do they have any interest in rehabilitating psi events into their doctrines. Premonitions remain suspect and often are placed in opposition to a spiritual life in religious organizations.

So where do you go to find out about your premonition if you can't talk to your friends about it? If premonitions are not taught in school, if your minister or priest or rabbi or frowns on it, if science can't explain it and the church won't accept it and your family doesn't talk about it, where do you go to learn what a premonition means or how to respond to one of your own?

In North America you go to pop culture, of course. There are plenty of images and stories about premonitions in the movies, on the Internet, in books, with television magicians and the television skeptics that debunk magic, and they all have something to say about premonitions.

Pop Culture to the Rescue

You may wonder why anyone would rely on popular entertainment for understanding anything, but popular culture can open our lives to experiences we might never have dreamed about. Movies, television, the Internet, and books take us inside the daily lives of people we would never meet otherwise and show us the consequences of decisions we will never have to make. At its best, popular culture can show us another way of being human, give us another way to experience and understand daily life.

I have seen images of the top of Mount Everest and they are spectacular. I almost feel like I have been there, the images are so clear. I know the people who have actually stood on Mount Everest will tell me the pictures don't do it justice. They'll say that seeing it on television is nothing like seeing it in person, and I believe them. I also know I will never climb Mount Everest, so this is my next best thing. I will never be a surgeon or take down a criminal mastermind. I will never wander the desert on my knees or fly across the African savannah in a biplane. The books that describe these adventures help me imagine such things. The images from television and movies help transport me in my imagination.

Popular culture can give us views of other people's daily lives. We see our concerns and hopes reflected in their stories and through those reflections we know we belong, we are part of the culture. I shudder when I write this, but popular culture teaches us how to behave in both ordinary and highly unusual social situations. Pop culture holds up a mirror to show how we live right now and at the same time lets us imagine how we might live, what the world could be like if things were just a tiny bit different. I have learned how to greet someone who speaks a different language, how to de-clutter my house before selling it, how to dress for success, and how I could get the most from my garden if I had a garden. Popular entertainment has it all. Or nearly all.

I can also pick up a lot of nonsense. With television shows set in police precincts and hospitals to guide me, I have learned just enough about the law and medicine to get myself into real trouble. Still, from movies I feel ridiculously sure of what to do if my car ever explodes. I would toss my identification into the fire, go underground and off the grid, avoid the corrupt government and corporate evildoers dogging my footsteps, and track down the killers using my trusted inside sources. In the movies there is always an inside source. If I come down with some strange disease I will consult a real-life professional. If my car explodes, I know just what to do.

What helps all of us sort out the good ideas from the nonsense is the steadying force of our daily reality. Real daily life is a satisfying counterbalance to the fluff and gives us the common sense we need. Really, if my car ever does explode I will do what I've learned from my parents, my teachers, my friends, and the fire marshal who visited my second-grade class. I will call 911 and ask the fire department to put it out. We each have our own experience with love, work, family, sleep and getting up and getting dressed, bills, grief, embarrassment, failure, hope, surprises, and physical aches and pains. In these and in so much more we are all experts. We understand the difference between what true pain feels like and how it is portrayed in the movies. We have our favorite actors who echo, magnify, and illuminate our emotional lives, which is great, and we all know actors we don't ever believe. That's not what real pain looks like, we scoff. We all earn our commonsense wisdom from our daily lives with our memories of what worked and what didn't last time and our plans for how we will handle the next day.

The Perils of Pop Culture

When the experience being depicted is something we don't yet understand, however, the line between fact and fiction is harder to find. Some people live for years without ever having the need for hospital-level medical care. All they know about this intense medical environment comes from television shows that are set in hospitals but mostly focus on the social lives of medical residents and doctors. The illnesses these shows contend with are generally treatable. Even the shows about medical mysteries manage to wrap up each mystery with a solid explanation by the end of the episode. If you have never had a life-threatening illness or been the main support for someone you love who is ill, your view of hospitals may be a little skewed. You might know intellectually that medicine can't solve all problems, but you might only have experienced medicine on television. If you ever do need to enter the hospital or the legal system you will quickly learn the difference between reality and the fantasies these shows depict.

My time as a social worker in hospitals has taught me that medicine is more complicated and filled with more hope, anger, loss, prayer, and fear than can ever be shown on television. Like the mountaineers who have climbed Mount Everest, I know real medicine is more powerful than anything the movies can depict because I have seen it up close in my personal life.

Premonitions fall into this camp of something we don't encounter every day. Premonitions are still uncommon enough that we haven't yet sorted out all the ways they might appear in daily life. We haven't yet decided as a culture whether premonitions are fact or fiction in daily life, so we have trouble finding the difference between reality and fantasy on the screen. If we never had a premonition then we might forget to question whether the made-for-TV movie is portraying a premonition accurately. Instead we might actually look to pop culture for direction, which is where we get into trouble.

Western culture long ago categorized all premonitions as a supernatural force or fantasy, and our popular entertainment followed suit. If I never had a premonition, I would think from television and movies that premonitions carry only the worst kind of messages about disasters and death. I would think any sane person could be driven mad with a premonition's visions of suffering. I would think the only people who think they have premonitions are eccentric, shawl-wearing, patchouli-smelling hippie renegades, and they are always wrong. If I relied solely on pop culture for what premonitions feel like, I don't think I would be able to distinguish a genuine premonition from a psychotic episode. In short, premonitions in the popular culture are frightening.

If we never talk about psi events and if we never share our ideas about what these events might mean for daily life, then all we have left is popular entertainment to tell us how they work. Without the solid foundation of our own personal experience to counterbalance the nonsense, premonitions remain something like a ghost story or a magic trick in our imagination.

When some movie spouts nonsense about premonitions, nobody calls the script writers on their lack of fact-checking and no one complains to the directors that that's not the way premonitions work in real life. And sadly, some audience members who have experienced premonitions will wonder secretly if the movie is depicting how it actually works for others. Should they be worried? Will they go insane? Should they start wearing macramé shawls over flowing skirts?

Finding Our Way

Premonitions in daily life counterbalance the premonition nonsense just as daily life provides a counterbalance for the rest of pop culture. I am going to examine three of the most familiar storylines for premonitions, the meanings that have frightened my friend Helen and so many others like her. I want to trace back to these stories' origins and show how premonitions in ordinary daily life offer us more richness and calm steadiness than their fictional portrayal.

Pop culture uses three basic dramatic themes to exploit premonitions. First, premonitions are portrayed as an overpowering supernatural force that is dangerous, potentially evil, and very real. Second, following the lead of those scientists who take a hard-line skeptical stance, psi events are portrayed as magic tricks performed by frauds and liars who make money off the gullible and weak-minded or cover some other crime they are committing. And third, premonitions are included in storylines as a sign of mental illness. People who believe in the reality of psi events are portrayed at best as superstitious and lacking scientific rationality and at worst as emotionally or mentally unsound for believing in such nonsense. Each of these three stereotypes has a foot in our collective history. Each can easily be countered with the reality of ordinary premonitions in daily life.

1. Premonitions as an overpowering supernatural force. A month's viewing of television programs could lead anyone to believe premonitions deal only with the most brutal aspects of life. Programs link almost every premonition with images of death and destruction. Fictional characters (predominantly women) are haunted by images of brutal crimes. They see ghosts of the dead or help police investigate horrific crimes that haunt their dreams. Sometimes even death isn't enough to create chills, so the heroines must battle against evil or malevolent ghosts. Some fear for their safety; most fear for their mental health; almost all isolate themselves because what they know is dangerous or because they fear being rejected by the larger community.

Characters (again, mostly women) who experience premonitions in the movies fare no better. They are almost universally portrayed as being overwhelmed with horror or driven crazy by the images they cannot control. Often the only people who believe our heroine can see the future are the killers, who now have to kill the heroine to keep her quiet. The people with premonitions end up alone, terrified, and up against impossible odds to save the world—it all makes for riveting entertainment.

In one successful horror movie franchise (Final Destination series), the hero follows the warning of a premonition and narrowly escapes being blown up in the first fifteen minutes of the film. But from that moment on he is hunted down by Death (a malevolent presence) because he was supposed to die in the explosion. The moral could not be clearer. He cheated Death by following his premonition and now he has to pay with his blood. Friends who were foolish enough to trust him (or her—there are four installments at this writing) and save their own lives from that first explosion also spend the rest of the movie being stalked by Death, and they all die in horrific, gruesome ways.

These movies warn viewers of the dangers awaiting anyone who goes looking for the future. It is much better to push into an unknown and possibly dangerous future than to receive a premonition and know for sure that danger is coming. In the world of horror movie premonitions, a premonition only prolongs the agony and sets up its hapless victims to be stalked by Death. Who needs premonitions like that?

These movies focus on our culture's fear of knowing too much, too soon. They are influenced by the many Christian doctrines that insist any event not specifically sanctioned by holy doctrine is inherently evil. It is no wonder so much popular entertainment sets its horror stories around the early Catholic Church, with its inspired use of exorcists, demons, and witches under the spell of Satan.

Even the scientific community has assumed that most premonitions are about terrible future events. Researchers have found some plausible explanations for why so many premonitions foretell dangers and trag-edies. If premonitions are signals from an event catapulting backwards in time (a big "if," but bear with me), then perhaps the more tragic events send back stronger signals, making them easier to recognize. Or if our internal, hard-wired danger detectors search the future for trouble (another big "if"), then perhaps the more tragic events elicit a stronger emotional reaction from us, making those events more easily seen.

Certainly the majority of stories reported to researchers have been about tragedies, but those studies did not use random samples. Tragic events have an enormous emotional impact on all concerned, which may lead more people to search for clues in the days leading up to the acci-dents and find the premonitions. Perhaps because tragic events are more incomprehensible than daily life, more people question the occurrence and so send such anecdotes to researchers.

Researchers forgot to ask themselves how many other people may have had premonitions but didn't contact researchers. Perhaps so many stories wind around tragedies because those are the stories researchers can most easily use. Tragedies and accidents are also most often unexpected, meaning no one could have predicted them beforehand, which makes any premonitions about them easier for researchers to verify.

Some researchers started with a tragedy and then worked their way backward, looking for premonitions in the days leading up to the event. John Cox studied train crashes a year after the events took place. J. C. Barker was stunned along with everyone else by the Aberfan disaster and only later asked people to send him their premonitions about it. Researcher Mary Stowell studied the meaning of precognitive dreams by conducting in-depth interviews with people who had precognitive dreams, but she chose to interview only those people who had dreamed of at least one death.[48] These researchers decided premonitions are most useful in avoiding accidents and are more likely to show up in the aftermath of tragedy. Each needed compelling anecdotes that could stand the test of a skeptical audience. They built on the knowledge of past generations without stopping to wonder if the knowledge was accurate.

In recent years people have countered the evil supernatural storyline with a positive supernatural storyline. Professional psychics tell their audiences, yes, this force is overwhelming and supernatural, but it is a spiritual force for good and not evil. It is angels and saints and ascended masters, not demons or Satan; a gift, not a curse. It is bestowed by God to be used in service to others.

The idea that a higher power can interact directly in our personal lives for the better has been making a resurgence in the past few decades. Smaller religious communities emphasize direct prayer to God for interventions in daily life and are taught to look for signs of God's presence in synchronicities and psi events. In these circles premonitions still warn of disasters but this is understood as a way to protect us, keep us safe, and bring about a brighter future than might otherwise happen.

The question most often overlooked in this conversation is whether most premonitions really do show us visions of death. The answer is no, not really. Despite all the published stories, most premonitions are much smaller, both in their intensity and in their connecting event. Premonitions connect to ordinary life events. I have had premonitions of a red sweater, a lost wallet, a box of breakfast cereal misplaced on a grocery aisle. I have talked with people who foresaw an out-of-service elevator, a handful of wilted lilacs, a missed dinner date with friends, and an unexpectedly emotional business trip. These connecting events are concerned with our daily life. The premonitions are important because they exist, not because of the importance of the event.

The idea of an overpowering and malevolent supernatural force can't compete with the counterbalance of our daily life experience with these ordinary premonitions. If we had a common understanding of how premonitions move through our daily lives, we would no longer fear the horror stories, just as we have little fear of real vampires walking the streets after dark.

2. Premonitions as magic tricks Popular culture supports another oversimplified, dressed-up version of premonitions as well. Rather than a powerful supernatural force, many storylines portray alleged psi events as magic tricks used to fool a gullible and superstitious public. People who claim to have experienced a psi event are dismissed as charlatans who are abusing their friends' trusting natures to make a name for themselves. The characters in these stories who didn't fall for the charlatan's deception sniff and say, "How could Casey be so foolish as to be taken in by this superstitious nonsense?" And we, the viewers, don't want to be like Casey, so the next time the subject of premonitions arises among our friends, we make sure we show our skepticism.

Two television shows today play with this theme. *Psych* follows the adventures of a man with exceptional observational skills, who pretends to be psychic because (a) people can't believe he's that smart, and (b) criminals will dismiss him as foolish until he solves the crime.

The Mentalist also features a man with exceptional observational skills who used to work as a mind reader and magician but quit to work with police. He is an expert at reading human behavior and manipulating others, and insists all psi events must have a logical explanation.

I grew up with the cartoon *Scooby-Doo* and I used to love watching smart teenagers solve mysteries involving the superficially supernatural. One character believed all the nonsense and ran around terrified, while another remained skeptical, rational, and figured out how the trick was done. And it was always a trick. Ghosts, mummies, prophecies, and ancient curses were all designed by the criminals to provide the perfect alibi or frighten poor gullible people away from the treasure or away from the crime scene, depending on the episode.

Most regular television series have at least one episode in which mysterious happenings turn out to be the work of a fraud or deluded individual. Even the venerable *Law and Order*, which strove for ripped-from-the-headlines realism, included an episode in which a man claimed to have a psychic vision of a murder. In the end the police discovered the man had been an actual witness to the crime (or maybe he had committed the crime) and had a mental breakdown about it.

Skeptics come by their distrust honestly. Magicians have confounded and delighted audiences for centuries with their seemingly amazing mental abilities. With time-tested skills in illusion, such as cold reading and sleight-of-hand, plus the technological wonders of hidden microphones, magicians can create a near-perfect illusion of mental telepathy and precognition. They tell their audiences such gifts are a sign of their connection to another dimension and audiences love it. Magicians often challenge their audiences to either find the illusion or admit the magician is truly psychic, and audience members happily comply—many will agree the magician has a gift if they cannot find the trick by the end of the show.

These artful illusions become fodder for professional skeptics who will hold up a magician's performance as proof the genuine experience does not exist. They argue that if magicians can fool the public into believing their magic act is a genuine psi event, then that means every instance of psi is nothing more than someone's artful illusion. Skeptics warn us not to trust the experimental studies because magicians can fool researchers, too. They warn us not to believe the stories of friends and colleagues because people can fool themselves into believing the impossible. If magicians can produce the illusion of psi, then there can be no real psi.

The argument that magic tricks done well means that psi events are not real requires a big leap in logic. While some may genuinely believe the magician has a gift, most audience members don't believe the magician as much as they agree to suspend their disbelief in order to appreciate a magic trick done well. They don't want to look for the magician's trick; they want to be entertained. They want to revel in the possibility of real magic in the world, if only for a few hours.

In these settings the manufactured psi events may confound their sensibilities and tweak their assumptions about reality, but only in the context of a fun evening out. They know from their own daily experience that cars and people don't levitate anywhere but on a magician's stage. They know only elephants and young women in spangled dresses disappear in the flash of an eye. Everything else in daily life stays put. If they can't find their car keys the next afternoon, they will retrace their steps, and not wonder if someone else made the keys vanish.

This is how we make the distinction between fantasy and reality. We hold on to our personal experience as our foundation for how the world actually works. We may find truth and new insights from actors portraying strong emotions in the movies, but we don't confuse those illusions with our own emotional lives. We don't think actors call into question the reality of our personal lives. If I followed the skeptic's argument that all psi is simply a magic trick because magicians can fake them onstage, then it follows I might have to question my own emotional life if so much of it can be manufactured by performers. But I know this is not a reasonable argument. I don't mistrust my own feelings or the feelings of my friends simply because some people can fake it.

And so it goes for premonitions. A magician's skill at "mind reading" and "prophecy" has nothing to do with my premonitions in daily life. My premonitions might not look as glamorous or smooth as the magician's, and might not connect with the earth-shattering revelations of disaster movies, but they remain powerful because they are my personal experience.

3. *Premonitions as mental illness.* In much of popular entertainment the characters who believe psi is possible are portrayed as indecisive, gullible dreamers who can't tell the difference between their own fantasies and objective reality. In the entertainment industry the belief in psi nearly always means there is something wrong with the believer.

For decades characters in the movies who had glimpses of the future were driven insane by their visions or considered insane for believing their visions. They fight to get their warnings heard like modern-day Cassandras, begging the police (or security or strangers—whoever the heroes might be) to believe them, but to no avail. Inevitably disaster strikes and they are held responsible or dismissed as deranged. Heartbreak and emotional breakdowns follow.

In the past several decades, being psychic on television has been played for laughs. When a character (usually female) exclaims, "I am a little bit psychic," the audience knows to laugh at her. When characters earnestly believe they have seen the future, they often turn out to be mentally or emotionally unstable or sort of wacky with a good heart, but always, always they are proven wrong. By the end of the episode, we in the audience are reassured they were not psychic, no matter how much they wanted to believe they were.

The lead character in the comedic television show *Psych* turns this stereotype on its head. He tells people he is psychic so that he will lose credibility in their eyes, which he then uses to his advantage. Calling himself psychic opens doors for him. At the same time the audience trusts him as a lead character only because he knows he is not actually psychic. We are in on the lie and that puts us inside the magic trick. We are smarter than the baffled criminals and police detectives who can't figure out his trick but also can't accept his goofy explanations.

Where did such fears of mental instability come from? My guess is most of these fears are rooted deeply in Western culture, in myths such as Cassandra's story. The twentieth century saw a resurgence of these fears in the field of psychology, which by many reports has been more adamantly opposed to psi events than any other scientific field of inquiry. Around the middle of the twentieth century, psychology researchers began asking why some people might believe in psi experiences when everyone (at that time) already knew psi could not happen. They began a search for the mental and emotional defects that must exist—why else would such believers hold on to their irrational beliefs? In one research project after another they asked: Are people who believe in the paranormal more likely to be psychotic? Are they less rational than skeptics? Do they lack skills in critical thinking? Are they more self-absorbed and narcissistic than skeptics? Have they been traumatized early in life or abused as children? Are they more likely to be poor, uneducated, or superstitious? Have they been deprived of a sound scientific education? Do they feel more out of control in their lives or fear death more than skeptics do?

Most of these questions were settled with a convincing "No." Researchers could not find a significant difference between believers and skeptics to account for their differing beliefs. The psychological studies showed no consistent correlation between a belief in psi and any mental, emotional, or personality defect. People who believe psi is possible have the same level of critical thinking skills as skeptics; they have the same level of education and the same understanding of scientific principles. Believers and skeptics alike come in all races, ethnicities, religions, ages, and socioeconomic classes. Around the world believers and skeptics live by similar spiritual beliefs and connections to organized religions.

The only significant difference between people who believe in psi and those who don't is that believers are much more likely to have had a psi event of their own. They believe psi is possible because they had a psi experience.

This should have been good news for people who had a premonition. All these negative results should have helped the national conversation move away from ridiculing believers, but that didn't happen. Instead, people became even more confused. A study looking for psychological deficits that has persistently negative results means—what exactly? The two negatives didn't translate very easily into a positive. Each study was dutifully reported but still carried the caveat that given enough time some deficit would emerge. More than that, most people remember the questions better than the results. People question why psychology researchers would ask the questions about mental illness if they didn't already know mental illness was to blame?

All of these studies have trickled their way into the general public in the form of skeptical questioning rather than reassurance. We hear a friend's story about a psi event and can't help wondering if perhaps he is a little less rational or a little more gullible or possibly more fantasy prone than we are.

This idea that psi believers must have something wrong with them or else they would know psi is nonsense permeates mainstream culture. People who never had a psi event accept the skepticism without much thought. If they do find themselves face-to-face with an event for which they can find no logical explanation, many feel confused and even panicked. Dr. Arthur Hastings, former dean of faculty at the Institute for Transpersonal Psychology, counseled many people who ask for help after a psi event. Often these people were skeptics before their psi event who found themselves thrown into confusion when a direct experience contradicted their sense of reality. Many feared they were going crazy because they knew only crazy people believe in the fantasy of premonitions.[49] They felt defective, foolish, vulnerable, and uncertain about their ability to manage their lives. They feared their experience hinted at a serious mental illness, such as psychosis.

At first glance premonitions do appear to blur the invisible but potent line between sanity and psychosis. The fear is built on two large gaps in the common experience of the people being studied. The first gap is in their experience with premonitions, as these people have not had enough premonitions to trust them. The second gap is in their experience with mental health. Most people have not had the experience of a psychotic break to fully understand the differences between a psi event and a psychotic episode. For people who have not had either, the visions and voices of a premonition might seem much like a hallucination.

Fortunately the differences between psi and psychosis are clear and unmistakable up close. I have worked with people who suffer from serious mental illness, and I have talked with people who have had a psi event, and there is no mistaking one for the other.

Psychiatrist and neurologist Vernon Neppe dedicated his career to studying the intersection between psi, psychosis, and neurological disorders. After years of research and clinical work, he distinguishes between a psi event and psychosis based solely on a person's ability to function in their life. "No matter how strange the patient's experiences are, they are not perceived as abnormal unless they distinctly interfere with the patient's functional and coping skills."[50]

Functional and coping skills are those skills we use to navigate through our lives. We use functional skills to help us find and hold a job, shop for groceries, clean our house, and cook our food. We use coping skills to recover from disappointments, appreciate moments of joy and humor, and handle daily minor frustrations. When we fail at something we use coping skills to talk ourselves into trying again.

People can struggle with any of these skills for reasons that have nothing to do with mental distress—the economy makes it hard to find a job, a physical disability or medical illness makes it impossible to maintain independent living. Sometimes people suffer a tragedy that tests all of their coping skills, and they can feel overwhelmed by the emotional demands of living.

People who live with psychotic delusions may think they are psychic, but their belief often reaches out beyond a specific moment to encompass their entire lives. The following passage, quoted by Richard S. Broughton in *Parapsychology: The Controversial Science* was expressed by someone suffering from a psychotic delusion during treatment at the Institute for Parapsychology.

> I know what you people are doing. You're beaming thoughts into my head—trying to make me go crazy. Don't tell me you're not. I've read about your lab. My ex-wife's paying you to do this, isn't she? Well, it's going to stop. When I get through to the CIA, they'll close you down in a minute. You just wait. [51]

This person has not had one specific event he finds unusual. He is not looking for an explanation of one discrete experience. Instead, he is convinced the Institute can beam thoughts into his head. He is sure his ex-wife has paid the Institute to attack him personally. He believes he can convince the CIA to stop the Institute from its primary work. His beliefs are ongoing, and they affect his relationships and most likely every part of his life.

The visions and voices of psychosis often feel intrusive and can continue for months and years. They disrupt people's ability to attend to the world around them. Sometimes the visions and delusions block out the good intentions of people they know and trust. People with an untreated psychosis have trouble managing their daily lives. They have trouble distinguishing between their internal thoughts and what is happening in physical reality. They lose friendships, jobs, and their ability to concentrate on the task at hand. Without treatment, every aspect of their lives can become disrupted and tormented.

Premonitions in daily life, on the other hand, appear as a fleeting moment, barely long enough for most people to notice them. People who accept the psi event as real don't often find their acceptance interferes with their ability to function in the rest of their lives, a key test of

any mental illness. They may feel confused and go on a search for meaning, but they remain connected to their family and friends, and continue
to work as they did before.

Even the way people talk about a psi experience is remarkably different from people who are living with delusions. The staff at the Rhine
Research Center have many contacts from the public every day. The calls
about psi events like premonitions follow a typical pattern: "I didn't
believe in premonitions, but then I had a dream (or heard a voice or saw
a vision) about an event, and two days (or hours or months) later that
very thing happened. I was able (not able) to change what happened.
Can you tell me if it is real and what it means?"

The vast majority of psi events do not bring anything like a breakdown in function or coping. Most are too random, too fleeting, and too
trivial to do anything more than startle us. Even the initial confusion and
search for meaning that many people go through after a premonition are
all healthy ways to integrate the experience back into daily life.

In recent years a few researchers have looked for possible emotional
benefits of psi, and they have found several. Some psi events have been
linked to positive mental health, especially for those people with a spiritual worldview. Psi events can bring an "increased belief in life after
death, belief that their lives are guided or watched over by a higher force
or being, interest in spiritual or religious matters, sense of connection
to others, happiness, well-being, confidence, optimism about the future,
and meaning in life."[52]

Any event, psychic or otherwise, that causes a painful disruption in
your daily life or your sense of identity, deserves attention. If a psi event
disrupts your ability to cope and function in your life, it is time to talk to
someone. If premonitions bring you such a sense of overwhelming hope-
lessness that you can no longer work or concentrate, or if a psi event
causes you to isolate yourself from everyone, including trusted family
members, then it definitely is time to talk to someone.

Dr. Arthur Hastings eventually wrote guidelines for counselors who
work with people who have had a psi event. He wants to help counselors

emphasize their clients' functional abilities, specifically their ability to think and act according to their values and their common sense, no matter what they have experienced. He advises counselors to name their clients' experiences as potential psi without pestering them for proof and assure them that others have experienced something similar, that they are not alone. Sometimes simply knowing there is a name for the experience brings enough reassurance. Hastings wants to help people reconnect with what he calls "reliable reality,"[53] the reality of daily life. He believes we can all keep our rational brain working on each psi moment without losing our sense of awe and wonder at the possibility of psi.

So where do we go from here? We can find new ways of describing and accepting premonitions and other psi events that will help us balance our personal reality against entertainment's hyper-dramas. We don't have to choose between shutting down our experience as impossible and allowing a psi event to run away with our fears. If we stay with our direct experience of premonitions, we will find there is less drama (fewer exploding cars) but more emotional intensity as we acknowledge its importance. All we need is a meaning for premonitions that respects both the experience and the realities of daily life.

PART THREE

Meaning of Premonitions

CHAPTER 7

But What Does It Mean?
Making Sense of Premonitions

The prevailing popular stereotypes of premonitions do not capture the creative, playful, sometimes frightening, and always complex psi events people find. Premonitions in daily life are more flexible and more engaged with our ordinary concerns than popular entertainment can imagine right now. Once we step away from the glib stereotypes of premonitions in popular culture, we will have more room to find a new story about premonitions that will help us hold, explain, describe, and eventually use our experience.

Today the quest for meaning usually moves along two distinct paths. The first is a more general path used by scientists, philosophers, psychologists, and evolution experts. They are looking for a meaning that explains how premonitions are possible within linear time, or what internal mechanism makes them work. So far no one has come up with an acceptable answer. Scientists have found evidence for premonitions in the laboratory, but they still have no idea where premonitions come from, how they work in our brains, or what ultimate (evolutionary?) purpose they might have.

Fortunately we don't have to wait for a scientific explanation before we look for our own meaning for premonitions, and therein lies the second path. We can always ask, what does this premonition—my premonition—mean for me, what is its message for me? This question centers on how a premonition interacts with daily life, how it influences and is influenced by our daily concerns. It won't be a definitive answer; it won't give us the one definition for all premonitions. But the answer will put the demons of pop culture to rest. We can find answers to questions like:

- What does this say about my well-being?

- How will this premonition help me make a good life for myself and for my family?

- How do I find community with this experience? How do I protect those I love?

- How should I—how can I—respond to the insights I find?

We have plenty of examples of personal meaning forging ahead of our scientific understanding. A surprisingly large part of daily life trundles along just fine without having any scientific explanation for how it works. As I've mentioned before, scientists don't know how three pounds of unfeeling, unthinking matter suddenly leaps into the stratosphere of self-reflection, imagination, and play. For right now they have to be content with the answer that it just does. Scientists will keep searching for an explanation, but they don't expect anyone to relinquish the responsibilities and joys of consciousness while they work. And after work they roll along with the rest of us in their own ordinary days.

The question of personal meaning is answered by each of us individually, and that holds its two greatest attributes. First, the question of personal meaning can be answered by anyone who has had a premonition. Second, the experience of a premonition can hold more than one meaning or explanation. The question of personal meaning has many answers already, found by people who decided for themselves how they would make sense of their experience.

A Wealth of Individual Meanings

Dr. Louisa Rhine once combed through the premonition anecdotes she had collected, looking for one single meaning for the experience of a premonition and discovered instead almost as many different meanings for premonitions as the number of people who described them—thousands of meanings from thousands of events interpreted through thousands of different perspectives.[54] She was looking for an answer to the meaning of the phenomenon of premonitions, however, so her findings looked like a failure. The thousands of interpretations people had given to their experience didn't have enough in common with each other to develop one satisfying, overarching picture of premonitions.

I think these different explanations and descriptions of premonitions hold promise in our present-day search for meaning. The fact we can find thousands of personal meanings for premonitions holds an important insight into how we make sense of the rest of our lives, which will in turn help us each find a satisfying meaning for our own experience. The meaning for any single premonition is always embedded in each individual's life and is subject to each individual's choices. When we look more closely we can see connections emerge between our life, any given singular event, and the meaning we find for it.

And isn't this just the way all of daily life works? Every event, every object, every moment can hold so many different observations from different perspectives. Something as basic as an orange will change before our eyes as its background changes. An orange on a wooden plank of a table surrounded by Dickensian orphans or in a bowl of oranges in a tasteful Miami beach house or on an artist's table with a blue pitcher and flowers nearby or on a farmer's market cart or in the hands of a senior with Alzheimer's who can't quite remember what to do with it. The orange is an orange, but it becomes its particular orangey self through context and through our beholding eyes. Each perspective adds color and understanding to the whole. One brings out its sweetness, one its color and texture, one its nutritional value, one its provenance.

And so it is with premonitions. Each meaning brings to the fore new potential for how we understand premonitions. Each meaning gives us another angle from which to view our own experience. And each individual meaning helps us fill in the gaping holes left by our popular culture's limited (riveting, but limited) understanding of psi events.

Six Volunteers

I interviewed six people who had at least one premonition to find out how they made sense of their experience. I found these six people by sending a letter to fifty-five people who sang with me in a community choir. Nearly 20 percent of them contacted me.[55] Eleven out of fifty-five people had experienced something like a premonition at least once, although some had never considered the idea of a premonition before they read my letter. I also forwarded the same letter to a doctor I had met at a conference earlier that year who shared my interest. He talked to his patients and within a few days I received calls from four more people. From these fifteen volunteers, I chose to interview three men and three women.

During two long conversations with each of these six people, we investigated together their experience and meaning of premonitions. They responded with an astounding assortment of theories, questions, fears, jokes, rants, and religious and spiritual beliefs.

Evelyn has two young children and talks with enormous energy. With her long brown hair, she looks younger than her thirty-four years. She is the first in her family to get a college education and now runs a daycare business out of her home. When she was a teen and still a dedicated member of the Mormon Church, she was suddenly bombarded with premonitions that continued for nearly two years. She dreamed of simple school events and of a warning that helped her avoid a terrible accident, but she needed her mother's help to find a positive explanation.

Charlie is a police officer, on the force for over ten years, who is uncomfortable thinking about where his premonitions come from. All he can tell me is how he uses them to remain safe and catch criminals, something he does very well. He is quick to laugh at his own expense and especially at the puzzlement of colleagues who can't figure out how he manages to find so many criminals. One premonition helped him prepare for the emotional upheaval of helping young people after a fatal car accident.

Roger is a writer and an intellectually precise man who approaches life rationally, making him wary of discussing an experience that he does not understand. Physically he is small and wiry, with short gray hair and an intense gaze behind his glasses. He had one premonition about a tragic accident that happened more than thirty years ago, but that one moment remains sharp in his memory and as inexplicable as ever.

Julie describes herself as a bold and brassy blond, and loves to think about the bigger questions in life. She was delighted to find premonitions entering her life through her spiritual practice of meditation and is learning how to trust and follow them. As a social worker she helps people with physical and mental disabilities find and keep steady jobs. Her premonitions guide and support her, and include an insistent message to call her mother and a sudden command to meditate just before her car spun out of control.

Phillip is a division manager in a large software company, but he wears his hair long to remind himself of his creative passions as a writer and musician. Over the years he has developed his ability to catch glimpses of the future; he knows that when he has time to clear his mind, the premonitions will be waiting for him just below the surface of his awareness. He has used his premonitions to help him prepare for accidents, fender-benders, and missed dinner dates.

Olivia is a hospice chaplain who considers her premonitions a vital part of her Catholic faith, even if she doesn't mention them to the people in her church. She learned about premonitions from her mother and feels grateful for their presence. Premonitions have helped her prepare for news that would have been unexpected, giving her time to find a graceful response.

These people aren't famous or flashy. They are not professional psychics—most balk at the label of psychic. They all have jobs and careers they enjoy, but none have jobs that put them in the spotlight. Some are married to people who trust them; some are still looking for the right person. They haven't studied the research literature about premonitions, and none have discussed their experiences beyond a few trusted people.

Most of their premonitions are vague and fleeting, without the kind of visual details researchers need to verify them, which is very much like most premonitions. Their premonitions circle around their personal lives rather than signal world events, which again is true for most premonitions. They have had premonitions about such ordinary moments as a missed dinner date, as well as moments that saved them from potentially devastating accidents, but most of their premonitions could seem trivial if they weren't so rich in personal meaning. These are the premonitions of ordinary life.

Evelyn, Charlie, Roger, Julie, Phillip, and Olivia all accept the possibility of psi as real, *and* they critically evaluate each potential experience. It might seem like a delicate balance between belief and skepticism, but that is only because we too often limit our responses to either accepting everything without question or admitting nothing in a hardened skepticism. These six people have learned to compare the connecting events to their initial moments and to look for patterns, for chance, and for a connection that defies their usual explanations. They are willing to learn from their mistakes, from their successes, and from every time they claim (even to themselves) that a particular moment might connect to a future event.

Most importantly, they fit their premonitions into their whole lives, as one experience among many. This helps them balance their premonitions with every other way they think about the future. They evaluate their premonitions in the light of their common sense, life experience, spiritual beliefs, scientific understanding, and help from family and friends. They do not see themselves as at the mercy of an overpowering supernatural force, and they refuse to believe premonitions are dangerous to their mental health.

They trust that their premonitions are acting in their best interests, even if the messages they receive occasionally frighten them. They decide how they will respond to each premonition, based on the information they receive, the possible future event, and their values. They change what they can and forgive themselves for their inevitable limits. They can do all these things because they have found a meaning for premonitions that allows them to trust their experience. Their meanings help them understand that their premonitions are trustworthy and fallible, mysterious and limited.

A Short List

Here is a short list of personal meanings these six people have found or made for their premonitions. These are not the only meanings available for premonitions; doubtless thousands of meanings have been created or discovered. These meanings give a hint of the range and depth available to those who accept their experience as real.

....

MEANING OF PREMONITIONS
1. Practical Tool
2. Transformative Experience
3. Glimpse of the Future
4. A Little Bird
5. Flower
6. Ability
7. Anomaly

1. A premonition is a practical tool. This idea comes from Charlie, who uses his premonitions as one tool in his work to keep himself safe and to catch criminals. This meaning prioritizes Charlie's work-related needs over any supernatural element.

If premonitions are a practical tool, then they exist for our purpose. The reason for a premonition's existence depends solely on its usefulness to us, just like any other tool. If the premonition stops being useful we can shut it off. We don't have to worry about who created the tool or if we have the right to use it for our daily concerns.

2. A premonition is a transformative experience. Olivia described her premonitions as a transformative experience. One moment her world is ordinary; the next that same world feels saturated with new meaning. Premonitions give her a glimpse into a spiritual reality beyond her physical reality and in doing so they transform her life.

Transformative experiences are those that shift our entire perspective about the world or our lives. Almost anything can become a catalyst for a transformative experience, like the birth of a child, war, marriage, sudden poverty, or winning the lottery. Some people use the term "being born again" to describe a religious transformative experience.

If premonitions are a transformative experience, they can change our relationship to the world simply by showing up, no matter what the connecting event may turn out to be. Even the most trivial premonition can transform someone's entire worldview.

3. A premonition is a glimpse of the future. Phillip sees premonitions as his glimpses of a future that is already set in place. His premonitions give him time to prepare emotionally for what he knows inevitably will happen.

If a premonition is a glimpse of a predetermined future, then we are catching a sneak peek into our own future. How we caught the glimpse or what we will do about what we know becomes less pressing. Some have felt deeply comforted to know a terrible future event was out of their hands and all they had to do was prepare for the inevitable. It gave them a sense of being held through the worst times.

4. A premonition is a little bird, something tells me. Charlie's phrases are nonspiritual, nonscientific, nonskeptical, and nonbelieving. He avoids the spiritual or scientific implications of the most often used cultural images. The little-bird image conveys a friendly, even chummy feeling. Charlie hears a little bird, not an eagle screeching from above. Charlie gets "a little feeling of something not quite right" instead of a physically jarring vision of disaster. He said "Something tells me," which is less frightening than something warning or commanding. The words are devoid of power, force, or even mystery and instead emphasize the control and power of Charlie, the person who hears the little bird and makes decisions accordingly.

5. A premonition is a flower. A former colleague of mine thinks of premonitions as flowers that need careful tending, and she is the gardener. This meaning emphasizes the rarity and delicacy of premonitions, and their need of protection and encouragement.

If a premonition is a flower, then maybe it has no other function in life apart from its beauty and sweetness. In this meaning a premonition's importance lies in the fact that it exists at all and not that it is useful as a warning system.

6. A premonition is an ability. Phillip considers his premonitions an ability to catch glimpses of the future. He can nurture and develop his ability through practice and attention or let it dissipate through lack of use.

If a premonition is a human ability, then it becomes one more part of our human potential, neither greater nor lesser than any other human ability. While some people will have more natural talent, almost everyone can improve with training and support. Just like other abilities and skills, it will diminish if we don't give it our attention and passion.

7. A premonition is an anomaly. Roger understands his one premonition as a scientific anomaly, so he doesn't have to find a better explanation for it. He can let it remain as yet unexplained, while holding on to its reality. He knows something happened to him while in graduate school, but he has no need to work at figuring it out any further.

An anomaly is something that deviates from the normal order of things. In scientific circles anomalies lie outside the expected results; they are little bits of data that don't fit. One anomaly has little to no importance, and most researchers leave them out of their final results. An anomaly that appears in multiple experiments, however, raises new questions about the subject. Parapsychologists like the word anomaly because it lets them acknowledge the vividness of a personal experience without having to give it a specific meaning or explanation.

8. A premonition is a family tradition. Olivia grew up in a family that treasured and respected premonitions despite their church's warnings against premonitions. Olivia's mother had premonitions of her own, and she helped Olivia learn how to appreciate her experience.

Some people learn how to respond to premonitions from older generations. If premonitions are part of a family tradition, then each generation learns what to believe, how to act, and what to accept about premonitions.

9. A premonition is an inherited trait. Evelyn once wondered if she inherited her premonitions from her father, who also had premonitions. A premonition that is inherited has less to do with what we believe or how we look for them and more to do with basic human physiology. Inherited premonitions mean we did not search them out and we are not responsible for what we see. Inheriting the trait of premonitions means to some people that they belong to their families more deeply or in a new way.

10. A premonition is an additional—an extra—sensory perception. Dr. Joseph Rhine, the first person to devise a method to study psi in the laboratory, also was the first to call these phenomena extrasensory perceptions, or ESP. He worked to pull premonitions out of the supernatural realm by emphasizing premonitions as a natural perception, along with vision, hearing, smell, touch, and taste.

If premonitions are a human perception, then they pose no threat to the people who notice them. If they are a sensory perception, then our scientists can study them like other sensory perceptions and test for them rather than taking the word of people who claim them as their own. For the past eighty years researchers have done just that.

A premonition is surprisingly supple, yielding almost effortlessly to any number of meanings we find. These meanings are just a few out of the thousands, maybe hundreds of thousands of possible stories for premonitions. They are unique to the people who live them, and they each express a truth about premonitions, even as they contradict each other. They build on each other and offer us choices. If premonitions are as flexible and inclusive as other human experiences, as I believe they are, then we can learn something important from these many different aspects. Each meaning highlights a different aspect of the premonition experience, and each meaning highlights a particular truth.

Premonitions and Worldview

As much as premonitions may disrupt our notions of free will and the flow of time, I have discovered that how we make sense of them comes as much from us—from our beliefs and our assumptions—as from the actual premonition or its future event. The meanings we find may have less to do with the premonition and more to do with how we see the world in general, or our worldview.

A worldview consists of our most deeply held assumptions about the world and our place in it. Worldviews answer the fundamental questions of life such as, how did the world come into being? How do we find truth? What makes a good life? Is there a purpose or meaning to life? We find answers from our own unique balance of spiritual beliefs, scientific understanding, habits of thought, family traditions, professional training, education, common sense, and life experience. Our worldviews help us understand and integrate new experiences by giving us an automatic frame for all experiences.

Any new experience automatically gets plugged into our internal set of rules, explanations, and assumptions about the world. When a new event fits easily within our worldview, we know what to expect from it and from ourselves, because we understand the rules that govern it. When a new experience doesn't fit our internal rules or challenges our worldview, we can feel out of control, afraid, and confused.

This idea of worldviews can help us understand why we have such a range of reactions to premonitions. We don't react to the shape and size of premonitions, we react to what we believe premonitions mean. Some people are terrified by even small premonitions that connect to the smallest of future events. A man I met on an airplane recounted his premonition of knowing the elevator he was waiting for would not—would absolutely not—be the right elevator for him and his mother to take. He was a child at the time, and he told his mother they could not get on that elevator. When its doors opened they found workmen inside who told the waiting crowd the elevator was off-service for repairs. "How did I know that?" he asked me, his eyes wide. "I shouldn't have known that. Why was I so sure?" He already knew—his worldview had already insisted—that premonitions were not supposed to happen, leading him to feel challenged.

Others speak of their premonitions with awe and gratitude, even for warnings of terrible future events, because they already know premonitions are real and can help them. When Julie was driving home one evening from an afternoon party she felt a sudden and strong urge to chant a protective meditation song she had learned (and forgotten) more than ten years earlier. As she describes, "It was as strong as a voice right in my ear, *Turn off the radio and chant.* My intellect was saying, *This is silly, why would you need to do that?* But the voice said, *You need to do this now.* I had a choice, but I knew that if I were smart I wouldn't override this feeling. I turned the radio off and I began to sing." Less than a minute later Julie's car hit an oil slick on a bridge and began to spin out of control and into oncoming traffic. She could have felt terrified in that moment, but instead she felt held by a sense of calm, from the chant she still heard in her head. She knew she escaped unharmed because her internal voice protected her by helping her remain calm in the midst of a frightening situation. She has no doubt, "What I was being told to do helped protect me."

Another person might hear Julie's story and wonder why the premonition didn't protect her from the accident, that maybe the premonition hadn't done its job, but Julie doesn't see her premonition that way. In Julie's worldview, premonitions bring directions that hold and protect her through life's troubles, not keep all troubles away.

Science and Spirit and Daily Life

In 1997, Dr. Mary S. Stowell interviewed five women about the meanings they give to their precognitive dreams.[56] Like Louisa Rhine, she found each person had a unique view of her premonitions. When she looked more closely, she also found each personal meaning was rooted in one of three distinct worldviews; one relied on spirituality, one relied on science, and one she left unnamed, but that seems to balance somewhere between science and spirituality. I call this third worldview daily life.

Science and spirit find different answers to life's questions because they pose different questions to begin with and use different methods to find their answers. Science studies the material world, the part of the world that can be measured or categorized. Science asks, what is the universe made of and how long has all this stuff been here? Someone whose worldview relies on science can experience awe and a deep humbleness at the astonishing complexity of the physical universe and trusts that the answers to life's great questions can be found within this same brilliant universe. People with a strong science worldview often think of life's purpose in terms of chance, evolution, or perhaps the biological imperative to reproduce, rather than religion or spirituality.

Science offers an enormous range of explanations for premonitions. At its most limited, a scientific worldview states unequivocally that psi does not exist. People who rely on this limited view often see premonitions as a direct challenge to everything they know to be true. As part of her research Mary Stowell interviewed two people who had precognitive dreams and who shared this more limited scientific worldview. She found both volunteers felt distressed and overwhelmed by their precognitive dreams, primarily because their dreams contradicted what they already believed about how the physical world works. Stowell observed, "It was almost as if there was so strong a template for a rational worldview that the [premonition] experiences seemed alien and frightening."[57]

At its most expansive the scientific worldview encourages an open and curious engagement with the world in all its complexity. Scientific researchers study psi events and consciousness, and let their data lead them forward rather than dismissing data that seemed to contradict previous knowledge. People who live from this more expansive scientific worldview may look skeptically at premonitions, but they also are more willing to trust their direct experience, even if they do not yet have a satisfactory explanation.

Roger looks out on the world from a well-established scientific understanding of the universe. His one premonition, a warning about riding with his friends in a plane that subsequently crashed, didn't disrupt his worldview as much as it wedged itself between the way he thought the world should work and the way the world presented itself to him. His premonition shocked him, as the crash and its aftermath shocked him, but his rational brain quickly settled it into the category of a perplexing problem, an anomaly yet to be solved. He won't dismiss his experience just because his facts don't fit the prevailing scientific theory. His ability to hold on to his experience and think about it as just one more bit of data comes directly from his scientific worldview.

As Roger put it, "My feeling is that at some point, the process that we call science is going to find a rational explanation for it. I can't propose metaphysical suggestions for this. That's not part of my worldview. I just accept that it's real."

Roger didn't see a spiritual experience in his premonition, but instead saw a scientific puzzle. He felt no need to find spiritual significance because in his worldview he didn't have a spiritual experience. He saw science at work in the world.

A worldview that relies on spirit asks why the universe was created, who created it, and what its ultimate purpose may be. People who live from a spiritual worldview may see themselves as spiritual beings on a physical journey. Physical life is a classroom or a reflection of God's plan or a part of God's creation, but physical life gathers its meaning from beyond physical existence.

Premonitions that rise out of a spiritual framework have little need for proof. People who live from a primarily spiritual worldview already understand scientific proof will not help them accept or explain their experiences, so they have no need to look to science for further clarification. In some religious traditions even the desire for proof can seem like a lack of faith.

In the most conservative religions, the idea of premonitions can challenge holy doctrines. This challenge has led many religious leaders to condemn premonitions and all forms of psi as unholy, part of the occult, or a temptation to evil. These condemnations are remnants from the early Christian wars, when anyone who questioned official church doctrine was condemned as a heretic.

Evelyn grew up in a very small, tight-knit Mormon community that feared such things as premonitions, and her sudden influx of impressions when she was sixteen nearly overwhelmed her. She wanted help under-standing what was happening to her, but she knew she couldn't go to her church for support. As she explained, "I had it brought up in me as a belief that anything like a premonition was kind of—if it wasn't God it was something else, and the other something else would have to be Satan!"

Just as Roger saw a scientific anomaly, Evelyn saw the devil at work. Her foundation for her life at the time belonged to the church, and sud-denly she was looking at the world with the eyes of a wavering believer. She was not seeing a scientific anomaly that she then interpreted as potentially evil; she was seeing the presence of evil in her home and in her dreams, and it frightened her, no matter how innocuous the future event might be. She began sleeping with the bible under her pillow as a protective talisman.

At its most broad interpretation, the spiritual worldview extends beyond any particular religious doctrine and into a more universal sense of human spirituality. Spiritual worldviews have helped many people welcome their premonitions as ultimately good and beneficial, and even a significant part of their spiritual life. Julie left her Protestant Church when she was a young woman to follow a more informal and personal spiritual journey. She practiced meditation as one part of her spiritual discipline and learned to quiet her internal chatter long enough to hear a quieter voice giving her directions. When these directions helped her avoid or cope with disturbing future events, she accepted it all as part of her spiritual journey. Her premonitions connect her to a higher, guiding spirit. She said, "There are other things that if you quiet down enough you can hear, other connections. My tendency is to say that it is spirit connected. I have no other way of viewing it."

Julie is spiritual; she sees a spiritual presence moving through her life. Just as importantly, she lives in a world in which human beings have free will. Her premonitions come as warnings that feel like suggestions, nudges, pushes in a certain direction, which she then decides how, when, and if to follow. She works in partnership with her guiding presence, and she always keeps the last word.

I love this about Julie's premonitions, or rather about how Julie understands her premonitions. She knows her guiding spirit is present to help but never command. The inner voice nudges her in a certain direction, but she is free—always—to choose a different response. She has even turned her guides down when the timing wasn't right, when she was busy, or when she wasn't in the mood. And because she knows her premonitions exist to give her life added richness and meaning, the choices and warnings they present do not frighten her.

The third worldview model is less often noticed, but can be every bit as powerful as the first two. I call this third model daily life, as it grows out of daily life experience through family and family traditions. Whereas science builds its knowledge over centuries through experiments and studies and spirit reveals its knowledge through religious doctrine or spiritual practice, daily life transfers knowledge from one generation to the next within the intimacy of family. Daily life is built on family traditions, cultural teachings, and common sense.

Those who lean on the daily life worldview learn from direct experience, families, teachers, and friends. People who rely on family traditions to help them make sense of premonitions may be very comfortable with science and may belong to a religious community. But they have seen how their premonitions can be an extension of their family traditions using the habits and beliefs of past generations to ground their lives.

Charlie calls his job the best career he could have ever found. Charlie accepts his premonitions because they work for him, just as his father taught him they would. He also learned from his father, who was in law enforcement before him, that when working in a dangerous profession any warning should be heeded, even warnings that can't be readily explained. He explained, "It's helped me be successful at catching bad guys, and it's helped me stay alive. That's it. That's the bottom line." He found a meaning for his premonitions that grew naturally out of his family tradition.

Charlie has no need for metaphysics or for scientific research. He has no need to explore the origins of his warnings or figure out how they interact with his brain. He won't philosophize about meaning or follow the research to prove its existence. He doesn't worry about who created this tool he uses or if he has the right to use it for his daily concerns. Its reason for existence depends solely on its usefulness, just like any other tool he uses. He accepts his premonitions because they work for him.

Not everyone who sees the world through this daily life model looks like Charlie. Phillip is in many ways a mirror image of Charlie. He is deeply religious, philosophical, and intensely interested in the world of scientific research as well as metaphysics. But when he talks about premonitions he draws upon the lessons he learned—and rejected—from his family traditions. He views the world as an artist (musician and fiction writer) and outsider in today's society. Premonitions are one more marker of his difference in his family and society, and as such he welcomes them.

I have mixed and matched these three models for worldviews for most of my life, and I imagine most other people have as well. Our spiritual beliefs can add purpose and direction to scientific discoveries; our family traditions can either soften or sharpen the doctrines of religious communities; science can either confirm or poke holes in the family lessons we learn about the world.

Olivia might have had the same trouble with premonitions that Evelyn had. But Olivia's mother taught Olivia that premonitions are a part of God's love, even if the church was not ready to hear it. Olivia sees her premonitions as a window between this physical world and a greater, transcendent, loving reality. She explains, "If it has always felt like a loving, open connection, then why wouldn't I trust it? It wasn't something to be feared. It was something to be embraced." Olivia's meaning for premonitions is deeply rooted in her worldview within the Roman Catholic Church, but it was her mother's acceptance of premonitions that gave Olivia permission to welcome and embrace her experience.

These three perspectives are not mutually exclusive. We might feel more confident viewing events from one perspective, but we all have the ability to mix and match. We can use ideas from all three perspectives— science, spirit, and family tradition—to explore events and activities in depth. We put each perspective on like a different pair of glasses, giving ourselves permission to view the same experience from three (or more) different angles.

For instance, sports announcers often shift between science, spirit, and daily life when they work a game. They describe the techniques the athletes use, the specific training many athletes go through, the way their muscles move under particular stress—all very technical and scientific. They also talk about the athletes' hearts and aspirations—their passion for winning, their love for the game, the spirituality of play. Finally they talk about the athletes' work ethic, their family support, their community's pride, any tradition of the game that runs in the family. Each aspect gives more understanding of the player, the game, and the sport.

I was never much of an athlete, but I knew singing in much the same way—as a spiritual, technical, and familial experience—and each perspective deepened my overall understanding of music. I studied theory and vocal technique, practiced scales and arpeggios every day, learned each note and where to place it in my voice, and memorized the tunes. But if I performed with just the technique I missed making actual music, which lay beyond the notes. I had to let go of technique and throw myself into the heart of music, where the audience and I could feel transformed by its meaning. The technique was necessary, but so was the art. Finally, I practiced music out of habit, out of the work ethic I learned as a child, out of my parents' reassurance that practice makes better, if not perfect.

What Makes a Meaning Work

How will you know which meaning is the right one for you? Vernon Neppe, a neurologist and psychiatrist who has studied the experience of déjà vu, takes a pragmatic approach to all psi events. While he doesn't address how a psi event might be helpful, he maintains any psi event that does not cause psychological harm should be considered within the range of normal, healthy human events.

Arthur Hastings, a psychologist who has written on how counselors can best help people suffering with a psi event, has the same clarity. Keep the experience as long as you can think for yourself. Keep it if you can see more options instead of fewer, if it opens your life to possibilities without overwhelming you. Learn how to live with it using your life experience, your common sense, your own good judgment. Push back if you have to. Shut it down if you must. But always remember you have control in your life, even in the face of something as yet unexplained.

A meaning that restores confidence will not make the culture's stereotypes go away, but it can armor you against the worst of its habitual fears. With a personal meaning that gives you confidence—maybe even joy—you will have less need to look to popular entertainment for another explanation.

Most importantly, your willingness to enter into a conversation with your experience, by naming it and finding a meaning for it from your own life, will reinforce the control you do have with premonitions, even the ones that scare you. You do not have to live at the mercy of an unknown force; you can be in conversation with it. You have no more to fear from a premonition than you have from a powerful dream.

I, too, take a pragmatic approach to this question. A good meaning allows me to feel competent and strong, and to not worry too much about my sanity. A good explanation will allow me to stay connected with the people I love and not push me to abandon my life, my friends, or family. A good meaning is one in which I get to keep my common sense, independence, values, and worldview. A good meaning allows me to make more decisions because of the premonition and not fewer, even if the only options I can see involve how I will respond emotionally. A good meaning gives me peace even if there is nothing I can do to change what is coming. A good meaning helps me function in life.

The six people I interviewed all forged their premonition meanings from their personal worldviews that were built upon their life experience, spiritual beliefs, family traditions, professional training, education, and friendships. They allowed premonitions into their lives, neither shutting them down as impossible nor allowing them to take over. Despite all the popular images of people being driven to distraction with gruesome visions of terrible murders, these people have no fear their premonitions will one day fill them with images they cannot control.

Compare them to my friend Helen in chapter 6, who lives in fear of having another premonition, largely because of mainstream culture's depiction of premonitions as messengers of death. Helen fears her premonition not because its connecting event terrified her, although she was saddened for her friend. She fears her premonition because fear is the only reaction she has learned.

The meanings we choose give us more than just an acceptable explanation for a premonition. Our personal, idiosyncratic meanings help us make peace with an otherwise unknown and incomprehensible event. More than that, the meanings we find will help us know what to expect from premonitions and how to respond to one with integrity and trust. The meanings we find, perhaps even more than the experience itself, will propel us forward into a more trusting relationship with the unknown.

In the next few chapters we will see how meanings help define who we are and what community we want. The meanings we find will give us new choices or limit our responsibility. The meanings will tell us if we can use our premonitions to keep ourselves safe or if we need to wait for an inevitable future.

CHAPTER 8

What Does It Say About Me?
Premonitions and Self-Identity

If the first question about premonitions is "What does it mean?" then the second question, "What does it say about me?" follows so closely and comes wrapped so tightly around the first that the two questions could be mistaken for one. Whatever we decide premonitions mean—what causes them, why they appear, what they offer—will affect how we see ourselves as well. The reverse is also true: how we see ourselves will affect our meaning for premonitions, in a quickly spinning circle.

"What does this experience say about me?" is the second most frequently asked question of psi researchers. When people have asked parapsychology researchers about premonitions, they don't want only a scientific explanation for the event. They want to know what kind of a person could have had such an experience. They want assurance about their own self-identity.[58]

In the last two chapters I listed roughly fifteen different meanings for premonitions: a powerful tool, a delicate flower, a punishment, a moment of transcendence, an ability, and an anomaly, among thousands of other meanings. Looking back over the list of premonition meanings it is easy to see the way each one helps shape our self-identity. If a premonition is an ability, then I am talented. If a premonition is an anomaly, I am its objective observer. If a premonition is spiritual guidance, then I am spiritually attuned to that guidance. Besides giving us a way to accept our premonitions, these meanings say something important about each person who has the premonition.

My colleague Andrea described her premonitions as a flower and without ever stopping to think it through, the image of a flower carries an identity of Andrea as gardener. This is a strong image, giving her some control with premonitions. As a gardener she can nurture or neglect the flowers, making her more powerful than any single premonition she may find. The image of premonition as flower allows her to think of herself as a caretaker.

When Charlie sees his premonition as a practical tool he becomes a tool-wielder, maybe even the tool-maker. He judges the premonition by its usefulness in his daily life, and he has a say in how and when he puts it to use. A practical tool could never be confused with a curse or punishment, so Charlie never sees himself as a victim of, or cursed by, his experience. He is not a victim, and he is not a spiritually attuned person because a tool has nothing to do with spirituality. He is instead a pragmatic man who has put his premonitions to good use.

Of course, Andrea may think of her premonitions as a flower because she already is a gardener, and already sees her world in terms of flowers. Charlie may already have seen himself as a pragmatic man, which helped him see his premonitions as a powerful tool he could use. The meanings we find have their roots in how we already see ourselves. If I see myself as talented, I may see my premonition as one more talent I can develop. If I am already an objective observer of the world, I am likely to see a premonition as an anomaly. If I have a strong spiritual belief that allows premonitions, I can then easily see premonitions as one part of my spiritual journey.

Meaning and identity spin around and around, both leaning on and influencing the other. Each meaning carries a frame through which we see ourselves; each meaning reflects our self-identity. As long as the meaning we find and our self-identity match in a way that helps us in our daily life, we will have no troubles. Our trouble comes when our experience directly contradicts or challenges our view of the world, or our self-identity.

If I already know a premonition is not possible, if I already see myself as someone who would never deal with such nonsense, then a premonition is going to cause problems for me. Evelyn enjoyed school and was active in her Mormon church. She also knew from her church and from her family that premonitions were evil, spiritually dangerous, a punishment from God, or a temptation from Satan. See how quickly her meaning for premonitions became a new aspect of her self-identity:

I thought that somehow Satan had gotten in my home and I was being possessed. I kept thinking, "What have I done wrong? To put myself in this position I must really be bad. This must be an evil possession of some kind, for not going to church enough." I started going to church fanatically, and slept with my Bible under my pillow. ~Evelyn

Evelyn's meaning for premonitions had an immediate effect on how she saw herself. If premonitions come from Satan, then she must be possessed. If premonitions are a punishment from God, then she must have done something wrong to deserve such punishment. Looking back, Evelyn now can see there was no reason for God to be angry with her, but at sixteen she was convinced she must be guilty of something, or else she wouldn't have been punished with premonitions.

Premonitions are most upsetting to those people who already hold the firm belief that premonitions can't, or shouldn't, happen. If a premonition contradicts how they see the world, no matter how delicately it appears or how useful they may find it, they can feel personally threatened by it.

They won't think to themselves, "Wow, I guess I have to re-think my self-identity and views about how the world works." No, most people will wonder along with Evelyn, "What is wrong with me?"

It takes courage to accept those aspects of our lives that don't conform to our expectations. Evelyn had been taught to fear and reject premonitions, which led her to wonder if she had to fear and reject herself. She couldn't stop having the premonitions.

If premonitions cause a rift in how we see ourselves, if they unbalance us with their appearance, what do we do? Fortunately for us, premonitions are not the only events that stray close to the edge of what the culture finds acceptable. Daily life is full of such new events and experiences that challenge how we see ourselves, and most of us have developed habits that allow us to integrate these new experiences with a minimal amount of disruption.

Here are three ways in which we manage the interplay between a new, jarring experience and our personal identity. Each strategy most likely will be familiar to you, even if you haven't thought it through before now. Each strategy is more like a habit really, to help us keep both our experience and our worldview without sacrificing our self-identity in the process. Each habit/strategy reminds us we do not live at the mercy of any one experience, no matter how much it challenges our sensibilities.

First, we can look for explanations we like better that already exist within the worldview we do trust. Second, we can find a safe emotional distance between what we experience and how we identify ourselves. Finally, we can identify closely with our experience but fold it in with all of our other identities, which lessens its impact on us.

Find Another Message Within Your Worldview

The first option is to look within your own worldview to find another message. Every system, whether it be religious or family or a school of thought, learns how to incorporate a wide range of interpretation. The range of ideas that exist within current scientific thought and within spiritual/religious traditions is immense. It is possible to hold firmly to a core belief while still interpreting that belief along a never-ending continuum. Even among the cozier confines of family traditions you might be able to find someone who shares an interest or question of yours.

If you live within a predominantly scientific worldview you still have a choice about which scientific interpretation, which theories, and what kinds of research you eventually will trust. Carl Sagan (*The Demon-Haunted World*) uses the scientific language of discovery, exploration, and a fearless reliance on data, wherever it leads:

> The scientific way of thinking is at once imaginative and disciplined. Science invites us to let the facts in, even when they don't conform to our preconceptions. It counsels us to carry alternative hypotheses in our heads and see which best fits the facts. It urges on us a delicate balance between no-holds-barred openness to new ideas, however heretical, and the most rigorous skeptical scrutiny of everything—new ideas and established wisdom.[59]

Sagan's words lean toward scientific exploration, imagination, and openness to new ideas (balanced with skepticism). Other scientists describe science in less lofty terms, calling science a method that helps us explain, predict, and control whatever it is we want to study, such as weather prediction, and medical explanations that lead to control and eradication of disease. Individual scientists push forward new ideas and reconsider old ones all the time, even as they argue about which ideas will lead somewhere promising and which are nonsense. Open the scientific journals to any subject and you will find multiple studies that contradict each other until a consensus slowly and painstakingly builds over the years.

So how does a strongly scientific-minded individual see herself when a premonition appears? Certainly some scientists insist premonitions have not yet been proven to exist and turn their attention to other projects, but other researchers find the evidence for premonitions both credible and convincing. If this person learns only the negative message for premonitions, and isn't willing to consider alternatives, she may be in trouble.

Mary Stowell's two volunteers who held strong scientific views found their premonitions didn't just disrupt their view of how the world works. The premonitions disrupted how they saw themselves. They had no positive image for people who had dreams like theirs, and as a direct result they doubted their own sanity—a highly distressing thought for professionals.

It is possible, however, to keep a scientific worldview and accept an unusual experience. Roger frames his experience as scientifically unexplainable rather than scientifically impossible, and this makes all the difference. He prides himself on his rational, scientific worldview, *and* he accepts his direct experience of a premonition even though he cannot explain what happened. He bases his reasoning on a philosophy of science very much like Dr. Sagan's, one that allows for the emergence of new ideas.

In this meaning his identity becomes one of possessing a fearless open curiosity, something he values. He can accept his premonition as real data—facts that didn't conform to his preconceptions, but valid nevertheless. He has found a message within the science worldview that helps him trust his experience and maintain his identity as a rational man who is both open to, and questioning of, all human experience. He trusts the scientific process will make sense of it eventually.

The spiritual paradigm is as wide-ranging as the scientific paradigm, with room for every belief from the most conservative religious doctrine to the most far-flung dreams of the New Age. Church communities frequently splinter off and form new identities as leaders push for either more reform or a return to tradition. Open the holy books and you can find support for almost any social or theological position you want to make.

Within the spiritual worldview a premonition need not bring automatic condemnation. While some religious communities firmly believe premonitions are the mark of evil, like Evelyn's church taught her, other religions and spiritual communities accept premonitions easily. The sacred

texts for Judaism, Christianity, and Islam all include early stories of premonitions that marked the spiritual path of leaders, even if later doctrines
discouraged their followers from doing the same. Eastern philosophies
teach some form of meditation to help clear the mind and focus on
the present moment. While premonitions are not considered signs of
enlightenment, most meditation practices lead to an increased awareness
of premonitions.[60]

As a child I learned the biblical story of Joseph and his many-colored
coat. Joseph was favored by his father because Joseph had extraordinary
dreams and a gift for interpreting them as signs of future events. He
eventually interpreted the Pharaoh's dream of seven fat cows being eaten
by seven lean cows as meaning Egypt would have seven years of good
harvest followed by seven years of poor harvest. Joseph's interpretation
of the dream, and the Pharaoh's willingness to act on that interpretation,
saved the Egyptian people from starvation.

Even the more conservative traditions within the Christian faith are
wide enough to include and celebrate those rare moments of knowing
a future event. I once met a woman who was attending an Evangelical
conference. She understood premonitions as God's personal answers to
her prayers. She asks Jesus for help and receives messages from Him—
warnings and guidance to help her understand her personal future. By
understanding those moments as answered prayers and a direct communication with Jesus, she feels blessed and enriched. She doesn't worry
that other religious traditions might reject her experience, and she
doesn't pay attention when more mainstream Christian beliefs contradict
what she knows. Each communication about her future strengthens her
identity as a deeply religious and devoted person.

If we believe premonitions come as a spiritual gift, then we may feel
gifted, or spiritually connected to a higher power. Olivia names her premonitions as spiritual moments of transcendence. Their presence—her
momentary flashes of knowledge—tell her she is blessed and this meaning for her experience reinforces her self-identity as a spiritual person.

Even if our families have no connection with psi events, the power of family lessons to name and hold our experience is unmatched by either science or religion. Our parents are our first teachers, our first and primary lens through which we view the world. We grow up and move away, find our own values and explore other cultures, but the lessons we learn first run the deepest, and those are the ones we trust first when confronting something new. My earliest lessons about how the world is put together came from my family. I looked at my premonitions not through the eyes of the scientific tradition alone, but through the eyes of my parents' interpretation of science. I understood my premonitions not from my church, but from my parents' interpretation of our church.

Evelyn shows the power of these family messages. By the time she was seventeen she had suffered through premonitions of small and large events for more than a year. She had tried a few times to explain to her mother what was happening, but her mother resisted the very idea of premonitions. She didn't call Evelyn a liar exactly, but she was sure Evelyn was mistaken. Her mother's refusal to believe her frightened Evelyn, and she retreated from friends and her church in misery.

Finally one morning Evelyn told her mother about a dream she had had of her boyfriend showing up unexpectedly at their house, holding wilted lilacs behind his back. Her boyfriend had never brought flowers before, so this tiny event seemed highly unlikely to both of them. Later that day he did show up with wilted lilacs held stiffly behind his back, and her mother finally saw the connection between Evelyn's dream and a future event for herself. From that moment on she was on Evelyn's side, and was able to give Evelyn a new way of seeing herself. When Evelyn reached a crisis point later that year, fretting that her premonitions meant she was going crazy, her mother was able to give her a new meaning for her premonitions and for herself.

[My mother] told me, "You're not crazy! You're one of the smartest people I know, you're not crazy!" She said, "Some people just have this ability, I guess." She called it an ability and you know, it was a little easier to take after that. ~Evelyn

The difference between thinking I have an ability versus thinking I am going crazy or being punished by God is profound. An ability carries the meaning of creativity and power. If a premonition is an ability, then I am capable of doing a premonition (in language we don't have yet). I can develop an ability, like I develop my ability to play a musical instrument or throw a ball. Most importantly, I can safely wrap my identity around an ability, much like athletes and performers find their identity in their actions.

Evelyn's mother didn't reach for scientific studies or for religious beliefs to help her daughter. Instead she held firm to her belief in Evelyn's intelligence and sanity. She named Evelyn's experience an ability and the power of her naming it helped Evelyn grab hold of this identity too. Evelyn now could see herself as someone strong enough to have an unusual ability, something that might help her have a better life. Evelyn's mother helped her reclaim her inner strength.

Evelyn accepted this meaning for premonitions because it came from her mother, someone she trusted to understand the world. Her mother's interpretation of premonitions carried enough weight to balance against her church teachings, and gave Evelyn the solid ground she needed to view her experience and herself in a positive light.

A strong positive meaning can help us accept ourselves with premonitions even as we remain connected to this skeptical culture. We can keep our common sense, our rational decision-making, and our spiritual or religious values, while still accepting our premonitions as one part of who we are.

Find a Safe Distance
Between Premonition and Self-Identity

Just as some people identify themselves closely by their premonition, other people make a point to avoid a connection. Not everyone wants to go through the work of re-evaluating their identity or their worldview in light of a new or unusual experience. That is where the beauty of keeping a safe distance between experience and identity really shines.

Rather than rejecting the premonition outright, or identifying ourselves as someone who has such an experience, we hold on to the premonition as something that happened around us, but is not us. We hold it out away from ourselves, a little bit at arm's length. We don't throw it away, exactly, but we also don't say this is who I am. Instead we say this is something I have, or this is something that happened to me. A premonition can be something that just happens to us, and not necessarily something that implies anything about us.

This kind of distance happens all the time as we pick and choose how we want to see ourselves. It is not possible to completely identify with every experience and event that comes our way. The question of identity is more complex than just events and experiences as well. Our identities are influenced by ethnicity, race, religion, financial status, gender, and sexual orientation, as well as fashion and aesthetics. We each decide on any given day which parts of our lives will be fundamental to our identity. One day I might be an American and the next an American *writer,* with the emphasis on what I do rather than where I was born.

Work and self-identity often wind together, but not on all days. I have been a student, a mental health therapist, a social worker, a singer, and a writer, and have defined myself at least in part by all of these jobs, but I haven't identified myself by every job I ever worked.

While in college I worked as a waitress in a pizza joint, but I defined myself as a student waitressing for money. I kept a distance between what I did and my self-identity. I had a job but I had the choice to keep that job separate from me, and not let it define me. My choice was made easier because I had parents who could help me with college tuition, and because every other person working in that pizza joint was doing the same thing. No one identified him- or herself by their job. Even the manager was a struggling artist. We were all struggling artists, dancers, musicians, writers, and students, who all worked at that pizza joint for money. Work was work, satisfying because of what it brought us, but in no way did the work define us. We made sure of that.

Even a frightening event like a new cancer diagnosis can be felt as either a life-changing experience or merely a temporary setback in a person's life that is crowded with other goals. I have met people whose lives have been transformed by chronic illness, who have chosen to let it transform them into someone new, hopefully better and wiser and stronger. These are the people who join or start up support groups, who delve into education and advocacy work, who find ways to challenge and even change the healthcare system.

But for every person who takes on the identity of illness, others will take the opposite approach and say, I will not let the illness define me. I have the illness, it does not have me. They keep a distance between how they see themselves and the experience they must go through. They are not transformed by the illness, but see it instead as just one more obstacle to overcome. Both of these approaches can work for the people who choose them, and both are respected choices in the culture. These choices can show every person with a new diagnosis that there is a wide range of strong responses he or she can make.

Charlie is married with kids, but when I was interviewing him the identity he chose to bring to the fore was his professional identity. His career both defines him and calls for what he considers the best part of himself. He is proud to wear the uniform and grateful he can protect his community. He has frequent premonitions, but he would never consider himself psychic. He doesn't consider himself anything in relation to his premonitions; he doesn't allow the experience to define him in any way. A premonition is something he uses in his work, something he *has*, and not something he *is*.

I'm sure I don't look at myself as being extra like ESP-ish! I don't look at myself as being someone that can read a mind or anything like that. I don't believe my intelligence is above anybody else's. I'm an average person, I'm kind of a fat boy and I'm a crummy housekeeper. There isn't anything special about me with the exception that I have an intuitive thought into what's going to happen. ~Charlie

Charlie loves the help his premonitions bring, but he will not build his self-identity around his premonitions, and that distance gives him important benefits. The distance helps him keep the vitality of his premonitions without making himself vulnerable to the larger culture's reflexive skepticism.

Researcher Vernon Neppe knows that when people closely link their self-identity to psi events like premonitions they put themselves at risk of being personally rejected by the larger culture. He has worked with people who were not able to handle the distress of such rejection, some of whom grew embittered. They were unwilling to reject the culture that rejected them, but also unwilling to surrender their identity as experiencers. They isolated themselves from friends and family, and struggled more with work and relationships. In short their psi experience, or rather their primary identity as a psi experiencer, caused a level of distress that threatened to disrupt their lives.

If we don't identify so closely with the experience, we will not feel as strongly the sting of personal rejection. Charlie understands this well. He does not feel personally rejected just because he can't talk about his experience with his colleagues. When the other officers laugh at an occasional psychic-type joke he knows they aren't laughing at him. And because he doesn't feel personally rejected by his colleagues, he feels no pressure to reject his premonitions in turn. He gets to keep his premonitions—at arm's length, but still present—and keep his place within his community.

This kind of distancing ourselves from our experience also gives us more room to explore the experience. If our identity doesn't depend on this one moment being a premonition, then we can question it more closely without fear of disrupting or challenging it. A little bit of distance helps us remain more honest with ourselves. We can hold it up to strong light, knowing whatever we find will not challenge our identity, because the experience doesn't affect how we see ourselves.

Use Multiple Roles to View Premonitions

Neppe's warnings about the perils of living with a stigmatized experience come from a spirit of helpfulness, I know. I am sure most researchers would rather people not feel personally rejected due to an unusual psi event.

But the warnings also come from a certain blindness to the power of holding on to a personal experience despite cultural pressures to conform. People often go out of their way to identify themselves by aspects of their lives that don't quite fit within accepted standards for the community, and they do so for a host of good reasons. Some value nonconformity. They like the personal integrity that comes with self-acceptance in the face of opposition. Some even create new communities based on their (slightly) nonconforming life choices. Artists and writers congregated in New York's Greenwich Village, Toronto's West Queen Street, and the Left Bank of Paris in the 1920s. Each new community builds strength in numbers, when like-minded souls find and nurture each other.

In the past few decades we have seen many previously marginalized groups become more visible and demand more respect from mainstream culture, and as a result everyone has benefitted. The culture has become more flexible and accepting of diverse opinions, traditions, and beliefs; there is more room for all of us to learn from the wisdom other cultures and perspectives offer. And the groups that had been shut out of a common, mainstream daily life find themselves fitting into the social fabric at last, their needs addressed by the whole.

There is another common strategy people use to incorporate a stigmatized experience into their self-identity while still fitting into the mainstream. Rather than putting all their identity into one experience-basket, they simply add the new experience to an ever-expanding pile of multiple identities they enjoy.

They enjoy the spinning conversation between experience and identity, and don't want to distance themselves from any of it. They take each experience into their identity to see how it changes the way they see themselves and the world. They say, I bowl therefore I am a bowler and the world is full of lanes. I cook therefore I am a cook (and a bowler) and the world is a feast. They enjoy a flexibility of spirit that lets them put on and take off any experience. Most of us spend adolescence trying on the trappings of many different identities, looking for a fit between our experience and a community.

I had a friend in graduate school who enjoyed his life in just this way, and it drove me crazy. Now I think I was probably jealous of him, but at the time I didn't understand how he could be so casual in his presentation to the world. I remember one night I met him at a bar to hear a jazz/soul singer. When I first walked into the bar it reminded me of the old movies from the fifties, where all the cool cats and beat poets wore berets and turtle-neck sweaters, and smoked cigarettes while writing in their journal, the music swirling about them. And then I spotted my friend in the back, wearing a black turtle-neck and beret, cigarette and journal in hand. He had jumped with both feet into the world of 1950s jazz music, trying on the fashion and the passion of the beat generation, only thirty years too late. I couldn't jump into the jazz scene like he did. I was too carefully settled into my identity as a student. I was not going to let a night of jazz change my life, not even for an hour.

If my friend ever has a premonition, I have no doubt he will consider himself psychic (and a therapist and an artist and a poet) and immediately seek out ways to develop his gift. People like him open their arms wide and embrace their experience as their newest self-identity. They will be linked with their experience no matter what it is, because that is how they live in the world. They don't worry about rejection because they have so many other ways of being in the world. If the world rejects them for one identity they can pull up another one and fit right in again.

My friend is a slightly amplified example of how most of us navigate through multiple identities. No matter how closely we identify with any one experience, we all have a good twenty or so other identities at our disposal. Phillip considers himself psychic, even though he knows the word carries negative connotations. He knows he runs a risk of being personally rejected when he identifies so closely with an experience that is rejected by the larger culture, but this just makes him draw his experience closer. He can do this because he defines himself just as passionately with his other interests, other roles, and other abilities. He is a writer, a musician, and a devout Christian. He is American, Scottish, a goof-ball, a science fiction enthusiast, an avid reader, an entertainer, and a person with his own secrets to keep.

By having so many roles to choose from, rejection by the larger culture for any one experience is less likely to throw him off-balance. Premonitions are just one part of his overall identity, one perspective on the world. If a premonition conflicts with his understanding of himself as a Christian, it does not conflict with his identity as a musician or a science fiction writer. He simply switches his perspective to that of another role that can accommodate the premonition more easily.

He is well aware of how many scientists have rejected claims of psi events, but he also knows many scientific discoveries were ridiculed before becoming common knowledge. As a musician he plays music written hundreds of years ago by people whose work was rejected initially as too odd, too discordant, too weird for popular taste. From this history he takes comfort that a time will come when premonitions are also widely accepted, once the veil of cultural disapproval lifts.

We can find multiple meanings for our premonitions. We can lean on the multiple ways we define ourselves without premonitions. And we can keep a little bit of distance between a premonition and who we are. Most importantly, we can explore the meanings found by other people, who live from other worldviews, who have made other choices. With each new idea we gain more choices for our own lives. I don't think we can fully adopt a meaning that doesn't somehow fit with what we already know of the world, but just knowing these other meanings exist can help us stretch our own imaginations to find positive meanings, meanings that help us have our best lives possible.

Finding a meaning you can trust is key. You don't have to be victimized or haunted or overwhelmed. You don't have to fight against your perception or doubt your sense of reality. You only have to find a way to live well with what you have, and fold your experience into your life just as you have done thousands of times before with other ideas, other experiences.

When you find a solid meaning for your premonition, that meaning will help you see yourself in a new light as well. A positive meaning can help you find the person you want to be—adventurous, pragmatic, curious, deeply spiritual, skeptical, questioning—whatever it is that upholds your values. Just one acceptable meaning can help you trust your experience as both real and relatively benign, and give you the courage to trust yourself.

With that trust you will have an easier time finding others who share your experience, or your worldview, or both, in community. You will have an easier time deciding how you will respond to the premonitions you find.

CHAPTER 9

What Do I Do Now?
How to Respond to a Premonition

If you find a premonition early, before its connecting event, you might find a new choice waiting for you. When you know—or think you know—what is coming next, then you have time to think about how you want to respond to it, which is no small thing. Louisa Rhine once looked at thirteen hundred premonition anecdotes from her Rhine Collection and found more than half of the people didn't know they had had a premonition until the future event happened, making the question of how to respond irrelevant.[61]

So we've established you are lucky to find a premonition early, but now what? How do you decide what to do? If the premonition is about some small moment you might not feel in a rush to do anything. But if you wake from a dream filled with intense images or feel a rising anxiety about some unknown impending danger, you might want to know exactly what your options are.

I have found three different factors that have helped many people figure out what to do with a premonition. The first is to know exactly what information you have. No premonition is perfect, as we have seen. Gathering the details from the initial moment or what you already know from the rest of daily life will help you know what kind of response is possible. If you dream the winning numbers of a lotto ticket, for instance, your response is pretty clear. A vague, uneasy feeling that won't go away, however, gives few clues about what you can do next.

The second factor rests on what you know your premonition means. The meaning you have found for your premonition—what it's for, how it works, why one is appearing to you right now—offers a working template of what you can expect, what options are open to you, and the extent and limit of your responsibility.

The final factor is how your premonition fits in with the rest of your life. This last factor isn't talked about much in the literature. Premonition anecdotes often make it sound like people make their choices based solely on the strength of their premonition, but in my interviews I found this isn't the case. The people I interviewed always balanced their new information against what they already knew, their plans for their day, how their decisions would affect the people around them.

A premonition can be accurate in its details and still not give us the reasons why such a future was shown to us. We still get to decide whether the information is practical for us. When I was sixteen I decided not to take the upstairs bedroom in my parents' new house, even though my premonition clearly showed me living there. I trusted my premonition's accuracy, but I didn't trust it knew which room was right for me. If I had believed my premonition was showing me my destiny, what *must* happen, I would have lost out on the bedroom of my teenage dreams, and that would have been a tragedy.

I also know something as mysterious as a premonition can exert a sudden and powerful force on what had been an otherwise ordinary day. Because we don't yet understand premonitions, we sometimes make the mistake of assuming the premonition's message is beyond our ability to question it. Our regular concerns pale in comparison to the urgency of a premonition. This leads some people to believe a premonition's message (or directive or warning) is always right, or rightly interpreted, which can be a mistake.

A college friend of mine once met a man she had dreamed about twice the week before. She was sure the man she met was the same man as in her dreams, which astounded her. She then decided this man must be her soul mate—why else would she dream about him? She felt an intense connection between her dream image and the man in her daily life, and she decided this connection could only mean they were destined for each other. She just knew she would eventually marry him.

Unfortunately they didn't have much in common and after a few months she broke off the relationship. She told me later she was shocked by the whole episode. How could he have been so wrong for her when he had been in her dream? What was the dream for, if not to point her toward her best and brightest future?

Premonitions can be just this accurate in details and this intense in connection, and still not give us perfect answers about our lives. No matter where premonitions come from we still have to respond to them from the middle of our daily lives, with our daily concerns and ambitions intact. How we respond is only helped when we use our common sense, rational decision-making, intuition, and life experience as well as the information we receive.

Six Common Responses

I have found six common responses to a premonition, gleaned from the research, conversations with friends, my own life, and from the people I've interviewed. No single response works in all situations. I think I have used every one of these options, based on the information I had, how much time I had to act, and the possible consequences I could see if I acted or if I did nothing. And each decision I've made has been built on what the premonition meant to me. I have ordered the responses here from the simplest action we can take to the most complicated.

The first three responses to premonitions seem almost passive. They don't challenge the future as much as they wait for it to happen. People wait and watch as time unwinds into the future event, or they disregard the warning in favor of some other daily concern, or they prepare themselves for an inevitable future event. Researchers who noted these responses in the past considered them non-responses, but I see each one as a conscious decision. The importance of these decisions lies not so much in what people didn't do, but in each person's reasons for acting as they did. The reasons show a careful weighing of options and clear decisions—not passive at all.

The last three responses challenge the future event in some way, giving us hope that any future is changeable and open. Some people avoid the future event, which may not change what happens but does change what happens to them. Others warn friends and family in order to protect them from danger, which again changes who is involved in the future event. The last choice, the most difficult and the least understood, is to change the future event before it happens.

Choices That Wait for the Future

Researchers like Louisa Rhine have not paid much attention to the reasons why someone would choose not to act boldly on a premonition's warning. Most researchers want to see responses with actions and behaviors involved, responses they can verify through observation. This focus on the observable has limited our understanding of the more passive-seeming responses. People choose these first three responses based in large part on what they know their premonitions are for. Even the most passive-appearing response can be an active engagement with premonitions from within a particular meaning for them. Sitting back and waiting can come from as clear an understanding of premonitions as the more active responses.

1. Wait and watch. Of the nearly six hundred people in Rhine's study who wondered if that first moment was a premonition, about 25 percent simply waited and watched the initial moment slowly unfold into the connecting event. They had noticed the initial moment and wondered if that moment would wind its way into a future event, but they had no reason to do anything else.

Many waking premonitions focus on such tiny, harmless future events, and there is no need to do anything but watch them blossom. I met a man once, an engineer, who told me that he often wakes up humming a particular song and when he leaves for work thirty or forty minutes later, that song will be playing on the car radio, in exactly the same spot he had been humming. If this had happened only once he would have considered it a chance occurrence. Twice in a month might be a remarkable coincidence. But he has been doing this for years, and he can find no logical, or technological, engineering reason for it. It doesn't fit with his understanding of sound waves, radio mechanics, or how playlists are constructed for each morning drive.

Apart from challenging his technological expertise, this simple premonition does him no harm. He knows he could refuse to turn on the radio and avoid any chance for a connecting moment, but he doesn't see the point of hiding. He could also scan all the radio stations looking for his song, but he doesn't do that either. Instead he turns on the radio and listens. Such a small decision may not change his world, but turning on his car radio is a reflection of his curiosity and sense of fun, and his confidence in his personal experience. When he decides to turn on his car radio he is responding by agreeing to look, to watch for the connecting event.

When the connecting event is positive, no harm comes from sitting back and watching. Olivia once had a sudden and unmistakable certainty that two of her friends, who had not yet met each other, would meet and very quickly get married. Over the next year she watched from a distance as they did meet, fall in love, and get married. She felt immensely satisfied, as if she had had a glimpse at her kitchen table of a higher purpose for these two people.

Others wait and watch out of fear. In Stowell's study of precognitive dreamers the women who lived from a scientific, rational worldview could not accept their precognitive dreams into their picture of how the world operates.[62] They had no framework to help them make sense of their dreams, which felt disruptive and meaningless and threatening. They waited for each connecting event with fear and dread. The disconnect between their direct experience and their belief was so profound they could not think of what else to do but wait.

Sometimes waiting and watching is the only response available. Charlie knows his premonitions help him in his job, but sometimes he can't do anything but watch and wait. One afternoon in his rookie year he had had a sudden thought that he would be on the scene of a fatal accident that night. He recognized the moment as a premonition, but he also knew he didn't have enough information to stop an accident from happening. He waited and watched because he knew that was his only available option.

2. Disregard. Saying no to a premonition gets little attention because taking no action *on purpose* is hard to understand. Disregarding a premonition is different from ignoring it. People ignore their initial moments when they don't recognize them for what they are. When people disregard a premonition they have recognized the initial moment for what it is, but they make a deliberate choice to take no action. They decide not to allow the premonition to impact their plans.

Julie feels free to act upon a premonition's warnings, change direction mid-stride, or say no when it suits her. She recognizes the importance of prioritizing her daily life over a sudden insight, no matter how intriguing that insight might be. By choosing which warnings she responds to and which she lets pass by, she asserts her daily life concerns over her psi events.

Charlie weighs his little warnings against the legal ramifications of acting on them. He knows he needs a legal reason for every action he takes, and he refuses to follow any warning that conflicts with this fundamental legal imperative. Sometimes this results in him waiting and watching for events to unfold, ready to respond but unwilling to intervene without a legally just cause. He knows sometimes his refusal to act will allow criminals to slip past him on the highway but he takes pride in his decision to follow the law first. He expects his little-bird warnings to work within the law he is sworn to uphold.

3. Prepare emotionally. About a third of the people in Rhine's study had premonitions about a disturbing future event.[63] Rhine was sure these people would have wanted to change or avoid that event, but she was again surprised to find fewer than half of them made any attempt to do so. Some did nothing more than prepare for the future event as if it was inevitable.

I think such emotional preparation is not only valid but sometimes is the only response available. Some people choose this option when their premonitions show future events that lie outside of their control. Rather than simply watching it unfold or disregarding the premonition's warning, they prepare themselves emotionally for what is coming. When a future event appears inevitable and heartbreaking, this option can bring a surprising peace and comfort.

A woman I met told me how she once dreamed her middle son, not yet twenty-five years old, was killed in a hunting accident. The dream was so vivid she woke up crying. She warned her son and thought about begging him to stay home from the upcoming hunting season, but he promised to be extra careful and not take any risks. Her husband told her she shouldn't take a bad dream so seriously. So she stopped trying to keep him home, and began to prepare herself emotionally for a grief no parent wants to endure.

When her son died in a freak hunting accident two weeks later, she realized her premonition had given her a saving grace. She had appreciated her son in those last two weeks in a way she hadn't for a long time, from the perspective of having (perhaps) a limited time left with him. She let go of her worries that he wasn't finding the right job or the right person to marry, and saw again his good heart, his fearlessness, his playfulness, and his ability to love others. Now she feels comforted by the warning her dream brought her, because she was given time to cherish her son.

Some people prepare themselves emotionally for a threatening future because they believe the future will happen no matter what they do. Phillip and Olivia both understand their premonitions as glimpses of a future that already exists, something that cannot be changed. They have never questioned what other actions they could take to avoid or change the sometimes-troubling futures they see. They know their premonitions exist only to help them emotionally prepare for an inevitable future.

One morning Phillip's wife drove him to work as usual. But this morning, when he stepped out of the car and turned back to say goodbye, he suddenly knew she would appear to him in tears at the end of the day, crying about their damaged car. He hesitated for a moment then said goodbye as usual, and didn't warn Wendy to take extra precautions. Instead, he spent the day slowly adjusting to hearing bad news about their car. I asked him why he chose not to warn her, and he was surprised by the question.

> All I knew was something was going to happen to the car and, while I was a little anxious, I didn't have an overwhelming fear of disaster or anything. Maybe if I had said something she wouldn't have driven the car that day. She might have gone back to the apartment complex and just waited, afraid to go anywhere. She would have come out to pick me up though, which is when [the accident] happened, so it wouldn't have helped any to warn her. It would have ruined her day for nothing. ~Phillip

Phillip used the strength of his premonition to evaluate how serious this particular future event would be. He didn't tell his wife because he didn't want to upset her, and because he didn't want her to think that she could somehow avoid the accident, something he knew was inevitable. Because his premonitions bring him information from a future he believes already exists, he had no thought about turning away from it, avoiding it, or changing any aspect of it.

Choices That Attempt to Change the Future

People who have a premonition about a frightening future event face more troubling decisions. They may try to avoid the event, or influence it in some way to keep themselves or their loved ones from danger, but these choices are rare. Only about 12 percent of the people in Rhine's study attempted any kind of change.[64] Of those who tried to influence the future a third of them failed, most often because they did not have enough details.[65]

Premonitions of a future danger can frighten us. Knowing a terrible future event is coming and knowing what to do about that event are two different things. If a premonition brings enough details we can confidently step aside and let the danger pass. We hear a voice telling us to stop the car, or stand back from the curb, or turn down the invitation, and we obey without much thought, because directions like these are unambiguous and come without a specific future event attached to them.

But most premonitions aren't that clear. Not all situations can be turned aside with a simple command, and not all premonitions bring such direct messages. We need to make choices about how much we will risk to avoid a future that does not yet exist. Whatever we decide to do must lie within our personal ability or control. We can't make an airline cancel a flight just on our say-so—unless we are in charge of flight cancellations, but even then I imagine there are protocols.

The next three options are listed in order of their complexity. First, we can avoid the future event by changing our actions. Second, we can warn others away from the future event. Finally, we can try to change or eliminate the future event altogether. This last option is the most complicated and the most controversial. All of these options bring up questions and challenges that have weighed for centuries on researchers, philosophers, and people who have premonitions, testing each generation's most cherished beliefs about fate and free will.

4. Avoid the future event. Books on premonitions are filled with stories of people trusting their premonitions enough to get out of the way of some approaching catastrophe. People successfully have avoided car accidents, shipwrecks, hotel fires, and freak accidents in the home, but all those events still occurred.

Researcher William Cox studied commuter train crashes in the 1950s, comparing the number of passengers involved in the crashes to the number of people on the same scheduled runs in the days and weeks prior to the accident. He found significantly fewer people on the trains that crashed than anyone expected, and fewer than chance alone would predict. The missing passengers made him wonder if some people had avoided the accidents through what he called an unconscious premonition, meaning people changed their travel plans without being aware of a premonition.[66] Although Cox could not know the decision-making process of those missing passengers, he assumed they changed their plans unconsciously because otherwise the newspapers would have reported the people who recognized and trusted a premonition. Today we know many people could have acted on warnings, visions, or a steadily increasing uneasiness without ever talking about their decisions publicly.

Avoidance changes the impact of a premonition's connecting event on the people involved, but does not interfere with the event itself. The missing passengers on Cox's trains didn't change what happened, but they did change what happened to themselves. When the *Titanic* sailed in 1912, several passengers had premonitions of disaster and stayed away; their concerns did not stop the ship from sailing, or from sinking, but they avoided almost certain death by staying home.

Avoiding a future event allows the event itself to happen on schedule, which in turn helps uphold one of the popular theories about premonitions. Some researchers wonder if these people had a sensitivity to the future accident, as if the accident sent out a distress signal backward through time, like ripples from a rock thrown into water. The ripples travel in circles, spreading out from the event in all directions at once. When the ripples move forward in time we feel them as the emotional consequences of the event. When the ripples move backward in time we feel them as a premonition for the event.

Evelyn didn't have a specific visual image of a car accident in her mind the day she backed out of her friend's road trip to beauty school. She avoided her involvement in a tragic accident, but she did not stop the accident from happening. The future accident could have acted as a catalyst for Evelyn's premonition, the rock in her future that sent ripples of warning backward in time to her.

Deciding to avoid a future event brings two distinct emotional challenges. First, by taking action we put ourselves in the position of possibly bringing about the very event we are hoping to avoid. Second, if we do succeed in avoiding a terrible event that still endangers another's life, we can feel an enormous guilt for surviving.

Whenever we try to avoid a future event we run the risk of inadvertently bringing the event into reality. We live in a complex and incomplete world, and premonitions, like every other tool (or ability or gift or guidance) on which we rely, are also complex and incomplete. We don't always know which way to turn to avoid the disasters we see. If we don't have enough specific information we can run straight into the very event we wanted to avoid. Premonition books are full of anguished stories in which people try to avoid a terrible future but only succeed in bringing it about, or something equally disastrous.

Louisa Rhine wrote about a mother who woke from a nightmare about her young son being hit by a car. This mother kept her son inside all morning, then took him to her sister's home in the countryside. She didn't relax until he was safely in bed for a nap, which is when he snuck outside and sat beneath a tree in the yard. And a car, out of control, jumped the sidewalk and ran over him. The grieving mother was left with the horrifying question, if she had not had the dream, if she had not moved him to her sister's house, would he still be alive? The evasive actions she took made the event she was trying to avoid possible.

Some people will respond to this story with a shrug of fatalism and the thought that it was meant to be. Clearly the dream came from a future that would happen no matter what the mother did. For them, the mother did not bring about the event as much as try to outrun her son's destiny. If she had stayed at home and done nothing, this reasoning goes, the accident would have found her son anyway. A different driver perhaps, a different street, but the same fatal outcome.

Rhine firmly believed in an open future with free will. She decided the poor mother simply did not have enough details to know exactly what to avoid or how to change her future. The fault lay not in her belief that she could change an inevitable future, but in her lack of detailed information. Perhaps if she had seen her sister's yard in her dream, she might have avoided her son's fatal accident.

I agree with Rhine. I want to know that my future remains open, no matter what a premonition might bring. I want the freedom Charlie and Julie enjoy, who respond to their warnings in the manner they see fit, given what they know about the premonition and what they know about their own lives. I want premonitions that give me more options than ordinary time allows, that understand the future is open if I have enough information.

And when we succeed? When we follow our uneasy feeling and turn around, and avoid a terrible event that happens before our eyes but without us, we often run into the second challenge of avoiding a future event. We may see that event affect others. What are the implications when we avoid a devastating future that reaches out and devastates someone else instead?

Survivors of any disaster often feel guilty for living when others died, for escaping unharmed when others suffered injury, even when they had no control in the situation. Guilt is built into our capacity for empathy and concern for others. After several hurricanes wiped out entire neighborhoods in Florida, Louisiana, and Texas in recent years, many people whose homes were spared felt guilty. They didn't know why they still had a roof over their heads when so many others were left without anything.

When people survive a devastating event because they recognized and trusted a premonition's warning enough to avoid that event, this kind of survivor guilt can intensify. If they see their premonition as a protective, guiding spiritual force, they may thank God or their guardian angels for protecting them, but that doesn't help the people who did not hear a warning, who did not know they were heading into danger.

When Evelyn learned of her friend's accident and the death of her friend's grandmother, she was grateful to be alive, and grateful for her warning, but she also felt guilty because someone else had died. She wondered if she was the one who was "supposed to" have died. She wondered why her friend's grandmother didn't get a warning of her own. She wondered if she was supposed to have done more to warn her friends. She knew she had no specific images to tell anyone and knew her friends wouldn't have believed her if she said anything. But that didn't stop her worrying that she was in some way responsible for another person's death. She comforted herself with the thought that that accident might have been meant for her friend's grandmother after all, that her decision to not get in the car was part of the plan. It must have been the older woman's time to die. This explanation helped her trust she didn't avoid her own accident as much as make room for what was supposed to happen to someone else. The thought helped her let go of some of her guilt.

If we know our premonitions exist to help and protect us, we may wonder why premonitions don't protect other people as well. Why do some notice a warning and move aside and others receive no warning, have no sense of impending danger, and lose their lives? If premonitions rest on a spiritual understanding of the world, then the answer to this question can also be found within a spiritual framework. It is not unlike the question of why God seems to answer some prayers but not others, or why God protects some lives but not others.

The people I interviewed who found other meanings for their premonitions also experienced guilt. Even those who see life as a succession of moments of chance, or use their premonitions as a sneak peek into the future rather than a protection from life's hardships, still wonder about their responsibility. After thirty years Roger can walk all the way around his decision not to tell his friends about his misgivings before the plane trip that ended with their deaths. He reassures himself he didn't recognize his unease as a premonition, and even if he did, his friends would not have listened to him if he had said anything. He knows they shared his skepticism about psi events. But still there is a part of him that wonders what might have happened if he had told them about this one momentary misgiving. He comforts himself by remembering his premonition was not a warning for him, and he didn't use it to avoid the plane. He has decided he was lucky his friend the pilot had too many passengers. The premonition was simply an additional, inexplicable moment.

A different meaning for premonitions can soften the question of guilt. Phillip's premonitions do not bring him warnings or guidance, and therefore he has much less guilt about bad things happening to himself or others. When Phillip suddenly knew his car would be damaged he didn't see it as a warning, but as a glimpse into what was inevitably coming. He didn't worry about whether he could or should warn his wife. Even when he sat nervously on an airplane, preparing himself for an extremely frightening accident that undoubtedly would involve others, he had no thought of being protected by a guiding spirit, no thought about saving himself from the accident, and no thought that others on the plane needed his protection.

5. Warn others. Some premonitions come with information about someone else's future rather than our own, or the future event we see includes someone else as well. I imagine most people would welcome the ability to protect friends and loved ones from accidents or other unforeseen tragedies. Even Evelyn, who has struggled with nearly incomprehensible premonitions for years, knows the benefit of keeping her children safe outweighs every doubt or fear she has about these moments. She says, "If I foresaw something that I could have stopped, or stopped somebody close to me from being hurt or injured, then I definitely think it would have been a bonus."

Charlie's first premonition helped him protect his coworkers, which cemented his trust of his occasional warnings. His first job out of high school was gravity logging in the Pacific Northwest. Gravity loggers use a heavy piece of machinery called a carriage that is suspended high on a cable running up and down the hill. The carriage weighs several tons and drags logs down the mountainside. Loggers stand beneath this carriage to attach its hooks (called chokers) to the logs and are reminded weekly not to stand underneath it too long. It is dangerous work. If the bolt that attaches the carriage to the cable ever breaks off, the carriage could drop and kill anyone caught underneath. But as Charlie tells it, people often get lax with safety precautions.

One afternoon Charlie felt apprehensive about that carriage. " I don't know what it was that made me so nervous. I had a feeling that, *God, we better be careful today*." All of Charlie's fellow loggers teased him about his nervousness and assured him he was just new to the job. But Charlie didn't stop warning them. "I'm saying, *Man, stay out from under that carriage,* for a couple of hours. [Then one time] we went and grabbed our chokers and [the bolt] just sheared off. And that thing dropped in between the four of us. Missed us. And I was—we were lucky. We were just looking at each other, *Wow, weren't we just talking about that?*

Charlie was able to warn his coworkers for two reasons. First, he was telling everyone to take precautions they already knew and understood. He wasn't telling them to stop working or to change their routines, just follow the safety guidelines more carefully than they might have done otherwise. And second, Charlie's premonition didn't give him a glimpse of a future event. He didn't have to think about what might happen, only what he and his colleagues should be doing right now. His premonition gave him his response rather than showing him a future tragedy and letting him figure out what to do.

When a premonition does come with a picture of a disturbing or dangerous event happening to someone else, we face a more complicated response. We can't quietly step out of harm's way without saying anything. We can't take another train, or refuse to get into a car, or graciously give up our seat on an airplane without thinking of what will come to others. Instead we must decide if we are willing to risk looking foolish in order to warn—and perhaps protect—other people. Such warnings almost always include self-disclosure and a small possibility of losing friendships. Such warnings also are rarely accepted by others without questions and a certain amount of eye-rolling, especially when we can't offer convincing proof (always a sticking point) that something terrible is coming.

6. Change the future event. There are rare times when premonitions bring enough detailed information to not only avoid the future event or warn someone else to avoid it, but to actually change the future event, and maybe prevent it from happening in the first place. When this happens—so rarely—many will still hesitate to challenge the future as they have seen it. Our most popular theory is that premonitions are ripples of information traveling backward through time from a future event. Events that send ripples of information backward through time may sound unconventional, but it is still a fixed event that causes something else to happen—our familiar cause-and-effect thinking, only backward.

If a person uses a premonition about a future event to eliminate that event altogether, then what would have created the ripples in the first place? If there is no longer a future event to send a warning back, then there can be no premonition. And without a premonition to spur us into changing the event, the future we had first seen would (maybe) have arrived intact. It's a forward spin on the old time-travel paradox, which says I can't travel back in time and kill my grandfather, because then I wouldn't be born and I wouldn't grow up to kill him, so he would still be alive. For premonitions the paradox runs forward: If we eliminate a future event because of a premonition, then that future would no longer exist—which means it could not have sent us a premonition and then we wouldn't have changed anything. Whew!

Louisa Rhine recounted the story of a precognitive dream that most likely saved the life of a young woman's son. The woman dreamed she was washing clothes beside a river while her toddler son played nearby. She turned back to the house for soap when she heard a splash behind her and whirled back around to see her son flailing in the water. She tried to reach him but he drowned before her eyes. When the young woman woke she was overwhelmed with the emotional anguish of watching her young son drown. Later that summer she and her family went camping, and one morning, while she was rinsing her family's clothes in the river while her son played nearby, she realized she'd forgotten the soap. As she was turning back to the campsite her dream came flooding back to her in an instant. She whirled around and snatched her son back from the river's edge.

This story, recounted in *Hidden Channels of the Mind*, is used to show the paradox of changing the future. Since the woman's son didn't drown, can her dream still be considered precognitive? If she did indeed save her son, then no future tragedy could have sent its ripples back to her in the dream to begin with. Without a connecting event to validate her initial impression, some researchers insist the dream could have been only of an imagined future, but not an actual future event.

I see in Rhine's story the best gift premonitions can bring, the gift of another chance at decisions that affect our entire lives. The young mother's dream gave her a second chance to save her son, and she took it. Her dream carried enough specific clues to warn her of danger. She noticed the clues, remembered her dream, and used it to protect her son. She changed both of their futures for the better.

There are other scientific theories of premonitions, and one takes into account the possibility of an open and changing future. It says maybe our premonitions don't show us the one fixed future that must be, but instead show us just one possible future, maybe the one future that is more likely to happen if we continue on our present course. In this theory the future remains open to our present decisions, no matter what we base those decisions on.

Every single decision affects the future at some level, whether we have had a glimpse of that future or not. On the most mundane level of daily life countless futures are being created and erased with every decision we make, and the world continues on without taking much notice. Rather than box us into a future that must be repeated, premonitions offer us the chance to make a different decision, choose again, and possibly avoid or change a future we do not want.

The decision to follow a premonition and avoid danger, or warn others, or change the future is anything but simple. Anyone who wants to change the future even in a small way can run into any number of obstacles. We might not have enough details to know what to do. Our warnings may get brushed aside by loved ones (or strangers) who don't believe us. We might not have enough control or authority to change what we want. But the potential rewards—a longer life, the safety of loved ones, a potential disaster averted—encourage us to try.

These problems are exacerbated when premonitions bring images of community-wide disasters. Some people suffer from recurrent nightmares of future (possible) plane crashes, earthquakes, fires, and floods, all happening far from their homes to people they will never meet. What can these people do with visions of a fire that destroys half a town on the other side of the world?

Premonition Guilt and the Limits of Responsibility

When vivid and frightening dream images of a catastrophe such as a fire connect to an actual future event, the dreamers feel personally involved, no matter how far they live from the event. The intimacy of a dream burns an intense, private connection into our minds and hearts. A fire on the other side of the country becomes our fire, because it began as our dream.

For some people such an intense connection brings a sense of responsibility and guilt that somehow they let the disaster happen. They wonder if they should have called someone, warned somebody, even as they admit they had no idea who to call or what they could say to convince a stranger to take their premonition seriously.

This is not the same guilt as survivor guilt. People with premonitions live with the anguish of watching disaster unfold not once but twice, with nothing they can do to prevent it. The need to find a purpose or reason for their premonition can lead them into a misplaced sense of personal responsibility. Some will believe their knowledge, however vague, places on them a responsibility to protect others or to stop the events from happening. Even though the dreams connect to events beyond their control and beyond their community, some will wonder if they were *supposed to* respond in their waking life, if they were *supposed to* protect strangers, or stop the disaster from happening—why else would they have such a terrible dream? Their helplessness can lead to a sense of personal failure, as if they have failed the dreams' greater purpose for their life.

Some people feel as guilty as if they've caused the terrible events to happen in the first place. They forget the limits of their premonitions, and the very real limits they must also accept as human beings. If they don't have a supportive community that can help them both acknowledge the premonition and give them a reality check on the limits of their personal responsibility, some may feel lost.

This feeling of sacred obligation for the troubles of the world can wear a person out. There is no amount of foreknowledge that will keep everyone safe and happy. If images of faraway disasters pepper our dreams, we each have to decide how much we can do to help. Books have been written about people around the country who woke from disturbing dream images of planes and fires, and buildings crumbling in the weeks leading up to September 11, and didn't know how to make sense of them until they saw the same images on the television. Some dreamers might have even figured out an attack was coming but were still helpless to prevent it.

Most premonitions of major disasters don't give people enough information to change or avoid those events. And even if a premonition did give all the details needed to avoid it completely, what then? If you woke from a dream that gave you every single detail—the what, where, when, and how a disaster will happen—what could you do, realistically, with that information? Most of us still don't have the control or authority needed to convince the people most directly involved to change their plans. No one outside of fictional heroes on television and in film has the kind of natural authority that would make recognized experts change their plans based solely on a stranger's warning.

An aerospace engineer named Roger Boisjoly did not have a premonition, but his experience shows how difficult it can be to convince others to change their plans.[67] In the early 1980s Boisjoly worked at an engineering firm that was contracted under NASA for the Space Shuttle program. Boisjoly's job was to make sure the space shuttles' O-ring joints, a vital part of the shuttles' rocket fuel cylinders, remained in good working order. In 1986 Boisjoly and his colleagues discovered if the space shuttle was left out in freezing temperatures the O-rings would almost certainly fail, allowing massive amounts of rocket fuel to escape and causing a fatal explosion. In the days leading up to the space shuttle Challenger's disastrous flight in 1986, Boisjoly took several steps to warn NASA of the faulty O-rings. The shuttle launch had already been delayed, and he knew it had been exposed to below-freezing temperatures. The day before launch he met with his managers and NASA officials to explain the problem. After all his warnings, however, the people in charge decided to continue the launch anyway. The Space Shuttle Challenger exploded just seventy-three seconds after lift-off, due to a failure of the O-rings.

Boisjoly had direct access to the people who made the decision about whether to continue or delay the launch, and he was their acknowledged and trusted expert in O-rings. And he still could not convince them to delay the shuttle launch.[68] I try to imagine what would have happened if NASA officials had received a call, not from a respected engineer but from a respected opera singer, or a respected accountant, or a respected health care worker who wanted them to delay the launch because of a terrifying dream they had. No matter how powerful the images, no matter how finely drawn the specific details, such dreamers have no authority to change the event.

How do we learn to live within our limits? The people I interviewed each respect their very real personal limits. They don't expect their premonitions to save everyone, and they don't let their premonitions obligate them with a responsibility they cannot meet. Charlie best illustrated how this acceptance of his limits worked when he waited for a fatal car accident one evening. He knew he didn't have information to stop the accident. He had nothing more than his own expectation, so he gave no thought to avoiding or warning anyone. He prepared himself for an emotionally wrenching situation but he didn't berate himself that he should have known more than he did, and he didn't feel guilty when the accident happened. He accepted what he knew and he used the information according to his professional experience and his common sense.

Find the Personal Meanings Within the Public Images

Dream experts have another way to counter the emotional distress of seeing images of disaster. The Reverend Dr. Jeremy Taylor teaches that all dreams can be explored from many different perspectives at once. Even if a dream includes precognitive elements, we can still look at its other meanings for our daily life. If we witness a global catastrophe in a dream, we can still find personal significance for our own lives in the symbolic forms the dream uses. By helping people understand their dreams from many different viewpoints, Taylor helps them develop a sense of capability in their waking judgment and re-establish the primacy of their daily lives over these night terrors.

After the September 11, 2001, attacks in New York City, Jean Campbell, lecturer and founding member of the Association for the Study of Dreams, wrote about how easily people with precognitive dreams of disasters slip into a deep sense of personal guilt.[69] She also demonstrates how multiple levels of meaning can help us better understand dreams of the Twin Tower attacks. The night of September 10, 2001, she dreamed she was in an airport control tower that she identified as the JFK International Airport in New York, "watching a man talk somewhat frantically into a microphone. There is a feeling of something gone wrong." She considers this image as precognitive, but she does not see it as giving her enough information to change the events of that day or even to recognize it as precognitive until after she learned of the attacks.

What she does next with her dream image can help people hold on to their dreams with less fear. She allows her dream to be precognitive, but she also recognizes the images it uses could be personally significant for her. She wrote, "Why was I in the 'control tower' during my particular precognitive dream ... why did my dreaming self choose this particular thing to see? The image has a personal message."[70] Her dream emphasized her ability to be 'in control' (in the control tower) in many aspects of her life. Out of the ashes of a disturbing dream about a terrible day, her dreaming self gave her a message of competence and, by extension, hope. By exploring the dream images as symbolic of her personal journey, as well as holding precognitive images of a terrible tragedy, she drew her dream back into her personal life.

Campbell's insights show a genuine respect for the precognitive elements while maintaining her primary concern with her daily life. She understands our dreams can place us in the midst of real horror for our own personal reasons. How many of us have had nightmares of war only to wake and wonder what or who we feel at war with? Our dreams might rummage through our immediate past (called day residue) and our immediate future (called future day residue), looking for images to make their point about our personal lives, regardless of the suffering those images portray.

Louisa Rhine published a story about a woman who dreamed her husband went up on the roof to fix their television antenna and was electrocuted when a sudden gust of wind blew it into a power line. She told her husband her dream the next day and then told him again a couple of weeks later as he was preparing to go fix the antenna. Her dream did not stop him from going ahead with his plans but he stayed alert and, when a big gust of wind came up suddenly, he pushed the antenna in the opposite direction, away from the power lines.

Rhine's description ends here, but I want to draw attention to all the little decisions these two people made to avoid a terrible accident. First, this woman recognized her dream might be a premonition in its initial moment, while she still had time to respond. She trusted her dream appeared for her benefit, as a warning to her. She believed her dream showed her only a possible future and not a predestined tragedy, which gave her room to warn her husband. She trusted her husband to listen to her dream respectfully and heed its warning. She remembered her dream for the next two weeks, and warned her husband again as he prepared to fix their antenna. This woman did not stop her husband from continuing on with his day, and he did not take the warning to mean he must never, ever get on his roof. Instead he waited and watched, going forward with his day as planned. He trusted his wife's dream and gave her the respect she needed to share something so unusual. By the time he started up his ladder he had enough details to understand how an accident might happen. He stayed alert while he went about his work and when the wind picked up suddenly and pulled the antenna out of his hand he was ready, and pushed it out of harm's way.

There undoubtedly will be times when the response we want to make to a premonition is just not possible. We might do our best and find it wasn't enough to change or avoid the future we saw. We warn friends only to watch them casually bat our warning away, roll their eyes, and go striding off into danger.

My hope, however, is these options will give you more room, more options to choose from when you notice a premonition of your own. Premonitions of any size can be watched, or prepared for, or pushed along, or avoided, or changed in a small way. If you are worried that paying attention to your experience will put you on a collision course with horrible world events, I can assure you that you still have control over what you pay attention to and you do not have to save the world today.

If you want the challenge of interacting with your premonitions, test your strength and see the limits of your control, then I have just the exercise. Pick a small premonition—any premonition—and see what you can change about it. Can you head off the unexpected flower delivery at work by talking about your allergies? If you dream of a traffic jam can you go to work another way? You might miss a traffic jam, or you might never know if a traffic jam ever existed. It's a puzzle, this winding, loop-ing, goofy path of time through daily life.

I changed a very small future of mine once when I was eleven or twelve years old. I was walking home from the 7-Eleven with a school friend when I had a moment of déjà vu that rushed out to encompass the next several minutes, and I knew—I just knew—my friend would ask what my favorite color was and I would say blue. She would laugh at me because she liked green and blue was a stupid color. And I would watch her trip in a puddle and then we would have an argument.

I knew all of this in an instant and I decided this time I was going to try something new. I took my destiny into my two grubby little hands and waited. Two seconds later she asked what my favorite color was. I hesitated for an instant before saying green. My (new) favorite color was green. She said green was her favorite too and wasn't that amazing we liked the same color. I told her to watch out for the puddle and she jumped over it, and we kept walking home.

I never did tell my friend what had happened but that moment gave me enormous satisfaction. Such a small future event, I know, but it felt momentous to me. I had proved to myself that I always have a say in what happens next. I might not always have the control to make changes, and I might not have enough the details, but I am allowed to make my own best decisions anyway.

Premonitions don't take away choice. They won't force you to fol-low a script against your will. Instead they give you one more piece of information that might or might not help you make decisions about daily life. Use the information in accordance with your values, your common sense, your traditions, your family rules, your rational or spiritual (or both) view of the world. Choose carefully whom you tell, but find some-one who can help you sort out your options and your limits. Do the best you can and accept the outcome. Forgive yourself for not knowing everything all the time. No one does. Not even the premonition.

 CHAPTER 10

Who Can I Tell?
Finding Community

There is nothing more powerful to help with premonitions than a trusted community. The act of talking about a psi event moves it from a purely subjective experience into the shared space of conversation. Talking about a psi event does more than give us room to vent. It helps us understand the psi event and gives us room to explore what we think its message might be and how we can respond to its warnings. Talking to someone we trust can help us decide whether we will accept (or reject) psi events in the future.

In 2002, two researchers published a paper about a short-term conversation group they had gathered, of volunteers who had had a psi event. The researchers wanted to understand the emotional impact such events can have.[71] The volunteers discussed their psi event and shared their stories and insights, and by the end of their research something remarkable had happened. Many volunteers described these conversations as life-changing. In talking to others they discovered new language to help them clarify their experience, which in turn helped them better understand both the experience and themselves. Even the people who had already talked about their experience to a trusted family member found these conversations opening new insights for them.

The conversations gave all who participated in them a much-needed sense of community. The volunteers examined their psi event without having to prove it happened or verify their own sanity. They learned from the experience of others, including people who had different opinions and reactions to psi events. The conversations gave them a chance, many for the first time, to belong to a group *because* of their experience, and not in spite of it.

We are social animals. As much as we prize our individuality, we crave the companionship of belonging to a group. Health studies conducted over the past century consistently show people live longer and better when we share our lives with trusted friends. We laugh more often, we take better care of ourselves, we survive inevitable losses with more resilience. Community helps us find more hope, purpose, and meaning to our lives.

When I talk about this book with friends, colleagues, even strangers, I hear this same need for community. They tell me their stories of unusual events and then almost all will talk about their relief at discovering someone else is interested in these events. When they realize they are not alone, that others have described psi events and share their most pressing questions, they feel relief. They feel less alone, more connected, even to people they will never meet.

These conversations have shown me over and over again the importance of community in naming and understanding any experience, especially those events that have no easy definition. Connecting with other people who are dealing with the same hassles, facing the same demons, learning the same craft, suffering the same pain, or stretching the same muscles can transform a life of isolation into a life of friendship and inclusion.

Communities of Common Experience

Thousands of groups and small communities come together with nothing more in common than a single shared experience. Dream groups and book clubs, hiking groups and curling clubs, choirs and community theatre, quilting societies and rugby teams all organize themselves around a shared activity or interest. People gather to improve their skills, or find company, match wits, share ideas.

For most of these groups the members' differing beliefs about politics, science, or religion are considered extraneous and are rarely explored. I have sung in several community choirs over the years without ever considering the religious beliefs of my fellow singers. In other groups these differing beliefs and attitudes actually become the group's backbone. Support groups for medical conditions work better when different perspectives, life stories, beliefs, and meanings are shared. We can learn from each other's experience even if we disagree.

Phillip and his friends shared a grand experiment one summer, even though they didn't share a common belief about psi events. The summer before they went off to different high schools Phillip and his friends carried out ESP experiments they had found in the back of old books. They carefully set up each experiment, tracked their successes and failures, and looked for flaws in the designs. Phillip was always the test subject. He guessed which card the experimenter would turn over next, visualized target pictures, and drew pictures of objects his friends hid in another room.

Phillip remembers that was the summer he trained to become better at psi—telepathy, clairvoyance, and premonitions—with the support of his friends. His friends challenged him to improve by testing his skills.

His friends did not share the same belief in psi, however. While Phillip wanted to test his abilities, his friends wanted an experiment to help them understand statistics, probabilities, and equations. They weren't against psi, but they didn't exactly believe in it, either. They were there for the research, and like all good researchers they ignored the questions of what premonitions meant or how psi might fit into daily life. Despite their differences of opinion, Phillip knows those experiments helped him understand psi as a skill that can be developed and honed with practice. He learned careful attention helps premonitions remain present in his daily life.

Today people who have noticed psi events like premonitions have some choices in communities that gather based on their experience. The Internet provides new ways to find others who have had like experiences, even if they do not share our personal meaning for their experience. The Institute of Noetic Sciences offers discussion groups in 18 countries, including 150 groups meeting in 37 different states within the United States alone. Its website also features the latest research on the science of consciousness. The International Association for the Study of Dreams (IASD) hosts discussion groups on its website, one of which focuses on dreams that show psi events such as premonitions, as well as community groups. The International Association for Near-Death Studies (IANDS) was formed to gather people who want to explore near-death experiences.

Communities of Common Belief

Other groups organize themselves by specific beliefs and values. Most political groups, faith communities, and service organizations rest upon a set of shared beliefs, values, goals, or guiding principles. Members contribute a wide variety of skills, activities, knowledge, and experience, but they all move in accordance to the underlying values. If an experience fits within the broad definition of a community, then its members will support it, even if other members have not had the same experience.

Such groups, however, will not support any experience that directly challenges their foundational beliefs. Olivia knows her premonitions lie outside the foundational beliefs of her church, which historically has likened psi events to witchcraft, the occult, and devil worship, and today still maintains an uncomfortable distance from psi events. She has not found colleagues or friends within her faith who share her understanding of premonitions. She has never heard her colleagues or friends describe psi events, which makes her think she might be alone in her experience. Olivia's premonitions are so closely entwined with her deepest spiritual beliefs that the lack of support within her community leaves her feeling a little isolated.

Olivia may be right that her colleagues and friends are not ready to accept her beliefs. She may be right her colleagues' beliefs about premonitions may be too different for her to feel accepted. They may negatively judge her experiences and how she makes sense of them.

So she carefully avoids talking about any experience that deviates too far from the commonly held beliefs within her community. But by not showing this important aspect of her life to others, she creates an unintended emotional distance between herself and her spiritual community. She puts up a façade she thinks others will accept and in the process loses the vital sense of being accepted for who she is.

Religious organizations are hardly the only institutions to reject premonitions or to impose a set of beliefs on its members. Science also provides a framework for viewing the cosmos that exerts a similar pressure for conformity of thought upon its members. The scientific community as a whole sends out highly skeptical messages not just about psi events but also about psi research and those researchers who bother with it.

The scientific professional community pressures its members to reject psi events, not because of the research, but because the idea of psi challenges their conception of physics. According to sociologist Robin Wooffitt, psi experiences appear to "undermine the pronouncements of the scientific orthodoxy."[72] Scientists are more likely than any other professionals to reject, both professionally and personally, those people who talk about psi events or experiments.[73]

It should come as no surprise, then, that scientists are less likely to report their own psi experience than other professionals, or trust their own perceptions if something unusual does happen. Psychologist Charles Tart has spent decades talking about psi with professional scientists. He knows that psi events show up in the daily lives of scientists just as often as they do for everyone else. But when scientists are confronted by a personal psi event, they often react with a level of secrecy much like Olivia's. Tart reported how scientists sidled up to him after his lectures and surreptitiously told him their psi experiences while no one else was looking. "These were experiences that intrigued them and/or were emotionally important to them, but *which they could not tell to their colleague or friends for fear of rejection or ridicule* [Tart's italics]."[74]

Like Olivia, they do not trust their colleagues to believe them and fear any admission of such an experience might damage their careers. And like Olivia, they feel more isolation as a result. The steps the scientists and Olivia have taken to protect themselves from being isolated have actually increased their sense of isolation.

Self-disclosure is an essential tool for building community. Friendship isn't possible without risking some self-disclosure. We show a little bit of our inner lives and we respect what people disclose to us, and over time our trust and respect deepens into friendship. Olivia and Tart's scientists may all be right when they insist they can't risk disclosing such an important and vulnerable aspect of themselves. But as long as they remain quiet they miss an essential connection with the people in their lives.

The Power of a Shared Worldview

Why don't people like Olivia and Tart's scientists go find a community that shares their experience but not their worldview? Why don't they search out support in New Age circles, for instance, who would be happy to accept their psi events as real and deeply meaningful?

For Olivia, whom I've met and talked with, the answer rests in her self-definition as primarily a Roman Catholic. She doesn't want to leave her church. She needs acceptance, but she needs it from people who share her religious beliefs. The science of premonitions doesn't interest her—she already knows her experience is real and doesn't need another study confirming it. What she does need is someone who can understand what a premonition means to her as a spiritual person. She needs to find someone who shares enough of her spiritual beliefs to understand her personal meaning for her experience.

Tart's professional scientists are no different. They define themselves by their training, their education, their adherence to the scientific tradition. They are not about to feel comforted by strangers who don't understand or appreciate the scientific worldview. Tart eventually set up a website just for professional scientists who have had a psi event. They can post their experiences anonymously if they wish and connect with other scientists who have had similar experiences. Tart's website speaks not only of current scientific attitudes toward psi events, but also of the human need for community among people who share our worldview. These scientists wanted and needed community just like Olivia did, and just like Olivia they needed community that shared their worldview. They needed validation from the people they most trusted—other scientists.

With so many obstacles to finding a community for premonitions— fear of self-disclosure, friends whose worldviews don't allow premonitions, an inability to prove the experience is real—why should we go through all the trouble of finding someone to share our experience with?

What a Community Can Offer

Whether we find community based on our shared experience of psi or a shared belief about psi, a trusted community can help us in five distinct ways. First, community can validate the reality of premonitions, even if the community has no agreed-upon belief about what a premonition means. Second, a community can help normalize both the premonition and the person who reports having one; rather than isolating the experiencer, the premonition becomes a means of belonging. Third, a community of shared beliefs can help anchor a premonition into an agreed-upon story about what it could mean, which helps members know how to respond to one. Fourth, community challenges individuals to stretch their understanding of premonitions and build their skill level for having (or recognizing or accepting) future premonitions. Finally, community provides a safe place in which people can explore their own meaning regarding the experience and integrate it into their lives.

1. Community provides validation. Every time we turn to a friend and ask, did you see that?" we are looking for and forming community. We see a flash of light, a shooting star, or something odd and we turn to whoever is nearby and ask, "Did you see that?" "Am I crazy, or did that dog look like it was driving the car?" "Was that a funnel cloud?' "Did you see that? I wonder what it was." If the other person saw it too then we both know we are not just seeing things, because we have a witness, we are a witness to each other, and we can move on to the next question of what just happened, and what we think about it. If the other person didn't see anything, however, we lose our witness. Our little community shrinks back to just us, and we might have to consider that whatever happened was just our imagination.

Witnesses might not understand what exactly happened, but they can give us the first reassurance that something unusual *did* happen, even if they can't make sense of it. Their willingness to see it and name it as unusual gives many people their first stability. Yes, I saw it too. Yes, I saw you see it.

Evelyn's mother provided this fundamental validation for Evelyn. She reassured Evelyn that whatever was happening was real, even if neither of them could explain it. She brought Evelyn's inner experience back into the shared common room of their lives, where they stood beside each other and shook their heads in bafflement together. Her mother could see the premonitions and still hold on to Evelyn as part of her family, which gave Evelyn the one piece of solid ground she needed to stand on.

2. Community normalizes the experience. Whatever the hobby or passion, a group that devotes its existence to one particular interest will normalize that passion for all its members. People who feel set apart by interests that lie outside the mainstream come together and find strength in numbers. Community allows people to connect with others precisely because of the interest they share. Community imbues that interest with a new importance, which extends to anyone who shares that hobby (or passion). These groups often include novices and experts; casual observers, wannabes, and old-timers; and rules (upon rules) to help new members understand what it takes to belong.

Phillip's group of research buddies gave him a way to see his psi experiences as fitting in with his community's norms. When the group put their minds to the task of testing psi, they normalized psi events for all of them. Phillip could focus on his psi abilities without fear of ridicule because his abilities and interest were part of the norm for this group. His interest was more than simply tolerated; it became an integral part of how they bonded and of their work together.

3. Community anchors our expectations and our responses. In many ways community anchors the life events they form around. Community helps define the experience and teaches its members what to expect, and what is expected of them in return. Community reassures members there is an identifiable path they can follow, a well-defined and well-trodden ground.

Psychologist Arthur Hastings knows the importance of community in anchoring psi experiences such as premonitions. He advises mental health counselors to help their clients who struggle with possible psi events by naming the baffling experience. Giving it a name helps their clients know the experience is identifiable and nameable, even if it is not yet fully understood. "To give a name to something gives the person a raft in the middle of an ocean of chaos. The name indicates we have identified this as an anchor point."[75] By naming the experience Hastings invokes a previously invisible community of other interested people who have already charted these waters and know how to navigate them. Such a community can help clients choose their response by providing a range of options, along with how each option worked out for others. Such stories give confidence that premonitions can end well, without harm or guilt.

4. Community helps push the limits. Community can provide a safe place to explore psi events and maybe even push the limits of our understanding and abilities. Communities such as those surrounding sport teams, chess clubs, and community theater all include lessons, coaching, and competition to encourage members to improve their skills. Athletes need coaches and friendly competition from teammates to push them into the next level of play; performers need teachers and competitions to push them into the next level of performance; artists risk more when they see other artists taking risks. Expert members show novices how much is possible, how to risk more to improve, and how to learn from inevitable mistakes.

In the same way a psi ability can be strengthened through practice. Phillip's summer research buddies encouraged him to stretch his awareness as far as he could. That summer he learned psi events could be encouraged and cultivated. He learned a scientific approach will not hurt the experience. And he learned his curiosity and open-mindedness could help him strengthen his psi ability without jeopardizing his ability to evaluate his experience.

5. Community helps integrate premonitions into daily life. Researchers and enthusiasts alike create a safe community with journals, Facebook, blogs, and magazines. From birding and scrapbooking to physics and astronomy, regular communication between members offers a forum for people to share their ideas, submit their work for review, and get feedback from those with like interests and expertise.

Psi events are no different. We need a place we can explore our experience without fear of rejection, which gives us more room to evaluate their place in our lives.

If I feel defensive or protective about any aspect of my life, I tend to hold it close to me, to protect it from whatever insults or injury I imagine will come. I clutch it in my fists, prepared to defend myself. When I am in this posture, I don't have time or room to question whatever it is I am clutching so tightly.

I need a space safe enough that I can open my hands and evaluate the experience from all the perspectives I use in my life, such as my common sense, scientific curiosity, spiritual beliefs, family roles, my professions as writer and social worker, and personal history.

Olivia had her first opportunity to safely examine her premonitions when she talked with me for this book. As she looked at them from the context of our small, temporary community of two, it was as if she saw her premonitions for the first time. She could see herself, her struggles, her indecision, her joys much more clearly. She could examine her premonitions from many perspectives rather than only through her mother's acceptance and her church's disapproval, and her experience became more elastic. She talked about them from her childhood perspective and from her perspective as an adult. She examined them as her mother's daughter and as a helping professional, and she began to understand how her secrecy created a distance between her colleagues and herself that she was not comfortable with.

How Meaning Shapes Community

For most interests and hobbies, the communities that develop around them hold the shared interest or shared experience at its center. Choirs are full of singers who sing, regardless of what they think about religion. Hockey teams are full of hockey players who must play together if they want to win, but don't have to share the same politics. I could wax poetic about the beauty of quilting, but if I don't quilt I am not going to feel comfortable in a quilting group. I join communities of people who share an activity, and in that group I meet people with many different (mostly positive) views about it.

Many people who have had a psi event are looking for communities that not only share their experience, but also share their belief about what it means. Premonitions and other psi events may behave like a skill or an ability in the world of experimental research, but sometimes they are so closely entwined with our personal meanings that many of us will not be satisfied with a simple validation that such events exist. Scientists may not ever be comforted by support from the New Age communities, and people who struggle for religious acceptance may not ever find comfort from current scientific studies. People look for community from those who understand their worldview first, before looking for a similar experience. None of the people I interviewed—as lonely and isolated as some have felt on occasion—have gone looking for others who simply shared the experience. Most are more cautious, looking for someone who shares both the psi experience and the same general understanding of its meaning.

At first this puzzled me. Surely finding another person who had premonitions and could compare meanings would be enough to help people feel less isolated. But when I look back on my own search for community, I remember I did much the same thing. Certainly I looked for others who had premonitions, but I was leery of joining the many New Age groups doing brisk business in Seattle at that time. I held back because I disagreed with their explanations of what premonitions were for. Even though I searched for a spiritual understanding of my experience, I was not ready to consider a spiritual meaning that contradicted my predominantly scientific worldview.

The scientists who confided their psi events to Charles Tart needed acceptance not by just anyone, but by a community of their peers, other people who worked at a high level of scientific inquiry, who could approach these experiences from a scientific frame of reference.

This need for a shared worldview is just as true for the people who live primarily from a spiritual perspective. Olivia needs and wants a community of like-minded people who can help her explore the deeper questions of meaning and purpose in her life in light of her premonitions, which science does not address. As a hospice chaplain she offers an accepting, listening presence to help others explore the meaning of their lives and integrate even the most painful experience into their spiritual journey, and she understands the transformative power of such acceptance. She needs someone who shares her Spirit worldview to accept her with her premonitions intact.

A simple, shared belief in the reality of premonitions is not enough of a foundation for a supportive community. Two people can believe premonitions exist, but have such wildly divergent beliefs about what premonitions mean that the chance for real community is lost. Charlie learned this lesson when he warned his partner Jim about the fatal car accident he was suddenly sure was coming. Charlie was still a rookie and neither he nor Jim had ever witnessed such an accident. Jim laughed at Charlie, accepting his pronouncements in good humor like always, but not taking it too seriously.

Several hours later Charlie and Jim were the first responders to arrive at the scene of a terrible car accident. They were the first to see the devastation this accident had caused to four young lives. While Charlie had been preparing himself for this possibility, Jim's vehement negative reaction took him by surprise.

> From then on, Jim didn't want to hear me predict anymore. He'd say, "I don't want to hear it! Don't tell me! You're jinxing us!" He just didn't want to have to anticipate something bad happening. ~Charlie

It wasn't that Jim didn't believe in premonitions. After the accident he did believe Charlie was getting premonitions, but he did not share Charlie's meaning for the premonitions. While Charlie understood them as a necessary and even friendly warning, Jim saw them as menacing and something to avoid. Jim made it clear he would rather be surprised by an unknown future than somehow receive information ahead of time. Charlie stopped telling Jim about his premonitions after that.

Sometimes people who love their family but don't know how to accept a psi event will lean on the "I believe that you believe" statement of support. While it seems supportive on the surface, it cannot take the place of community. People who can only offer to believe that we believe are not providing validation that something real happened. They are not giving us ideas on how to accept it or encouraging us to push its limits. They are not providing an anchor or helping us name our experience.

They are loving us no matter what, which is kind, but they are reserving judgment on what we tell them.

When Julie started dating Michael, an engineer who had never considered the possibility of premonitions, she knew she needed to hear Michael's thoughts about premonitions before becoming too closely involved with him. Julie didn't need Michael to have had his own premonitions or to have a worldview that accepted premonitions. What she most needed from Michael was his acceptance that her beliefs were important. So she told him her premonition stories, dropping them one at a time into their casual conversations and then watching his reactions. And Michael did accept that Julie had experiences he did not understand.

> A lot of times he'd get a little bit of his puzzled look and then he'd bonk himself on the head like, "This just does not compute.'" He would tell me, "I accept that your beliefs are different than mine and I'd like to understand them, but it's not in my background, or experience, or lexicon."~Julie

Michael was able to believe Julie believed, but he could not accept her meaning for those experiences, something Julie didn't fully understand until she tried to help him avoid trouble.

In the days leading up to his annual four-day retreat in a secluded campsite, Julie noticed she was having a vague, steadily rising anxiety about his trip, which she understood was a warning for Michael. She asked Michael to stay home, but without more specific details Michael wouldn't cancel his trip. On the way to the campsite his group experienced a terrible accident. The van just in front of Michael's, the one carrying their gear, skidded off the side of a mountain, flipping completely over. The driver was hurt badly, and they were all shaken by what they had seen.

Still, Michael didn't recognize Julie's warning as help for him. Instead, he saw an opportunity to test one of Julie's anomalous experiences that had puzzled him for years. He tested the timing of her knowledge, compared her warning to the accident he witnessed (and barely avoided), and looked for any way Julie could have been wrong, all in accordance with his own scientific meaning for premonitions as an untested anomaly. He did find a surprising (to him) connection between the timing of Julie's warnings and the accident, which has helped him move a step closer to believing something unusual happened, but Julie was angry and frustrated by his response.

> Bless his really engineer, left-brain heart. He almost made it like a test. I thought, this isn't a contest to see who's right about these things! I was trying to protect him and he was trying to test me!~Julie

Julie wanted Michael to believe her psi events, which he did. She needed him to trust her when she said premonitions were important to her, which he also did. But she didn't understand until that accident how differently he viewed her experience. She didn't know how vital a role meaning could play in determining how Michael responded to a potential danger.

Benefit to Community

Researchers have long debated whether premonitions can provide a practical benefit to the larger community. Dr. Barker, the psychiatrist who studied premonitions surrounding the Aberfan mining disaster, was so intrigued by all the specific details he set up a premonition hotline, a number people could call to report their premonitions anonymously before any connecting event.[76] He hoped the hotline could harness individual premonitions to warn the larger community before the next national tragedy. The British Premonition Bureau ran for about five years, and several thousand predictions were sent in, but no community disaster was spotted ahead of time.[77] Instead, most premonitions focused on daily life.

The United States Intelligence Community tested psi abilities for more than twenty years, first at the Stanford Research Institute and later at the Science Applications International Corporation. They hoped they could use precognition and remote viewing (clairvoyance) in military applications.[78] Their studies showed strong evidence that both precognition and remote viewing work, but not well enough to make them reliable sources of information. Like premonitions, seeing at a distance happens most often spontaneously and without any conscious intention of the experiencer.

In September 2000, Dean Radin developed a series of tests for his website that allowed people to test their psi ability (or gift or tool or guidance or anomaly) online. The website tracked 428,000 precognition trials performed by 25,000 people between September 2000 and June 2003. After the September 11, 2001, attack on the Pentagon and World Trade Center in New York City, he wondered if such an intense, frightening event would show up in the website data. He wanted to know if the events of September 11 would influence the psi testing. He thought people's unconscious sensitivity to danger might have increased in the days leading up to September 11, which would look like higher numbers of successful hits on the tests performed on those days. He compared test results from early September to results taken from months before and months after the attacks. What he found was the exact opposite of what he expected. People's scores were much lower—significantly lower—in the days just before September 11, 2001. As Radin described it, "such thoughts [of warnings] were significantly *avoided* [Radin's italics]."[79] Without being consciously aware of having done so (otherwise they would not be testing their ESP online), they shut down their sensitivity to ESP. This sudden, statistically significant drop in test scores did not appear in any other time period in the year before or the year after the attacks. Radin described the results as looking like thousands of people throwing a blanket over their heads or suddenly covering their eyes in anticipation of something too frightening to witness.

The idea that individual premonitions can be gathered and used collectively to form a protective shield for an entire community is intriguing, but unlikely to work. Premonitions remain too personal and too spontaneous to provide the kind of protection researchers like Barker and the U.S. military had in mind.

Even if premonitions never become a global protective force, they still have important benefits to offer us. We can find those benefits by exploring premonitions as they are now, as they appear to us in daily life. Psychology as a field is making a similar transition now. Mental health has always devoted itself to the study of illness, disease, and public safety. But now the field is stretching to include research on more positive aspects of being, like happiness, forgiveness, optimism, creativity, and spirituality. Medicine is also studying wellness and longevity with new interest. Maybe it's time to move from premonitions in their most explosive, intrusive, and heart-wrenching forms, to the more benign, garden-variety premonitions of everyday life. Just like with positive emotions, we may find ordinary premonitions give more light and warmth than we had suspected.

Building and Finding Community

Where can we find a community to help us understand our premonitions? This is a difficult question to answer. Scientists have enough trouble finding acceptance within their own professional community, and have not found a way to help other people create an accepting community. Religious leaders might provide spiritual support but often they are limited by doctrine and training that ignores or devalues these experiences. Family doctors can perform medical tests to rule out organic brain disease, but they leave questions of meaning and community building alone. Mental health counselors may be able to help sort through some of the more perplexing questions of mental health, but very few have training in psi and many rely on the same negative mainstream cultural messages as everyone else.

In mainstream culture that leaves few professions that can support and affirm psi events. For right now at least, the one group that has done the most to bring people together has been the professional psychics.

Most professional psychics know their way around their bread-and-butter topics: health, wealth, love, and messages from loved ones who have died. But I think the professional psychics do good business for a different reason. Most people who visit psychics already believe psi abilities are real, or else why spend the money? And the most common reason for a person's belief in psi is having had a previous psi experience him- or herself. When I put these pieces together, I wonder if people visit psychics for the same reason others contact scientific researchers: They are looking for reassurance, validation, meaning, and community for their own psi event.

Professional psychics boldly assert their belief in psi and stand up against the culture's disapproval. Professional psychics allow their clients to be a little bit psychic themselves. They are role models for people too embarrassed to speak about their own experience. They offer an approachable meaning for premonitions, free of the more negative cultural messages, which includes a sense of safety and competence. They give their clients one way to make sense of a puzzling experience that still allows them to be fully functioning human beings, with both their intuition and rationality intact. In fact, the futures professional psychics predict may not be as important as their validation, support, and understanding for their clients.

Clients make a mistake, however, if they substitute a psychic's judgment for their own. Professional psychics advertise themselves as people who can consistently and reliably read the futures of strangers, which is a far step from reporting their own occasional psi event. They claim to have both a high level of natural ability and a high level of skill, both of which may be true, but both of which can be supplemented by the cold-reading skills of the magician. Whether they mean to gather information from the body language of clients or not, many become adept at finding the signs of agreement or disagreement in their clients' faces. They may call it looking for validation, but the skill has more to do with human psychology than psi.

What's more, even the best professional psychics have daily life troubles and emotional hurts just like everyone else. But unlike mental health counselors, professional psychics do not receive ongoing consultation to help them distinguish their own anxieties from those of their customers. As Dr. Hastings describes, "The psychic reader's own fears or angers ... may be presented as psychically received advice for the client."[80] Without some process to help them sort out their personal concerns from their psychic impressions, many pass those ideas and concerns directly to their clients.

Still, I think the validation psychics can give about their clients' psi events is a valuable service. Many psychics develop classes and groups to build their business that also help their clients build community with others who share their experience. I am not sure if these classes allow people to explore different meanings for their experience. The psychics I have met usually teach their own meaning for all psi events. But they give people the chance to find each other and perhaps develop their own community.

I found an unexpected opportunity to build community during the writing of this book. My project gave me a socially acceptable way to broach the subject in casual conversation, and people have responded in surprising ways. I have been amazed and pleased by the number of people who see me as someone safe to confide in. Strangers, relatives, friends, and colleagues all have had a personal story to tell about premonitions or other psi events they could not explain. Most have told their stories to just a few people, and some have not told their stories to anyone. Most have held their experiences secret, sure that friends would call them crazy if they revealed what they had experienced.

Even these casual conversations with strangers have provided the benefits of a welcoming community, however small and temporary. When we can tell the story of our psi events to someone who shares our interest, we gain confidence and a sense of belonging to the community. In agreeing to talk about our psi events we affirm such events are important and safe enough for us to discuss. In the space of such small conversations people find a little more elbow room for their own creative insights about the event, and more room to trust their own perspective, and even change it if they want.

Most people have expressed astonishment when they learned how many other people also had psi events. Most didn't know anyone else who talked about such things, leading them to suspect they were alone with their experience. Their surprise echoes Phillip's amazement:

> I guess I knew that other people have these experiences, but I knew in a more theoretical way. Mostly I don't bring it up and no one else seems to, either. Not everybody wants to talk about it, and not everybody wants to have experiences like that. Or it could be that everybody has those experiences but nobody talks about them. It could be premonitions are really normal, but our culture just ignores them. ~Phillip

Julie would like to find a community in which she can explore her premonitions, but won't bring up the topic unless she is sure she is talking to someone who will understand her. "If they say something like, 'Wow, I feel like I've been led by spirit or led by God,' then I think I can tell them about me. That doesn't happen very often, of course."

In fact, a conversation like this has never happened to her. She has never heard a friend or colleague use the language she is listening for, and she doesn't use that language in casual conversation. I sang with Julie in the same community choir for ten years. We sat next to each other Monday and Tuesday nights, talked before and after rehearsals, went out with the gang for beers and after-performance parties, but the subject of spirituality, let alone premonitions, never came up, She is waiting to hear words that people may never say because the topics are not considered appropriate for casual conversation in this culture.

Community brings more than a companion for the journey. Community brings hope and new confidence, and a sense of belonging that can include us within the human circle. Community brings both comfort and the encouragement we need to explore further.

So how do we move forward? We summon the courage to talk more openly about our lives. We acknowledge the hard truth that hiding our life experience in order to fit in doesn't feel like fitting in—it feels like hiding. We look for other people who have the same experience and compare their meanings with ours. Or we look for people who share our worldviews and compare their experiences with ours. We carry around a book on premonitions or psi events and talk to interested strangers about psi in general, keeping the topic at a safe distance from our personal experience. We talk to our religious leaders and ask for support and acceptance. We read books on the research, on psychology that can validate our experience, and we leave the naysayers behind for a while. We stop listening to the negative messages and start looking for the positive voices within our culture.

CHAPTER 11

The Stories We Tell

Every human experience, from the most ordinary to the mysterious, becomes experience only through the story we tell about it. With each story we draw events out from the background noise of insignificant moments and into our conscious lives. I agree with author Ursula Le Guin when she says, "We shape experience in our minds so that it makes sense. We force the world to be coherent—to tell us a story. Not only fiction writers do this; we all do it; we do it constantly, continually, in order to survive."[81]

We root our lives deep within stories. We tell each other, This is the story of my vacation, This is the story of how I met my life partner, of how I changed jobs, of how I lost my child, of how I survived a pain I didn't think possible, of how I came to be here. We tell our stories to new friends and old, at family gatherings, and to ourselves when we are alone, saying, "This is how I live in the world, and this is how the world comes to live in me."

We share our premonition stories in this same way, and can watch as our premonitions become love stories or horror stories, stories of perseverance, of dangerous situations and unexpected fortunes. With each re-telling we add another layer of meaning to our experience, another nuance of perspective, making it rich and varied. By telling our stories we can show premonitions as beautiful, awkward, threatening, fulfilling, heartbreaking, breathtaking, catastrophic, or graceful, all depending on who is telling, and living, the story.

Meaning and Experience

So which comes first—the event or our meaning for the event? I think most of us assume events come first, followed by their meanings in a neat linear progression. First comes the event and then we build our stories to make sense of what has already happened. When we look more closely, however, the link between experience and its meaning is more complex. Most of us look out at the world and see meaning everywhere. We see the world through the meanings we have already built up over a lifetime. Our worldviews have been colored and shaped and patted into place by a blend of family, culture, religion, personality, body type, gender, homeland. As quickly as we perceive the world, we perceive it through meaning.

Each ordinary event is so deeply entangled with the meaning we give it that the two cannot be separated. We just don't see random actions that are waiting for our interpretation. We see the meaning of the event as it happens. Our every description is infused with meaning that cannot be separated out.

This holds true for premonitions as well. We tell the story of what happened to us, and the words we use in our most basic descriptions carry meaning directly from the center of our worldview. Every description we use directly impacts the questions, so many people ask: What does it say about me? How can I respond? Who can I tell? Do I need to prove it in order to believe it? Do I still have free will? Whichever story we tell about how our premonitions appear to us will answer these questions.

A premonition and its meaning can't be easily untangled, even if we want to distance ourselves from a meaning we find negative. People who are primed to fear premonitions (as so many people are) most likely will experience their very first premonition as frightening and upsetting. Right from the first instant of the premonition they are living an upsetting and frightening event. Evelyn once dreamed of a classmate coming to school with "friends in her bag" and was frightened the next day at the sight of her friend holding a grocery sack. I can stand back and say that Evelyn's dream image was not that frightening in itself, that she could always go back and reframe this event as a simple moment with her friend that had frightening implications, but that was not what Evelyn experienced. Evelyn did not have a neutral moment with her friend that she mistook for something more sinister; her friend in that moment looked menacing to her. Her friend became part of a dream that threatened Evelyn's sanity and/or fundamental goodness.

Why does Evelyn have such fear while someone like Olivia reacts to premonitions with delight and gratitude? We live from the meaning we give to our experience, as much as from the experience itself. Olivia doesn't see in her premonitions the same danger to her mental health that Evelyn does. Olivia sees moments of spiritual connection to a world she welcomes.

Even when two people describe the exact same physical reaction, their meanings can differ enough to give them two distinct events. Charlie and Evelyn both describe an occasional spike in adrenaline which they both connect to their premonitions, but from there their meanings diverge until they describe two very different experiences. When Charlie feels his adrenaline rise he becomes more alert, more focused, and more excited, because he knows this rise in adrenaline is here to help him. Evelyn describes her adrenaline as a rising, tingling, anxiety, fear, and dread. It's not that she notices adrenaline first and then interprets it as fear; she feels anxiety first, just as Charlie feels excited first. Their meaning for premonitions becomes their experience.

When Experience and Meaning Fit Well

We have seen how the right meaning for premonitions can give us a sense of control and sometimes peace, courage, and hope. People who have had more than one premonition will recognize one more important aspect for the meanings we choose or find in our experience. Our meanings must account for all of our experiences. The best meanings have enough flexibility to make sense of the full range of our experience.

I have long admired people who have found one such perfect story for their premonitions. Of the people I interviewed, four—Julie, Olivia, Charlie, and Phillip—all had found a meaning that could describe and explain their every premonition. They each use (or see) a different meaning, but each one encompasses all the premonitions they have each encountered so far. Their meanings let them know exactly what to expect and how to respond to each psi event. Even when these four people make mistakes, they remain firmly rooted in their particular story for premonitions: spiritual guidance (Julie), moment of transcendence (Olivia), a professional tool (Charlie), glimpse of a set future (Phillip).

At first I wondered if they were exaggerating their claims, making themselves appear more assured with their premonitions than they felt at the time, but they weren't denying their lack of assurance. They still had questions, pushed back against premonitions they didn't understand, and made difficult choices based on not enough information. Throughout all their questions, however, their meanings for their premonitions remained stable.

Charlie, for instance, lives within a very particular story about premonitions, one that is deeply embedded in his worldview. He learned the meaning of premonitions from his father and sees that meaning reinforced in his experience. His premonitions always focus on his work and, in particular, on the most dangerous moments in his job, giving him a reliable tool to keep himself safe. He doesn't have premonitions about events that happen on his days off or about events that take place outside of his work environment. He doesn't wake up from dreams of earthquakes or plane crashes. Instead he goes to work every day at a job he loves, confident he will be given what he needs to make arrests and come home safely. He knows no one else in his family has premonitions, because no one else in his family works at a dangerous job. His story and his experience fit together smoothly with no overlaps and no gaps.

When Experience and Meaning Clash

As much as we define the events of our lives through the stories we tell about them and see meaning woven tightly into the fabric of every event, some events refuse to play by our rules. Life surprises us and confounds our best efforts to find a logical explanation for everything.

Premonitions are no exception to this rule either. Not all premonitions play inside the lines of our expectations for them. A new premonition can disrupt even the best explanations. Evelyn knows that not all premonitions play inside the lines we draw for them. She isn't sure her premonitions are useful, because so many of hers have involved ordinary events, like the lilacs in her boyfriend's hands or the candy in her classmate's grocery bag. She relied on a premonition to save her from a terrible car accident once, but she still can't be sure her next moment of anxiety will connect with any kind of future. She hasn't yet found that one consistent meaning to explain her experience, although she has been searching for nearly twenty years, and lives with an unpredictable experience.

When it comes to the search for a consistent meaning, I identify most closely with Evelyn. My premonitions also didn't have one consistent meaning when I was growing up. I tried to treat my premonitions like an experiment, an approach I learned from my parents, but many of my premonitions felt spiritual, as if they came with a greater purpose for my life. When I was seventeen, I applied for a job at a pizza place only because I had dreamed earlier about working there, and I figured that must mean I was supposed to work there because why else would I dream about it?

I wanted all my premonitions to guide and protect me, and I conveniently forgot that just a few months earlier I had rejected an upstairs bedroom one premonition had shown me. I have also dreamed of a joke that wasn't especially funny the day before I heard it from a friend and had a gut feeling about a new red sweater that another friend wore to class the next week. I had premonitions about comedy routines, a notice on a classroom chalkboard for someone's lost wallet, as well as premonitions that helped me find good jobs and new communities when I moved. I met my life partner through a premonition's gentle push. That premonition really did feel like a guiding spiritual presence.

When I was an adult, my mother confided that when she was a little girl her father had had premonitions, and for a brief moment I saw myself as continuing a family tradition of working with premonitions. But then I learned my grandfather was terrified of his experience. He taught my mother (who taught me) that a good Catholic fears premonitions because of their supposed association with evil. So maybe I had inherited a family propensity for premonitions, but I didn't want to take on the family story for them.

It troubled me I couldn't find one good explanation, one consistent story all my premonitions could roll into. The last straw came when I found myself in a grocery store swearing at a box of cereal that had been carelessly shoved into the tea section, just as I had dreamed about it the night before. I stood there for maybe a minute, waiting for it to mean something bigger than just cereal. But I couldn't find the significance. I didn't even like this type of cereal. I picked up the box and shook it, as if I could force more meaning out of it, but nothing more happened.

I'm sure I looked like an idiot that day, swearing and shaking a box of breakfast cereal in the tea aisle, but I didn't care. I vowed right then to ignore all premonitions as the complete nonsense they were. This pledge lasted only until another premonition brushed past me with enough information to protect me from a bit of danger, and I again found myself marveling at its mystery. Where did it come from? Why was it here? Why wouldn't my premonitions fit one meaning? Why couldn't I better control my own experiences?

Maybe we can take a lesson from our relationship to our nightly dreams, which are also part of us even as they perplex our waking selves.

Even if we don't consciously remember creating every dream, we know our dreams come from some part of us and remain connected to us. No matter how odd or upsetting our dreams become, we still know we have a hand in the creation of their images. Perhaps we have a similar relationship with our premonitions and other psi events. They are connected to us in a way we don't yet understand. What I do know is there will always be a sense of the mysterious with my premonitions, something that exists just beyond my grasp. The trick is to find enough meaning to trust either the premonition or my ability to handle the experience.

Change the Story

This brings us to what might seem like a new insight but is comfortingly familiar. It has rarely been mentioned as a possibility for premonitions, but it is true nonetheless. We can change the way we think about premonitions, and in the process we will change the way we relate to them. If we don't like our current understanding of premonitions, if we don't like how they treat us, we can always change the way we think about them, and our new meaning will in turn influence nearly every aspect of our experience.

The idea that we can change our relationship to a life experience by changing the way we view it lies at the heart of all mental health counseling. Psychotherapy is based on the understanding that when we change the way we look at our lives, our lives can change alongside our new perspective. This doesn't mean we can change past events, but we can change the emotional effect those events have on our present. We gain a new emotional past.

Two researchers, Genie Palmer and William Braud, saw the transformative power of people simply telling each other their stories of psi events. Just telling their stories out loud to interested listeners helped them understand their experience in a new way. Their psi events deepened from a disconnected event that happened to them into a more personal experience. Along with this deepening, hearing the stories of others gave everyone the chance to find a new perspective in their own lives. As Palmer and Braud noted, the conversations:

> ... can help individuals evolve in awareness, worldview, sense of the meaning of life, and appreciation of their very nature; and they can do this through ... encouraging a shift in the narratives used to describe oneself and the world.[82]

The shift in narrative Palmer and Braud describe is a shift in the story participants told about their experience. Such a shift does not need a new story. The shift may be much more subtle, a shifting of our balance from one interpretation to another.

We may not be able to control every aspect of our premonitions, but we do have influence. We have a say in how we make sense of them and in what we do with them, just as we have a say with our dreams. With each new meaning we find—premonition as professional tool, guide, comforter, human ability, skill, gift, flower, anomaly—we widen the picture of what a premonition could mean for us. We widen our vision of what is possible. This widening of perspective gives us more flexibility. Each new meaning carries its own impact on how we see ourselves and how we will choose to respond. A new meaning, in some respects, gives us a new experience.

With each new story we consider, we learn how to imagine our own premonitions from another perspective, which helps us notice again the role we play in what our premonitions mean to us. We gain a little more confidence in putting forward a new meaning. With enough practice we can learn that all premonitions need us to make sense of them, and all premonitions respond to the meanings we give them.

I noticed this after my little fit in the grocery store with my mixed-up box of cereal. I noticed that while I felt frustrated in my search for one meaning to fit all my premonitions, I also felt secretly pleased. I kind of enjoyed the mystery of my experience, as irritated as I became. I liked that my premonitions stayed one step ahead of my attempts to box them into one story, and I enjoyed trying to sort through my premonitions' erratic promises, red herrings, and occasional protection.

I still like that challenge. As much as I depend on a stable, consistent reality, my brain craves novelty, and premonitions bring me that novelty and a thrill of mystery that makes life exciting and unknowable. I want to always remain open to the possibility that I could be swept off my feet by the sudden emergence of mystery in an otherwise ordinary evening. Premonitions are a glimpse of something unfamiliar brushing past me, heading in the opposite direction of my expectation as if the wind had shifted for one second. And I catch my breath, skin tingling and alert. In that moment time slips out of metronomic quality and stretches into a mysterious fullness I still don't understand. I touch a moment of wildness that will never fit completely inside my well-ordered life. It feels like a gift, like a moment of grace that deepens and enriches my ordinary day.

We always have a say in how an event influences us, by taking note of the stories we choose to tell about it. A change in our story about any event can change the way we relate to it, and to ourselves.

Our new meaning may reach even further than that. We may have a say—not control, exactly, but more influence than we've previously imagined—in how premonitions appear to us right from the start.

Change the Premonition

Remember researcher Mary Stowell's two science-minded volunteers who were terrified by their precognitive dream? These volunteers could not make rational sense of their dreams about the future. They felt guilty for dreaming about tragedies, and then later were horrified to see the same tragedies unfold in daily life.[83] They felt like victims of their own dreams, as if they had no control over this unknown force that disrupted their lives.

And then they did something surprising. At the end of the study Stowell commented in an aside that both of these volunteers had put limits on their disturbing dreams:

After her last very frightening dream she did not want to have more of those dreams, *and apparently she had not had any since that time* [my italics]. [The other woman] could not tolerate having dreams about deaths or tragedies in her family and *apparently had not had such dreams* [my italics].[84]

These statements mark a deeper conversation happening between the women and their most troubling dreams. They each put their foot down, said *no* to the dreams they absolutely would not tolerate, and their dreams—somehow—complied with their demands. These two women stopped dreaming of tragedies and troubles involving their family. How did they control this force that they insisted was out of their control?

Stowell's volunteers show we can talk back to our premonitions and influence the type of experience we have. The volunteers no longer have dreams about terrible events, or dangerous events for their families, all because (possibly) they set a line against any further dreams of tragedies. If we change our expectations for premonitions as these volunteers did, then maybe our premonitions might change in how they appear to us as well, to meet our new expectations for them. If we can change our expectations, then our premonitions might be transformed, from warnings to insights, from tragedies to important personal growth moments, as we wish.

The idea that our expectation could change the details of what we experience is not so far-fetched as you might think. Daily life has plenty of examples. We can change the types of dreams we have through our conscious intention—maybe not all the time, but often enough to know we have a say in what dreams we experience. Much of mental health counseling is based on the belief that changing our expectations and beliefs can impact the events of our lives.

I've seen traces of this conversation between expectation and experience with the people I interviewed. Charlie sees his premonitions as a professional tool only, *and* he doesn't get warnings about anything except his work. He doesn't get warnings about his children's safety, as Evelyn sometimes has as an adult. He doesn't have his little bird whisper about his wife's travels, as Julie's rising anxiety pointed toward her husband's upcoming camping trip. He doesn't find warnings preparing him for the various accidents family members might find themselves having, like Phillip did when his fiancée scraped up the family car. He expects his premonitions to give him help in his job and that is what he gets. That is all he gets. Every time.

Stowell's volunteers raise the possibility that Charlie's premonitions are conforming to the meaning he has given them. Maybe Charlie is mistaken and just doesn't notice premonitions about his family life. Maybe he ignores his little-bird warnings when he's off-duty. But Charlie doesn't say that. He says he is simply describing how his premonitions come to him. His meaning might—*might*—influence the kind of premonitions he finds, and the type of connecting events they point toward (dangerous or criminal activity). Charlie's premonitions might in some way conform to the meaning he has given them—the meaning he has found in them.

I keep thinking about the old question, Which came first, the chicken or the egg? Did Charlie have work-related psi events and then find one clear explanation for them? Or did his explanation help mold his psi event into something useful for him? Does it matter which came first for him? Right now he has an experience that helps him, and a story that is grounded in his values and gives him confidence to recognize and use his psi events as he sees fit. He doesn't need to know which was first, as long as it works for him.

Evelyn lives with an unpredictable experience that defies her every attempt to fit it into a stable, protective, or comforting story. Her premonitions certainly are unpredictable, erratic, and frustrating. Sometimes she gets a rise in anxiety and can't find any reason for it. She will search her immediate environment for danger, check her kids, worry over her sense of impending doom, and then the feeling will go away without explanation. She can make no sense of it, and it frustrates her. Why do her premonitions defy her attempts at explanation? I wonder if her premonitions are conforming in some subtle way to her ambivalence about premonitions. She may in some important way influence the puzzling and erratic premonitions she now endures.

Olivia has never had a premonition about a dangerous future, and she has never had a warning voice steering her away from danger. She has no concept of premonitions taking on such tasks. She expects a transformative insight, and that is what she receives. Her premonitions appear to her as a grace-filled moment of near transcendence, and she welcomes each one as an illumination, a new understanding of what will happen in the future.

Premonition as Human Experience

It wasn't that long ago that people in Western culture felt vulnerable with powerful dreams. Before the Age of Enlightenment, Western dreams were often thought to come from a supernatural source, whether they were messages from God or from the Devil. People who remembered a dream were called dreamers, and having no dreams was a sign of mental health and a clear conscience.

Now we are not so easily frightened—or impressed—by our dream images. The Age of Enlightenment taught us a new, rational, scientific story about dreams that rooted them firmly within the human psyche and limited their divine power. In the past thirty years we have begun a new popular conversation about whether we have limited our appreciation of dreams too much, but no one is suggesting dreamers are dangerous to their community.

Premonitions today carry the same reputation as dreams did in pre-Enlightenment times. Premonitions often seem too powerful and too unknown to be safe. We fear a strong premonition can knock us off our rational feet, that just by accepting the reality of a premonition we will fall off a psychological cliff. We haven't yet allowed ourselves to take a good look at premonitions without all the fear and controversy.

But when we do look more closely, we will see that premonitions have a lot in common with dreams. We now know that premonitions appear more often, and in a wider range of sizes, than previously thought. And just like dreams, premonitions are dependent on us to pay attention to them and make sense of them, which gives us a say in how we live with them. Finally we can entertain the notion that premonitions—and all psi events along with them—belong within the boundaries of daily life.

So here is my final story for premonitions, the one that has fueled my passion and grounded my questions, the story that I have been telling throughout this book. Premonitions are *fundamentally* a human experience, understood only through our experience of them. In a sense, premonitions *are* us. They cannot exist apart from our living them, just as our emotions and thoughts cannot exist apart from us feeling and thinking them.

Yes, premonitions are extraordinary and mysterious, but we can pull at least part of this mystery back into daily life. We don't have to be scared or anxious about dealing with our psi events or a friend's psi events, because we already have the skills, habits, and knowledge built up over all our years of daily life to understand them. We can live with psi events as part of ordinary life, even when they seem extraordinary, because *we* are in ordinary life and they are part of us.

As a human event they are subject to our fears, hopes, mistakes, values, habits, and interpersonal skills. We might not discover the one explanation for all premonitions, but we can still explore what our personal premonitions mean for us, just as we figure out what our dreams mean for us. We can balance our premonitions with our intellect, moral and spiritual beliefs, work and family obligations, and common sense because that is what we do with every event in daily life.

Premonitions are mysterious, but we are not helpless in the face of this mystery any more than we are helpless in the face of our dreams. Through our stories we learn to trust premonitions' guidance, or use them in our work, or battle against their capriciousness and impossibility, or study their implications. We can let them hold us through tragedy or haunt us with what might have been.

No matter how mysterious premonitions truly are, we can still make sense of them when we tell each other our stories about what happened. Within our stories premonitions become beautiful, awkward, threatening, fulfilling, heartbreaking, spiritual, breathtaking, catastrophic, graceful— all depending on how we tell what happened. The meanings we choose can give us a sense of competence and safety in the face of premonitions rather than the habitual fear of low-grade horror movies.

We may never learn to control our premonitions enough to point us in the direction of the next winning Lotto numbers, but we do have a say in what premonitions mean to us, and how we will let them impact our daily lives. We have a say in how we respond to them and who else we choose to tell about them.

Premonitions tell us there is more to the physical world around us than we have let ourselves imagine. Premonitions tell us there is something more to know out there and then gently show us how "out there" in the universe truly lies "in here"—in our imaginations and memories, and in our emotional connections to others.

We will make mistakes along the way by following a premonition too literally or by turning away from its message, but we can learn from our mistakes just as we learn from all our other mistakes. And now we know we can even draw a line in the sand about what we will and will not accept from this ability. Premonitions will not make us superhuman or give us the answers to life's deepest questions. We will still need to accept limits with premonitions, the same way we accept limits with every other aspect of life.

With the right story we will find we can handle the occasional upheaval a premonition brings. At some point we will learn how to play with these moments without berating ourselves for knowing too much or for not knowing enough. At some point we will tell each other our stories and find new ways to make sense of them that let us grow into our best selves.

 APPENDIX A

Putting the Psi in Science

Most of the current research on premonitions is experimental and focused on the central question of whether or not precognition exists. I have included here a short description of some of the experiments that intrigued me as I was researching this book, along with a word of caution:

Whenever a non-science writer, such as myself, describes scientific experiments, something always gets lost in the translation. Scientific experiments are exacting, demanding affairs with multiple safeguards designed to weed out chance, error, and fraud. I have chosen not to write about the safeguards and focus instead on their conclusions. My intent is not to prove these experiments are accurate—other researchers have taken on that task. What I want instead is to give you a small sample of the kind of research being done. I have included references so you can read the original research if your curiosity is piqued.

An Overview of Premonition Research

Modern scientific interest in extrasensory perception (ESP) began in the late nineteenth century when scientists in the United Kingdom began examining psi events in a systematic way, by gathering anecdotes and verifying them with witness testimony and any artifacts they could find. Researchers knew these anecdotes could not prove the existence of psi, but the stories eventually helped them develop questions they could test. In the early 1930s an American scientist named Dr. Joseph Rhine developed a simple, quantifiable and repeatable experiment to test for the presence of telepathy and precognition. His research found evidence of a small, but statistically significant, psi effect which in turn set off a firestorm of criticism. Rhine spent the rest of his career updating and tightening his experiments with each new generation of technology that became available, and continued finding a small but significant psi effect.

Since Rhine's first experiments other researchers have put precognition to the test. They have used the scientific experimental method to develop some of the most rigorous and tightly controlled experiments used in the sciences. Early experiments that counted people's best guesses gave way to experiments that measured perceptions, and then to experiments that measured unconscious physiological responses. They developed their targets from simple cards, to places and pictures known only to one of the investigators, to computer images selected by a random number generator. Their volunteer subjects also changed, from a few psychically gifted people to people in the general public with no particular skill in psi.

Their work has been replicated in laboratories around the world, and the results have given evidence that psi exists, at least sometimes. Results vary (as they do in all scientific investigations) but taken as a whole they show a small but statistically significant positive effect.

The reaction from other scientists has not changed much in the past hundred years. Research results that do not find evidence of psi are trumpeted as proof psi does not exist, while results that *do* find evidence are met with hostility. Critics and skeptics have cried foul over methods, volunteers' and researchers' credibility, the analysis, anything that could create the perception of a positive result. The most hardened skeptics cling to an argument known as the "a priori" argument which goes like this: since we already knew psi is impossible, any experiment that purports to show evidence of psi must be wrong.

The most recent example of this controversy occurred in March 2011, when the *Journal of Personality and Social Psychology*, a prestigious professional journal of the American Psychological Association, published a research article that showed evidence for the existence of precognition.[85] The researcher, Dr. Daryl Bem, is a well-respected and often-published researcher. He ran four classic, well-documented experiments *backward* and found in his results a small but significant positive effect: evidence for precognition.

The regular version of one of these experiments gives volunteers a short list of words to copy. Later they are shown a longer list of words that includes the ones they have seen earlier, and then they are tested on which words they remember from the long list. This classic experiment demonstrates that volunteers more easily remember those words they have written down earlier.

Bem turned that experiment around. He tested the students on the long list of words first, then later had a computer pick some words and gave them to the students to study. At the end he found that students remembered more of the words from the long list that they would eventually practice later. Four experts who reviewed the research could find no flaws in Bem's methodology or analysis and recommended the work be published.

Science follows an exacting method for finding new truths about the world. All experiments must be repeatable, quantifiable, and provide consistent, statistically significant results before those results can be integrated into what is already known about the universe. But when experiments show evidence of something the field has not yet accepted, rational discourse becomes tinged with hidden (and not-so-hidden) emotions.

Psi and Controversy

Even before the journal published this paper the scientific community whipped itself into a frenzy of ridicule, threats, and accusations against all involved in the publication, including the researcher, the analysis, the expert reviewers, the editors of the journal, and the field of social psychology as a whole.

Skeptics object to the notion of precognition because it upsets their theories of time. Positive psi results challenge and sometimes threaten to disrupt too many long-held scientific assumptions. As researcher Robin Wooffitt explained, "Not only do [psi] experiences provide an implicit challenge to a common-sense understanding of the world, but they also undermine the pronouncements of the scientific orthodoxy."[86]

The scientific discussion about these experiments sounds like one long argument. Argument? I mean the decades-long feud between those who think psi has already been proven to exist and those who think psi is just not possible.

Today the argument plays in popular culture in its most simplistic terms. One side claims psi proponents are hacks who can't design a decent experiment; the other side sniffs that psi skeptics are frightened rabbits who are sure any evidence of psi will cause the world to crumble in front of them.

The truth behind these stereotypes is more complicated and much more interesting. Psi proponents have strong academic credentials and most have enjoyed successful careers in other fields of scientific research. They know what they're doing. They see themselves as courageous in their study of human consciousness and in their willingness to follow the data wherever it leads, according to the best scientific principles. Psi skeptics also have strong academic credentials and successful careers, and an interest in the field of psi. They also know what they're doing. However, their interest is tempered by a strong caution against accepting such a paradigm-changing phenomenon as psi. That interest is tested again when they duplicate the positive experiments but find nothing more than chance at work.

Psi Experiments May Mirror
the Expectations of the Researcher

A few psi skeptics have tried to replicate the experiments of psi proponents but haven't been able to repeat the same positive results. This has
frustrated and intrigued nearly everyone involved in psi research, skeptic
and proponent alike.

For decades now psi proponents have found more positive results,
more often, than psi skeptics. Skeptics more often get results that show
no evidence of psi, leading some to question the reliability of successful
experiments.[87] Proponents, on the other hand, become even more sure
psi exists and wonder if all researchers are using psi unconsciously to
influence their results, both for positive and negative outcomes.

In light of these findings, two researchers with opposite views decided
to perform the same experiment together.[88] Marilyn Schlitz, head investi-
gator at the Institute of Noetic Science (IONS) and a psi proponent, had
conducted several successful experiments. Richard Wiseman, a professor at the University of Hertfordshire in the United Kingdom and a psi
skeptic, had been unable to duplicate her findings. They agreed to perform
the same experiment on Wiseman's campus, using the same protocol and
method of analyzing data, and drawing from the same pool of volunteers.
They checked each other's results for error in method or scoring, cheating
by volunteers, or fraud by themselves. In the end Schlitz's subjects scored
significantly above chance, a successful experiment, while Weisman's subjects performed just at chance level, showing no evidence of psi.

The two researchers wondered if their personal convictions gave volunteers a greater (or lesser) comfort regarding the possibility of psi, and wondered if their beliefs could have had such a strong impact on the results.
They repeated their experiment two more times, once on Wiseman's
campus and once in Schlitz's laboratory. The second experiment had similar results to the first, with Schlitz's volunteers showing small but significant evidence of psi and Wiseman's volunteers performing at chance.
But the third experiment showed no evidence of psi in either test results,

leaving them with an open question regarding the force of an experimenter's beliefs.

A few years later, researchers Kevin Walsh and Garett Moddel gave two sets of volunteers, half believers and half skeptics, a one-page explanation of psi right before testing them for telepathy. Half of each group received a positive explanation of psi research and the other half received a negative explanation. The believers who read the positive fact sheets achieved test results that were significantly positive. The believers who read the negative fact sheet also had positive scores, but their scores failed to reach the level of significance. The group that scored lowest was the skeptical group who read the negative assessment. At the end of the experiment the researchers concluded that "belief and motivation produce success in psi tasks."[89]

Wiseman himself later ran a similar experiment but used college students to perform the tasks he and Schlitz had covered. Wiseman took one more step prior to his experiment. He quizzed all the volunteers about their beliefs regarding psi, and then chose the strongest believers and the most adamant skeptics to be senders. Results showed the people who believed in psi had a significant positive impact. People who were skeptical showed no influence.

What does it mean? Rather than pointing toward methodological flaws, these results seem to suggest that researcher beliefs and attitudes can influence the performance of volunteers.

Psi Experiments Are More Successful Than You Might Think

Researchers now have enough data to look at the overall picture of precognition research. These next two reports are not of experiments, but rather two analyses of the experiments performed so far.

In 1989 two researchers, Charles Honorton and Diane Ferrari, published a new meta-analysis of all forced-choice precognition experiments that had been published between 1935 and 1987.[90] Forced-choice experiments mean the subjects were given a limited set of answers to choose

from, much like Joseph Rhine gave his subjects the choice of five different cards from which to guess. Meta-analysis pulls together the existing
experiments and analyzes them as a whole. It quickly gained acceptance
for many fields in science, including medicine, and remains one of its
standard tools today.

Honorton and Ferrari found 309 experiments for precognition published by sixty-two different investigators, which tested fifty thousand
subjects in over two million individual trials. Their results show "a small,
but reliable overall effect" in experiments that have been replicated successfully around the world. They also noted four factors that appear to be
psi-inducive, meaning the presence of any one factor increased the likeli-
hood of that experiment finding significantly positive results. The four
factors: (1) volunteers who are chosen based on their past performance
on psi tests rather than a random selection; (2) testing volunteers individually, rather than in a group setting; (3) providing immediate feedback after each trial rather than waiting until the end of the experiment;
and (4) creating tests with short intervals between volunteer responses
and the subsequent generation of the event. Honorton and Ferrari found
eight experiments which included all four of these factors, and seven of
them had obtained significantly positive results.

The second meta-analysis was performed by statistician Jessica Utts
of the University of California Davis.[91] Utts was commissioned by the
U.S. Congress to evaluate the Star Gate program, a program designed
to find potential military applications for what researchers called remote
viewing. Utts evaluated the experiments run in the early days of the
twenty-year program as well as its latest research. In her report to Congress published in 1995, she gave the following assessment:

> Using the standards applied to any other area of science, it is con-
> cluded that psychic functioning has been well established. The
> statistical results of the studies examined are far beyond what is
> expected by chance. Arguments that these results could be due
> to methodological flaws in the experiments are soundly refuted.

Effects of similar magnitude ... have been replicated at a number of laboratories across the world. Precognition, in which the answer is known to no one until a future time, appears to work quite well.

It is recommended that future experiments focus on understanding how this phenomenon works, and on how to make it as useful as possible. There is little benefit to continuing experiments designed to offer proof, since there is little more to be offered to anyone who does not accept the current collection of data.[92]

Evidence of Time Reversal in Experiments That Aren't Studying Precognition

According to parapsychology researcher Dean Radin, scientists in classical mechanics, general relativity, electrodynamics, and quantum mechanics have all discovered time can and does flow backward, under certain limited conditions.[93] The scientists have created a new language to express these strange moments, such as exotic time-loops, reversals, symmetries, and acausal correlations. Most of these researchers continue to insist that time must move in one direction only, because they have no personal experience of time doing anything else.

Their argument starts winding around into a circle. Even if the science does support time moving backward, they say, it has to be wrong because we know time doesn't move backward in daily life. Of course, people who do see time moving backward in daily life via premonitions must be wrong because science doesn't support it. Radin adds his own speculation based on his research: Daily life may very well contain traces of the exotic time reversals physicists have discovered in their experiments, but we experience them as something else—precognition, intuitive hunches, gut feelings, and synchronicities.[94]

Radin became interested in our unconscious, physiological responses to the future (presentiment) after reading the work of Dr. Holger Klintman at Lund University in Sweden. In 1995 Klintman wanted to prove (or disprove) the theory that expectations impact a person's learning capability.[95] Like all good scientific researchers, he narrowed his question down to a single, repeatable experiment. He asked his subjects to name the colors they saw on a computer screen shown in sets of two: first a patch of color, and then the word for a color. The experiment measured the time it took the subjects to correctly identify the words.

Dr. Klintman predicted his subjects would have an easier time identifying the word if it matched the color they had just seen; for instance, they would have no trouble identifying the word *blue* if it came right after they saw a patch of blue. He predicted they would need slightly more time to identify the word if it didn't match the color they had just seen; if the word *yellow* followed a patch of blue, the volunteer would need extra time to identify it as yellow. And that is exactly what Klintman found. When the second word matched the first color, people had no trouble identifying the second word; when the colors didn't match, the volunteers needed more time to identify the second word.

Klintman was preparing to publish his results when he noticed his volunteers had trouble with the mismatched pairs right from the beginning. It took them more time to identify the first color of mismatched pairs than the matched pairs, long before they knew whether or not the following word would match. Klintman conducted five additional experiments, each one designed a little differently to examine this phenomenon, but was left with the puzzling conclusion that his volunteers were reacting to a color that would be shown to them in the future, and not to what was happening in their present.

We May Be Responding to Premonitions Unconsciously All the Time

Dean Radin designed his own experiments to study Klintman's unconscious precognitive perception.[96] In his experiment Radin took the cognitive process out of the experiment altogether and measured only the physical reactions people have to whatever they see. He showed his volunteers two different types of pictures: a picture of something calm, like a beach at sunset, or a picture of something disturbing, like a house on fire.

He then connected a pulse monitor and a skin-response monitor to each volunteer and asked them to watch the computer screen. The pictures were chosen by the computer at timed intervals, and no one— neither the researchers nor the volunteers—knew what the computer would pick each time. When the volunteers heard a beep they knew the computer would select an image in five seconds. Radin found that every person had a tiny increase in heart rate and sweat production in the five seconds before the computer chose a new picture, in anticipation of seeing something. He also found the disturbing pictures made the subjects' heart rate go up more and their skin sweat more than the calm pictures, all as he expected.

But more to the point, their physical reactions were stronger— significantly stronger—a good three seconds before the computer selected a disturbing picture. Their physical reactions were weaker in the three seconds before a calm picture was chosen. They seemed to be reacting physically to pictures the computer hadn't yet picked. These are intriguing results for what Radin calls *presentiment*, meaning a largely unconscious, bodily reaction to an immediate future event. His ongoing experiments show people can and do respond physically to events before those events occur.

Psi Can Test Like an Ability

Researchers have discovered that psi acts very much like a musical or athletic skill or ability. As with any new skill, volunteers learn more quickly when their training includes any of the following four elements: (1) the volunteers are interested in learning and relaxed; (2) the researcher who conducts the test believes the volunteers can succeed; (3) the researcher encourages the volunteers and makes it safe for them to take a risk; and (4) the researchers give the volunteers immediate feedback on their results.

Some of the highest scores on psi tests come from research that included all four of these elements. Conversely, the studies in which none of these conditions were met—when skeptics tested people who were not that interested in learning psi, and gave them no encouragement and provided no feedback—showed spectacular failures.

These results may seem obvious, even anticlimactic. After all, anyone who has had to step forward and put their abilities on the line has long understood the simple truth of these conditions. I remember learning this in high school gym class. Put any human ability to the test, and you will find positive encouragement works better than threats. Immediate feedback helps people learn more quickly. A positive attitude helps calm nerves and keeps volunteers, athletes, and performers relaxed and willing to take a risk.

What is new is the idea that psi testing follows the same rules. Psi events may in fact be psi *skills*, something anyone can learn given enough attention and practice. Researcher Dr. Pamela Rae Heath, medical doctor and psychologist, explained that psi most likely is an ability because it "appears to be influenced by ... mood, emotion, motivation, and belief. [And], the average college student or person off the street can often successfully perform psi. It would therefore appear to exist commonly, even if it is often weak in nature."[97]

Volunteers who do well on psi tests often believe psi is possible before they begin the test. This contrasts with low-scoring volunteers, who are more likely to have been skeptical before the testing. Many high scorers practice some form of meditation or self-relaxation, and as a group they are more relaxed during the testing process than those who scored lower.[98] Some researchers discovered high scorers were more likely to be extroverted, with a more outgoing personality. The high scorers paid more attention to their intuitive, gut instincts than low scorers, and they spent less time thinking analytically through the test problems. High scorers were more likely to be aware of emotions than the low scorers, and low scorers were more likely to focus on concrete facts and details. Low scorers were more likely to make quick decisions, while high scorers were more open to many points of view. Not every successful volunteer had all of these qualities, but when looking over large numbers of subjects and test scores, the people with these qualities tended to do better on the tests.[99]

Premonitions and Psi Events
Are Almost Common in the General Public

Far from being a rare event or the sign of a rare personality, psi events happen more often to more people than you might think. Whenever researchers ask ordinary people about their psi experiences through surveys, they nearly always find more than they expect.[100] In countries around the world, about half of the respondents report having had at least one psi experience during their lifetime. Researchers have surveyed general populations on nearly every continent, including Australia, Europe, Africa, Asia, and North and South America, and the results are remarkably similar. In 1987, a National Opinion Research Center survey found 67 percent of people surveyed in the United States reported having had a psi event of some kind. In most of these studies premonitions are included in the category of ESP, along with telepathy and clairvoyance.

When researchers look at countries and cultures in which psi is accepted as a normal or positive event, an even higher percentage of people report having one. The culture in Brazil accepts psi events as natural and beneficial, and more than 90 percent of the people surveyed reported having at least one psi event. Of those that report having a psi event, nearly 80 percent report both a high level of acceptance within their communities and a greater acceptance of themselves.

Richard Broughton of the Institute for Parapsychology estimated that "anywhere from one-half to three-quarters of the [United States] population claim to have had one or more psychic experiences."[101] This is an extraordinarily high number of people, considering these experiences have not yet been accepted by the culture as a whole. Even if many of these psi events could be explained through more conventional means, Broughton still estimates somewhere between 10 and 15 percent of the general population had had an experience that researchers cannot explain. And out of all the psi events reported, Broughton notes it is premonitions that are reported most frequently.

Some researchers have noticed that psi experiences are being reported more often now than they were thirty years ago, and have put forward a few theories as to why this might be. They wonder if psi experiences are more accepted now, making it easier for people to admit having one. Or perhaps psi is actually increasing in the general population, appearing more frequently in individual lives and more often in the community as a whole. One researcher noted the rise of Buddhism and other meditation practices in the United States and wondered if meditation might be affecting our awareness of premonitions.[102] So far there has been no research on this potential connection between meditation and psi.

Precognitive Dreams Can Be Cultivated

We already know dreams can be cultivated by setting our intention to remember them. Dream experts have written for years about how easy it is to cultivate dreams. We set our intention to remember them by telling ourselves at bedtime, *I want to remember my dreams.* We can make our intention stronger by putting pen and paper by the bedside so we can capture our first drowsy memories, or by joining a dream study group that expects and encourages us to bring in dream fragments.

In 2007, Dale Graff, a physicist and former director of Star Gate, the government program that investigated remote viewing, figured out how to cultivate his precognitive dreams by setting an intention to dream of pictures that would appear in one of three local newspapers within the next five days. He simply told himself firmly as he was falling asleep that he wanted to dream of these pictures. By the end of his experiment, he could focus his dream images on what would appear on one of the front pages within three days. He reports, "Psi/precognitive dreams can be experienced by setting a firm intention to experience and recall them, and to not recall any other type of dream that night."[103] That's all it took for him to increase his psi dreams. He only had to say to himself as he lay in bed, *I want to remember a dream about a front-page picture in an upcoming newspaper.*

I have included Dale Graff's research here to bring us back to the importance and vitality of our own daily experience. Anyone who is interested and has the inclination can easily follow Graff's example. We don't need a laboratory with random number generators or double-blind protocols to find our own premonitions. Graff shows how we can find our own premonitions and put them to our own test, for our own information and amusement.

APPENDIX B

How to Approach
Premonitions in a Clinical Setting

Mental health counselors could offer a safe emotional space for people to explore their puzzling or frightening psi events. They could prove even more helpful than the psychics, as they would not feel pressured to see their clients' futures. But so far most counselors have only learned to test for potential psychosis. And once they have determined their client is not psychotic, what then? Many will simply dismiss the experience as unimportant, and gently lead the client back to more ordinary concerns. They will encourage the client to dismiss the experience as nonsense or not worthy of their attention.

As we have seen, however, that response doesn't satisfy everyone. Many people find these experiences as powerful as they are mysterious. For some, the experience becomes personally transformative as it opens them to a wholly unexpected perspective, and they do not want the experience dismissed.

Fortunately, there are ways counselors can explore psi events without jeopardizing their clients' mental health or ignoring their professional training. Arthur Hastings, former dean of faculty at the Institute for Transpersonal Psychology and past president of the Association for Transpersonal Psychology, wrote guidelines for counselors who work with people who have had a psi event. Hastings has found that many people who seek mental health counseling for a psi event have three emotional reactions in common: fear of the event, fear they may be crazy, and confusion when their assumptions about reality are challenged.[104]

His primary goal for such counseling remains "to restore freedom of feeling, thought and action, to enable judgment and choice, and connect the person with reliable reality."[105] An unexpected psi event (as most are) can knock a person over with its implications for reality. Hastings' approach helps clients to their feet again.

1. Affirm and validate the possibility of their experience. While a spontaneous premonition is not an indicator of mental illness by itself, a quick succession of premonitions can stress almost anyone. A counselor's reassurance can dispel much of this fear. If the counselor can give their psi event a name and even the most general information about it, many will feel reassured.[106] Explain that such psi events have been studied, and direct them to the research available.

This is not the same as accepting their particular psi event at face value. Instead, counselors can reassure their clients that such an experience remains within the realm of human possibility. Such reassurance will relieve many people of a reflexive, fear-based questioning of their own sanity. Several books and websites do a good job providing a general overview of various psi events, and journals on parapsychology can be found in most libraries and on the Internet. Appendix C gives a list of the books and websites I have found most useful.

2. Avoid asking the client to prove the event actually happened. It is not fair to ask clients for something they cannot reasonably deliver. Clients already know how foolish they sound, and most will already know they can't prove it happened the way they are claiming. This may be the greatest stumbling block in counseling, as the search for evidence pushes everyone's desire to appear rational. But if counselors can work from their clients' descriptions, as they do with every other client description of thought or emotion, they will find an entire world of meaning opening up for exploration.

3. Look for the clients' personal markers for the event. Counselors can ask questions that help fill out the experience, such as: What told them this event was different from more ordinary events? What marked the event as unusual? Some may find similar markers to the ones people in this book found; some may find markers from their unique perspectives. By helping people examine their experience, clinicians may help frightened clients regain a sense of mastery, and help interested clients find a new path toward self-understanding.

4. Help clients distinguish their premonitions from the other ways they think about and imagine the future. This needs to be handled carefully. The reason for questioning is not to prove or disprove the existence of a premonition, but rather to give the client a way to begin making sense of his/her experience. Premonitions do exist, but they still need to know how to question their experience closely enough to be sure of what they know.

5. Help clients explore the possible meanings for their experience. Encourage them to use their rational skills, their common sense, their intuition, their dreams, and the life lessons they have picked up along the way to view the psi event from multiple perspectives. When clients can name and make sense of their experience, they are reasserting their place as the definer of their personal experience. They are also taking responsibility for evaluating their experience, rather than fighting against cultural expectations.

6. Help clients regain a sense of their individual power with a psi event. Some clients may need help muting psi events. They may want or need fewer psi events in order to remain emotionally balanced, and counselors can help them find ways to block the events. Other clients may want to find new psi events, which can be encouraged through meditation and relaxation exercises. Both approaches may help clients understand and increase the level of control they do have.

7. Help clients put the experience into perspective. Counselors can help their clients look at the psi event from the perspective of their whole life. Ground them in their strengths, their emotional resources, and their community ties. Help them pull the experience into their life, rather than feeling pulled out of their life by the experience.

Hastings noted some people respond to psi events not with fear, but with self-aggrandizement. While these experiences can lead some to a spiritual awakening or mark their progress along a spiritual path, the psi events themselves do not bring an automatic spiritual maturity.

8. Help clients decide how they will respond to the premonition. Counselors can help people with premonitions find their best response to a premonition, or help clients sort through past premonitions to find the extent of their culpability. Counselors can help them answer questions such as: What will happen if they warn a friend who doesn't believe in premonitions? How do they live with the limits of premonitions, even those that give detailed information? What steps can they reasonably take, and where is the limit of their personal responsibility? How will they react if they cannot stop future events? Imagine four possible outcomes: the event happens and you did nothing to warn or avoid. The event happens and you did what you could. The event doesn't happen and you warned people or changed your actions for nothing. The event doesn't happen and you have not warned anyone. Each outcome brings benefits and drawbacks, risks and advantages. Think about them carefully.

9. Help clients find a meaning that fits within their own worldview. Counselors can help clients view their experience through the lens of more than one meaning, to see how the event and their relationship to that event change. Allow them to talk about the fears and assumptions they have learned from the culture and how they can respond to those fears with dignity and grace. Questions to consider: Will this be a momentary curiosity for them or a marker of something more significant in their life? How closely will they identify with their experience?

10. Help them find company, and learn how other people have managed psi events. Counselors can help clients know they are not alone, and can help them figure out who they most want to tell about their experience. Counselors can remind their clients that psi events put them in good company, and wacky company, and dangerous company, and thoughtful company, just like with every other experience or event they face. Counselors can help them find their inner resources to choose who they will learn from and who they will trust. Even finding people they disagree with will help them figure out what they think and feel about their experience.

Premonitions deserve to be integrated into a full and rich life. One of the many graces mental health counseling offers is that anything can be talked about, any event shared and pondered and explored. When mental health clinicians can respond to psi events with the same attentive and compassionate interest they show other human experiences, their clients can only benefit.

Reading On

For those who are interested in exploring premonitions and other psi events in more depth, here is a list of books and websites I've enjoyed.

Books

Cardena, Etzel, Steven Jay Lynn, and Stanley Krippner, eds. *Varieties of Anomalous Experience: Examining the Scientific Evidence*. Washington, DC: American Psychological Association, 2000.

Dossey, Larry. *The Power of Premonitions: How Knowing the Future Can Shape Our Lives*. New York: Dutton, 2009.

Feather, Sally Rhine, and Michael Schmicker. *The Gift: E.S.P., the Extraordinary Experiences of Ordinary People*. New York: St. Martins, 2005.

Moss, Robert. *Dreaming True: How to Dream Your Future and Change Your Life for the Better*. New York: Pocket Books, 2000.

Radin, Dean. *The Conscious Universe: The Scientific Truth of Psychic Phenomena*. San Francisco: HarperEdge, 1997.

———. *Entangled Minds: Extrasensory Experiences in a Quantum Reality.* New York: Paraview, 2006.

Targ, Russell, and Jane Katra. *Miracles of Mind: Exploring Nonlocal Consciousness and Spiritual Healing.* Oakland, CA: New World Library, 1998.

Thalbourne, Michael, and Lance Storm, eds. *Parapsychology in the Twenty-First Century: Essays on the Future of Psychical Research.* Jefferson, NC: McFarland, 2005.

Ullman, Montague, Stanley Krippner, with Alan Vaughan. *Dream Telepathy: Experiments in Nocturnal Extrasensory Perception.* Charlottesville, VA: Hampton Roads, 2002.

Van de Castle, Robert. *Our Dreaming Mind: A Sweeping Exploration of the Role That Dreams Have Played in Politics, Art, Religion, and Psychology, from Ancient Civilizations to the Present Day.* New York: Ballantine, 1994.

Zohar, Danah. *Through the Time Barrier: A Study in Precognition and Modern Physics.* London: Paladin, 1982.

The Classics

These books mark the earliest systematic study of spontaneous psi events. They examine the evidence for premonitions in daily life, and offer some theories and alternative explanations.

Dunne, John W. *An Experiment With Time.* London: Black, 1934.

Lyttelton, Dame Edith. *Some Cases of Prediction: A Study.* London: Bell, 1937.

Rhine, Louisa E. *Hidden Channels of the Mind.* New York: William Morrow, 1961.

Saltmarsh, Herbert F. *Foreknowledge.* London: Bell, 1938. Reprinted as *Perspectives in Psychic Research.* New York: Arno, 1975.

Websites

Search the Internet for *premonition, premonition dream,* or *premonition meaning,* and you will find more than a million websites. Here are a few that are offered by well-established organizations. They offer solid information about psi and most invite the general public into their membership.

The Institute of Noetic Sciences (IONS) (www.noetic.org) focuses on consciousness research, human potential, and global transformation. They make a point of exploring consciousness from both a scientific and spiritual perspective.

The International Association for the Study of Dreams (IASD) (www.asdreams .org) explores the nature and function of dreaming. They do not offer interpretations of specific dreams, but their website provides forums for lively exchanges of ideas, including psi dreams and lucid dreaming.

The Journal of Scientific Exploration (JSE) (www.scientificexploration .org) is the quarterly, peer-reviewed journal of the SSE. Membership will give you access to back issues from 1987 to the present. The *JSE* publishes original research on consciousness, psi events and psi experiments, quantum and biophysics, alternative medicine, new energy, sociology, psychology, and much more.

The Parapsychological Association (PA) (www.parapsych.org/home.aspx) provides scientific investigation into psi. The association is intended for scientists and scholars who are professionally engaged in psi research, but the website also speaks to the general public who are interested in the topic. They have a membership category for non-professionals (affiliates), but their best feature may be their FAQs page, which gives a comprehensive overview of psi research, common criticisms (and responses) of parapsychology, and current psi experiments today.

Skeptico (www.skeptico.com) offers podcasts and transcripts of interviews with leading researchers in consciousness and parapsychology, both psi proponents and skeptics. I find the interviews engaging, frustrating, and informative.

The Society for Scientific Exploration (SSE) (www.scientificexploration.org) is a professional organization of scientists and scholars who study

unusual and unexplained phenomena. Associate and student member-
ships are available to the public, and everyone is encouraged to attend
meetings and participate with the society. The SSE publishes a peer-
reviewed journal, the *Journal of Scientific Exploration (JSE)*.

Chapter Notes

Notes for Introduction

1. Richard Broughton, *Parapsychology: The Controversial Science* (New York: Ballantine Books, 1991), 9–10.

2. Ibid., 10.

3. Fernando de Pablos, "Spontaneous Precognition During Dreams: Analysis of a One-Year Naturalistic Study," *Journal of the Society for Psychical Research* 62 (1998): 423–433. Nancy Sondow, "The Decline of Precognized Events with the Passage of Time: Evidence from Spontaneous Dreams," *The Journal of the American Society for Psychical Research* 82 (1988): 33–51.

Notes for Chapter 1

4. John E. Orme, "Precognition and Time," *Journal of the Society for Psychical Research* 47:160 (1974): 351–65. Orme analyzed 148 published, verified cases of premonitions from four researchers: Dunne (1927), Lyttelton (1937), Saltmarsh (1938), and Barker (1967).

5. Louisa E. Rhine, *Hidden Channels of the Mind* (New York: William Morrow, 1961).

6. In 1984 a researcher confirmed Louisa Rhine's decision when he analyzed both verified and unverified psi anecdotes, and found no significant differences between them. Sybo A. Schouten, "Analysing Spontaneous Cases: A Replication Based on the Rhine Collection," *European Journal of Parapsychology* 4 (1982): 113–58.

7. "These experiences are not mainly concerned with the fate of people, of governments, wars or the rumor of wars, but instead have to do with the ordinary doings of ordinary people. They are in fact mostly so personal, so mundane as to make incongruous the older supernatural explanations." Rhine, *Hidden Channels*, 38.

8. Orme, 351–65.

9. John C. Barker, "Premonitions of the Aberfan Disaster," *Journal of the Society for Psychical Research* 44:734 (1967): 169–81.

10. Ibid., 170.

11. Robin Wooffitt, "Analysing Verbal Accounts of Spontaneous Paranormal Phenomena: A Sociological Approach," *European Journal of Parapsychology* 10 (1994): 45–65. Wooffitt's study raised the possibility my interviewees might have this same desire to prove their trustworthiness to me. I tried to reassure them by explicitly telling them I trusted their ability to understand their experience and then focused on helping them articulate that experience. And still, with the exception of dreams, each person's premonition account included this sense of a sudden appearance.

12. Louisa E. Rhine, "Conviction and Associated Conditions in Spontaneous Cases," *Journal of Parapsychology* 15 (1951): 164–91.

13. Barker, 169–81.

14. Orme, 351–65.

15. "...a general non-specific feelings of unease, apprehension, depression, loss of concentration and in one instance a compelling thought.

Their distress was in all instances apparently relieved by the occurrence of the disaster or upon hearing news of it." Barker, 177.

Notes for Chapter 2

16. Sondow, 33–51; De Pablos, 423–33.

17. Daryl J. Bem, "Feeling the Future: Experimental Evidence for Anomalous Retroactive Influences on Cognition and Affect," *Journal of Personality and Social Psychology* 100 (2011): 407–25.

18. Researcher Dr. Pamela Rae Heath, medical doctor and psychologist, explained that psi most likely is an ability because it "appears to be influenced by... mood, emotion, motivation, and belief. [And], the average college student or person off the street can often successfully perform psi. It would therefore appear to exist commonly, even if it is often weak in nature." Pamela Rae Heath, "Experiential Research: Unveiling Psi Through Phenomenological Enquiry Parapsychology," *Parapsychology in the Twenty-First Century: Essays on the Future of Psychical Research*, eds. Michael Thalbourne and Lance Storm (Jefferson, NC: McFarland, 2005), 361.

19. Broughton, 103.

20. Ibid., 110–11.

21. John W. Dunne, *An Experiment With Time* (London: Black, 1934).

22. Jeremy Taylor, personal communication, Appleton, Wisconsin, November 14, 2003.

23. Dale Graff, "Explorations in Precognitive Dreaming," *Journal of Scientific Exploration* 21 (2007): 709.

24. Thich Nhat Hanh, *The Miracle of Mindfulness: An Introduction to the Practice of Meditation* (Boston: Beacon, 1975), 11.

Notes for Chapter 3

25. Carl Sagan, *The Demon-Haunted World: Science as a Candle in the Dark* (New York: Ballantine, 1996), 69.

26. Leonard Mlodinow, *The Drunkard's Walk: How Randomness Rules Our Lives* (New York: Pantheon, 2008).

27. Gavin de Becker, *The Gift of Fear* (New York: Dell, 1997), 31.

28. Sondow, "The Decline of Precognized Events," 33–51; De Pablos, "Spontaneous Precognition," 423–33.

29. Jeremy Taylor, *Where People Fly and Water Runs Uphill: Using Dreams to Tap the Unconscious* (New York: Warner, 1992).

30. Mary S. Stowell, "Precognitive Dreams: A Phenomenological Study, Parts I and II," *Journal of the American Society for Psychical Research* 91 (1997): 165–219, 255–304.

31. Andrew MacKenzie, *Riddle of the Future: A Modern Study of Precognition* (New York: Taplinger, 1974).

32. Ibid. Quoted in MacKenzie: "Let us imagine, for example, that as a result of natural anxiety in nervous people, one of such persons has a 'premonitory' dream of a car accident or a shipwreck just before starting on a journey. Let us also imagine that the person who had the dream (*or those people to whom it was told*), possesses telekinetic powers. As the impression of the dream is now in the subconscious it tends to come true (Freud). And on the very spot indicated by the dream, at which, of course, the impression is most vivid, the telekinetic phenomenon is set in motion by the person concerned, *or by the others*, by means of a fault produced in the vehicle or an explosion on the boat … In this way, the premonition is fulfilled. But it is not a case of premonition; it is simply a *telekinetic phenomenon* [Tanagras's italics]."

33. Dean Radin, *The Conscious Universe: The Scientific Truth of Psychic Phenomena* (San Francisco: HarperEdge, 1997), 111–12.
"The only way that we personally know that something is psychic, as opposed to a pure fantasy, is because sometime in our future we get verification that our mental impressions were based on something that really did happen to us. This means that, in principle, the

original psychic impression could have been a precognition from ourselves."

34. Dunne, *An Experiment with Time* (1927).

Notes for Chapter 4

35. Sagan (1996).

36. Ibid., 302. Quoted in Sagan: "(1) that by thought alone humans can (barely) affect random number generators in computers; (2) that people under mild sensory deprivation can receive thought or images 'projected' at them; and (3) that young children sometimes report the details of a previous life, which upon checking turn out to be accurate and which they could not have known about in any other way than reincarnation."

37. John Beloff, "On Coming to Terms with the Paranormal," *Journal of the American Society for Psychical Research* 90 (1996): 35–43.
"… we would once again be plunged into a cosmic anarchy where, at best, we would have to confine fundamental science to the normal workings of the physical universe while allowing that there are manifestations of mind that make a mockery of all physical laws and limitations, often in alarming, chaotic, and unpredictable ways. Given the public appetite for the marvelous and the sensational … given the ignorance, credulity, and superstition all around us, authenticating strong phenomena risks unleashing a spate of irrationality."

38. Stephen Wilson, *The Book of Mind* (New York: Bloomsbury, 2003).
"How memories are encoded, whether or not they leave permanent physical traces or engrams in the synaptic network, whether such traces are called into being by the act of retrieval, and how retrieval is accomplished are almost as much a mystery today as they were in Plato's time."

39. Elizabeth Loftus and J. E. Pickrell, "The Formation of False memories," *Psychiatric Annals* 25 (1995): 720–25.

40. Robert J. Sardello, "A Phenomenological Approach to Memory," *Existential-Phenomenological Alternatives for Psychology*, eds. Ronald S. Valle and Mark King (New York: Oxford Univ. Press, 1978), 136–51. "The present constantly influences and alters the past while the present is given direction by the past and is given possible form in the anticipation of the future."

41. Margaret Talbot, "The Placebo Prescription," *New York Times Magazine* (January 9, 2000).

42. Richard Wiseman and Marilyn Schlitz, "Experimenter Effects and the Remote Detection of Staring," *Journal of Parapsychology* 61 (1998): 197–208.

43. Ernest Keen, *A Primer in Phenomenological Psychology* (New York: Holt, Rinehart and Winston, 1975).

44. John Horgan, *The Undiscovered Mind: How the Human Brain Defies Replication, Medication, and Explanation* (New York: Free Press, 1999).

Notes for Chapter 5

45. Dame Edith Lyttelton, *Some Cases of Prediction: A Study* (London: Bell, 1937).

46. Sally Rhine Feather and Michael Schmicker, *The Gift: E.S.P., the Extraordinary Experiences of Ordinary People* (New York: St. Martins, 2005), 177–78.

47. Herbert F. Saltmarsh, *Foreknowledge* (London: Bell, 1938), reprinted as *Perspectives in Psychic Research* (New York: Arno, 1975), 9–11.

Notes for Chapter 6

48. Stowell, "Phenomenology of Precognitive Dreams II," *Journal of the American Society for Psychical Research* 91 (1997): 278.

49. Arthur Hastings, "A Counseling Approach to Parapsychological Experience," *Journal of Transpersonal Psychology* 15 (1983): 143–67.

50. Vernon M. Neppe and John Palmer, "Subjective Anomalous Events: Perspectives for the Future, Voices from the Past," *Parapsychology in the Twenty-First Century: Essays on the Future of Psychical Research*, eds. Michael A. Thalborne and Lance Storm (Jefferson, NC: McFarland, 2005), 252.

51. Broughton, 25–26.

52. J. E. Kennedy and H. Kanthamani, "An Exploratory Study of the Effects of Paranormal and Spiritual Experience on People's Lives and Well-Being," *Journal of the American Society for Psychical Research* 89 (1995): 249.

53. Hastings, 146.

Notes for Chapter 7

54. Louisa E. Rhine, *The Invisible Picture: A Study of Psychic Experiences* (Jefferson, NC: McFarland, 1981), 35.

55. This 20 percent return informally supports the Ross–Joshi data.

56. Stowell, "Phenomenology," 255–304.

57. Ibid., 278.

Notes for Chapter 8

58. Dr. Sally Rhine Feather, the daughter of Joseph and Louisa Rhine and a scientist in her own right, tells of many people who contacted her parents looking for reassurance that they were still sane and rational people despite their psi events. The Rhine Research Center still receives phone calls and emails from people looking for the same reassurances. They beg researchers to tell them psi events are real and that they are not crazy or making it up.

59. Sagan, 27, 302. As one of the country's most well-known astronomers, Sagan was frequently asked about alien visitations and alien abductions, for which he found no credible evidence. His concerns about the persistence of superstitious beliefs led to this book. Still he included a short list of ESP data he believed warranted further study:

"(1) that by thought alone humans can (barely) affect random number generators in computers; (2) that people under mild sensory deprivation can receive thought or images 'projected' at them; and (3) that young children sometimes report the details of a previous life, which upon checking turn out to be accurate and which they could not have known about in any other way than reincarnation."

60. Christine Hardy, "Tackling the Mind-Matter Problem from a Consciousness Perspective," *Parapsychology in the 21st Century: Essays on the Future of Psychical Research* (eds. Michael A. Thalborne and Lance Storm), 237.

Notes for Chapter 9

61. Rhine, *The Invisible Picture*. The Rhine premonitions statistics used in this chapter all come from chapter 10, 109–20.

62. Stowell, "Phenomenology," 255–304.

63. In Rhine's original 1,324 randomly selected premonition anecdotes, 433 people considered a premonition experience disturbing or frightening.

64. In Rhine's original 1,324 randomly selected premonition anecdotes, 162 people sought to change the outcome.

65. In Rhine's study, 60 people tried unsuccessfully to change the future out of the 191 who tried. (Rhine added 29 anecdotes to the original 162 to provide a larger sample.)

66. William E. Cox, "Precognition: An Analysis, II," *Journal of the American Society for Psychical Research* 50 (1956): 99–109.

67. Jenny Jones, "Challenger Engineer Boisjoly Tells Story Behind Disaster at Lecture Series Finale," *Madison Courier,* 18 Feb. 2005, www.madisoncourier.com; "A Management Decision Overrides a Recommendation Not to Launch," Online Ethics Center for Engineering, National Academy of Engineering, http://www.onlineethics.org.

68. Ibid. Afterward, NASA officials tried to claim they had no idea of the danger, but in the official investigation Boisjoly testified about

what he knew. He went on to found his own engineering firm and has told his story in the hope of helping young engineers understand the ethics of their profession.

69. Jean Campbell, "Dealing with Precognitive Dreamer Guilt," *Electric Dreams* 8.10 (2001). Available online at http://dreamtalk.hypermart.net/campbell/dreamer_guilt.htm.

70. Ibid.

Notes for Chapter 10

71. Genie Palmer and William Braud, "Exceptional Human Experiences, Disclosure, and a More Inclusive View of Physical, Psychological, and Spiritual Well-Being," *Journal of Transpersonal Psychology* 34 (2002): 29–61.

72. Wooffitt, 48.

73. Charles Tart, *The Archives of Scientists' Transcendent Experiences* (TASTE), Charles Tart, n.d., Accessed January 20, 2009, http://www.issc-taste.org/index.shtml.

74. Ibid.

75. Hastings, 143–67.

76. Barker, 169–81.

77. Danah Zohar, *Through the Time Barrier: A Study in Precognition and Modern Physics* (London: Paladin, 1982), 40–41.

78. Jessica Utts, "An Assessment of the Evidence for Psychic Functioning," *Journal of Scientific Exploration* 10 (1995): 3–30. Dr. Utts wrote: "Given our current level of understanding, [psi] is rarely 100 percent accurate, and there is no reliable way to learn what is accurate and what is not. The same is probably true of most sources of intelligence data" (22).

79. Dean Radin, *Entangled Minds: Extrasensory Experiences in a Quantum Reality* (New York: Paraview, 2006), 32.

80. Hastings, 158–59.

Notes for Chapter 11

81. Ursula Le Guin, *The Wave in the Mind: Talks and Essays on the Writer, the Reader, and the Imagination* (Boston: Shambhala, 2004), 264.

82. Palmer and Braud, 31.

83. Stowell, "Phenomenology," 277.

84. Ibid., 296.

Notes for Appendix A

85. Bem, 407–25.

86. Wooffitt, 48.

87. James McClenon, "Social Science and Anomalous Experience: Paradigms for Investigating Sporadic Social Phenomena," *Journal of the American Society for Psychical Research* 85 (1991): 25–38.

88. Marilyn Schlitz, Richard Wiseman, Caroline Watt, and Dean Radin, "Of Two Minds: Sceptic-Proponent [sic] Collaboration Within Parapsychology," *British Journal of Psychology* 97 (2006): 313–22. The Schlitz website includes this article: http://www.marilynschlitz.com.

89. Kevin Walsh and Garret Moddel, "Effect of Belief on Psi Performance in a Card Guessing Task," *Journal of Scientific Exploration* 21 (2007): 505.

90. Charles Honorton and Diane C. Ferrari, "'Future-Telling': A Meta-Analysis of Forced Choice Precognition Experiments, 1935–1987," *Journal of Parapsychology* 53 (1989): 281–308.

91. Utts, 3–30. "An Assessment of the Evidence for Psychic Functioning," The Utts website includes this article, a critique and argument from psychology professor Ray Hyman, and Utts's response to his critique: http://www.ics.uci.edu/~jutts.

92. Ibid., 3.

93. For more on the possibility of reverse causality and its implications, Radin suggested the following: W. M. Elsasser, "A Causal Phenomena in Physics and Biology," *American Scientist* 57 (1969), 502–16; C. W. Rietdijk, "Retroactive Effects from Measurements," *Foundations*

of Physics 17 (1987): 297–311; L. S. Schulman, "Opposite Thermodynamic Arrows of Time," *Physical Review Letters* 83.26 (1999): 5419–22; F. J. Tipler, "Rotating Cylinders and the Possibility of Global Causality Violations," *Physical Review D* 9.8 (1974): 203–20; J. Travis, "Could a Pair of Cosmic Strings Open a Route into the Past?" *Science* 256 (1992): 170–80.

94. Dean Radin, *Time-Reversed Human Experience: Experimental Evidence and Implications* (Los Altos, CA: Boundary Institute, 2000), Esalen draft, 12 May 2006, http://www.boundaryinstitute.org.

95. For a complete recounting, read Dean Radin, *The Conscious Universe: The Scientific Truth of Psychic Phenomena*, 117–18.

96. Ibid., 118–24.

97. Heath, 361.

98. Broughton, 103.

99. Ibid., 110–11.

100. The information for these two paragraphs comes from Elizabeth Targ, Marilyn Schlitz, and Harvey J. Irwin, "Psi-Related Experiences," *Varieties of Anomalous Experience: Examining the Scientific Evidence,* eds. Etzel Cardena, Steven Jay Lynn and Stanley Krippner (Washington, DC: American Psychological Association, 2000), 219–52.

101. Broughton, 10.

102. Hardy, 220–41.

103. Graff, 709.

104. Hastings, 143–67.

105. Ibid., 146.

106. Ibid., 147–48.

To Write to the Author

If you wish to contact the author or would like more information about this book, please write to the author in care of Llewellyn Worldwide Ltd. and we will forward your request. Both the author and the publisher appreciate hearing from you and learning of your enjoyment of this book and how it has helped you. Llewellyn Worldwide Ltd. cannot guarantee that every letter written to the author can be answered, but all will be forwarded. Please write to:

Jeanne Van Bronkhorst
^{c}/o Llewellyn Worldwide
2143 Wooddale Drive
Woodbury, MN 55125-2989

Please enclose a self-addressed stamped envelope for reply,
or $1.00 to cover costs. If outside the U.S.A., enclose
an international postal reply coupon.

Many of Llewellyn's authors have websites with additional information and resources. For more information, please visit our website at: http://www.llewellyn.com

Ignite Your Psychic Intuition
An A to Z Guide to Developing Your Sixth Sense
TERESA BRADY

Developing your psychic powers doesn't have to take a lot of time and patience. *Ignite Your Psychic Intuition* proves that we can easily tap into our sixth sense, even with the busiest of lifestyles.

In this innovative and easy-to-use guide, Teresa Brady demystifies psychic and intuitive development and step-by-step shows you how to unlock and heighten your extrasensory perception. Designed in an A-to-Z format, this book offers twenty-six practical teaching tools, one for each letter of the alphabet. Discover the four main types of intuitive communication—clairvoyance, clairaudience, clairsentience, and clair-cognizance—and how to use them to enhance your life.

Beginners and experienced practitioners looking for new ideas will enjoy developing their higher senses through white light bathing, energy scans, salt showers, directed dreaming, chakra cleansing, and crystal gazing.

978-0-7387-2170-5, 288 pp., 5 x 7   **$14.95**

KATHRYN HARWIG

The

RETURN

of

INTUITION

Awakening Psychic Gifts
in the Second Half of Life

The Return of Intuition

Awakening Psychic Gifts in the Second Half of Life

KATHRYN HARWIG

Natural psychic sensitivity is often associated with children. However, *The Return of Intuition* reveals a little-known, widespread phenomenon of profound intuitive awakening occurring in adults—usually around the age of fifty.

Bringing this remarkable trend to light is psychic medium Kathryn Harwig, who has helped clients nationwide understand, nurture, and embrace their newfound psychic awareness. Their inspiring stories highlight what triggers this life-changing gift—usually illness or the death of a loved one—and how it can be used to aid others, receive messages from friends and family in spirit, and begin life anew with confidence, courage, and clarity. Affirming the joys of aging, this unique spiritual guide offers comfort and support to the elders of our society, encouraging them to reclaim their once-revered roles—as the crone, shaman, and sage—by passing on spiritual wisdom to a new generation.

978-0-7387-1880-4, 216 pp., 5 $^3/_{16}$ x 8   **$15.95**

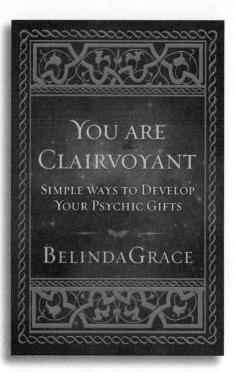

YOU ARE
CLAIRVOYANT

SIMPLE WAYS TO DEVELOP
YOUR PSYCHIC GIFTS

BELINDAGRACE

You Are Clairvoyant

Simple Ways to Develop Your Psychic Gifts

BELINDA GRACE

Clairvoyance is a gateway to unimagined possibilities—and it's within us all. Learn how to activate this powerful skill and use it to find greater happiness and fulfillment.

Anyone can connect with inner wisdom and divine guidance by following these simple techniques and easy exercises. On this enlightening path, you'll meet and talk to angels and spirit guides for assistance; gain insights into past lives to overcome negative patterns and find healing; conduct psychic conversations to get your point across; and get answers to important questions through automatic writing. This inspiring guide, written by a professional clairvoyant healer, features the author's true life stories and countless ways to use the gift of clairvoyance to transform your life—and yourself.

978-0-7387-2723-3, 240 pp., 5 $^3/_{16}$ x 8   **$14.95**

Extraordinary Answers to Finding Love,
Destiny and Balance in Your Life

Everyday
Clairvoyant

Cyndi Dale

Everyday Clairvoyant

*Extraordinary Answers to Finding Love,
Destiny and Balance in Your Life*

CYNDI DALE

This engaging book from professional clairvoyant and best-selling author Cyndi Dale features true personal stories and practical advice on how to handle everything from everyday concerns to major life decisions. Cyndi has provided intuitive consulting and healing to more than thirty thousand individuals, helping them lead more successful, happy, and prosperous lives. In this fascinating book, she shares what she's learned with readers in a fun Q & A format that is organized into three categories: relationships, work or destiny, and health. Heartwarming, humorous, and surprisingly down to earth, *Everyday Clairvoyant* also shows readers how to develop and make use of their own intuitive gifts.

978-0-7387-1923-8, 312 pp., 5 $^3/_{16}$ x 8   **$16.95**

To order, call 1-877-NEW-WRLD
Prices subject to change without notice
Order at Llewellyn.com 24 hours a day, 7 days a week!